9539

S0-AFO-933

OPENING NIGHTS

Theater Criticism of the Sixties

Also by Martin Gottfried

A THEATER DIVIDED
THE POSTWAR AMERICAN STAGE

OPENING NIGHTS

Theater Criticism of the Sixties

by
Martin Gottfried

G. P. PUTNAM'S SONS
NEW YORK

Copyright © 1963, 1964, 1965, 1966, 1967, 1968, 1969
by Martin Gottfried

"The New Theater Is Here. Isn't It?" first appeared in *Vogue* magazine. Virtually all the other material was originally published in *Women's Wear Daily*. Permission to reprint is gratefully acknowledged.

Library of Congress Catalog Card Number: 72-99284

FOR RAE AND IZ

Contents

7

8

CONTENTS

9

Foreword

A COLLECTION of theater criticism should serve two purposes. It should be a record of the significant stage events of the period it covers. And it should be greater than the sum of its parts. That is, if the critic is a good one, and if his opinions follow a controlled set of standards and attitudes, then the collection will become a *new* piece of criticism. It will be a critical continuum for a continuum of theater. I hope that *Opening Nights* serves these two purposes.

I have chosen the subjects on the basis of their importance to the theater from 1963 (when I became the senior critic for *Women's Wear Daily*) to mid-1969. When I say "importance" I don't mean commercial success, except in the section called "Rave Review (The Overrated)." There, the subjects are long-run successes in New York's show-business theater, most of which will be forgotten a few years after their movie versions are released. A climate of critical and public opinion is revealed by popular success, and I have used the section to indicate that climate. Unfortunately, at least half the best plays of any season are forced to close abruptly because of that same climate, and so the section called "The Unappreciated" is the other side of the coin. These plays are included so they *won't* be forgotten.

11

There are some obvious omissions. Not a single Neil Simon comedy is mentioned, though he was the most popular playwright of the period. I think Simon is more than a commercial hack and less than Molière (both opinions have been expressed). He is capable of more than he has done—a capability evident in patches of his writing (particularly *The Odd Couple* and *Plaza Suite*), but scanning the list of his plays, I frankly found none worth remembering.

Similarly, such Pulitzer Prize-winning plays as *The Subject Was Roses* and *A Delicate Balance* have been excluded. I liked Frank Gilroy's play but found it only a good example of an obsolete style of playwriting. Albee's, aside from being a mundane, unwell-made well-made play about a silly point, was also a safe play by a writer apparently frightened by a string of bad reviews.

The most significant theater developments of the period, I think, were the rise and sudden suspension of the unified musical (*Fiddler on the Roof* being the crucial success and *Anyone Can Whistle* being the disheartening failure); the degeneration of off-Broadway; the collapse of Broadway's frontline dramatists (Williams, Miller, Inge) and the collapse of the idea of "drama" along with them; the birth and development of off-off Broadway; and the extension by the Living Theatre of Brecht's production-creation methods, leading to the communal productions of the Open Theatre and the Polish Lab Theatre. In the spring of 1969 I was critic-in-residence for the annual Yale Festival of Undergraduate Drama, and a full half of the dozen productions were directly influenced by these companies. The most interesting theater development ahead will be the adjustment of playwrights to this form of production-creation and a reappraisal of the traditional idea of "literariness."

Finally, the period experienced a breakthrough in communication ideas, particularly demonstrated by the work of Marshall McLuhan and Andy Warhol. The theater was far too reactionary to be touched by these ideas, and one had to look to painting, sculpture, pop music, and an occasional film to find the influence. The only playwrights into such postexistentialism attitudes are Beckett and Pinter, and the subject is discussed in the last entry, "The New Theater Is Here. Isn't It?"

The Backword that concludes this book marks, for me, the end of a critical cycle and the start of another. Things have stayed the same for a long time, but I don't think they can anymore.

MARTIN GOTTFRIED

New York City
April, 1969

What Is
Called a Think Piece

Critics Be Cute (*June 13, 1966*)

S OMETIMES it seems to me that being a drama critic is no fit job for an adult. The reason begins with the drama critic himself—a man who makes a living off the creative work of other people. How easy it is to sit back and react, one way or another, and then have an ego gratified by the printing of that reaction. How easy it is to say this was funny and that was not, this was well done and that was sloppy. How easy to criticize.

It is, after all, the playwright who did the writing and the director who moved it to the stage. It is, after all, the actor who gets up there and plays it and the supporting creative people who give it looks. They are the ones who did everything.

And the critic? A cheap parasite, satisfying himself in the guise of public service. Public service! He is a layman presuming to be an authority. He is a printed mouth, a writer with no subjects of his own, and usually a bad one. He is either callow or pompous, dull or phony, insensitive or touchy, uneducated or pedantic, ignorant about theater matters or misstruck with his own knowledgeability and completely unaware of theater realities. If I were a playwright I would have nothing but a long, long laugh for drama critics.

But if I were a playwright, I am afraid I would be as foolish as all the others. Playwrights are as silly a lot as critics. They are not vain, but wildly insecure, which may not be so offensive, but is just as absurd. Their idea of what should be on a stage has little in common with what can be on a stage. Their thinking is muddled when it isn't adolescent, their language uncertain and disorganized. They have no idea of what they want to write or how to write it. Their awareness of the possibilities of theater is practically nil. They will write one play and cry over its desecration during production, but they will not begin to learn how to write for the stage rather than for the typewriter. And when foolish critics don't like their work, they cry. They blame it on the directors, who misunderstood the play. If I were a director I would have nothing but a long, long laugh for playwrights.

But if I were a director, I would be embarrassed to be one. Directors are now fancying themselves more creative than playwrights. They believe that they are the ones who make the production, not the writers. Directors now involve themselves with points of view, trying to project their college-line politics into totally irrelevant plays. The older-fashioned ones don't, being too busy looking for psychological motivation and pranks to mask nonexistent plays. They all sit down, terribly seriously, and proceed to analyze a script they have never understood. They act out the roles of directors as played in movies. Then they act out the roles of each actor, since they consider themselves brilliant performers. They take themselves terribly seriously, and in most cases, the actors go their own ways anyhow. If I were an actor I would have nothing but a long, long laugh for directors.

But if I were an actor, I would really be in trouble. Actors are interested in things like makeup and costumes and wigs. They talk about art, they drop names (Shakespeare, Shaw; like that). What they really want is a sword. Everybody wants to pose, everybody wants to recite. The critics are busy talking about interpretation and subtlety, but the actors are thinking about everybody watching them and do they look the way they looked in the mirror last night. They take acting lessons so that they can come to class in turtlenecks and talk show business. They study movement and yoga and do crazy vocal exercises taught by crazy teachers. And they dote over their costumes and wigs and ask the lighting designer to make them look pretty. If I were a lighting designer I would have nothing but a long, long laugh for actors.

But then, if I were a lighting and scenic designer I would be slouching around feeling terribly superior about all theater matters. I would be smug about style and cohesion and consistency. I would read a paperback a month and tell everybody how much I knew about dramatic literature and theater construction. I would insist on scenes being played in certain ways so as not to interfere with the looks of my gorgeous designs. I would explain how a production's physical look most impresses the theatergoer. If I were an ordinary theatergoer I would have a long, long laugh for designers.

But then, if I were an ordinary theatergoer I would be spending my money on orchestra seats for a stupidly dated kind of theater and keep away from the new stage excitement. I would be confused by the plainest ideas, laugh at wrong moments, and miss all the good jokes. I would consider going to the theater a very big deal and not a natural habit. I would be afraid to really express my reactions and perhaps be too sterilized to even have any. So I would repeat what the stupid critics said in the first place.

Children, children all. What self-respecting man would spend his life attending to such people and the theater routine that is masquerading as theater? Being a drama critic is no fit job for an adult, it sometimes seems to me.

Art **Is** at the White House (*June 25, 1965*)

If it had not been for the genuine involvement with art that John F. Kennedy had projected during his brief Presidency, the "Festival of the Arts" that President Johnson organized last week would have been just another Cultural Comedy from Washington. Political taste in art has always been a joke, whether it was Franklin D. Roosevelt choosing "Home on the Range" as his favorite song or the Johnsons wiring their Vice Presidential home and ranch for Muzak.

President Kennedy spoiled us in many ways. For the first time, we knew what it was like to have somebody bright in the White House—somebody who was interested—somebody who would be worth talking to at a party. It was also the first time, at least in a long time (probably since Jefferson) that we had a President who was broadly educated enough, and with the expanded and refined taste, to appreciate the importance of art. Not just for the tremendous personal enrichment it provides but for the stature that it gives a country in the historical perspective.

After the long steps that Kennedy had taken toward publicly thriving on art, it was obvious that his successor would have no choice but to continue. President Johnson, of course, recognized the Kennedy popularity, especially as magnified by the assassination, and it was good politics to create a sense of continuity. And even if he gives you the feeling of not having the least interest in literature or music or the theater, you can assume that he considers them "important." (Anybody, anywhere, will agree that art is important. After all, it's culture.)

So this Festival of the Arts, which in one long day was supposed to advertise the value of art to the administration. And advertise it did (with all the hollow sincerity of advertising).

The arts are as valuable to Washington as a single day out of the year. The arts are as valuable to Washington as the lumping together of music and theater and poetry and fiction and dance into thirteen hours. The arts are as valuable to Washington as the playing of several scenes from several plays (What? Watch a whole play?).

And look at the plays that were chosen. Tennessee Williams' *The Glass Menagerie* and Arthur Miller's *Death of a Salesman* were written about twenty years ago, and Frank Gilroy's *The Subject Was Roses* could have been. The other selection, Millard Lampell's *Hard Travelin'*, was a boost for Washington's local Arena Stage. Were these selections to represent contemporary American drama—when Robert Lowell's *Benito Cereno,* produced this year—and of this year—was so current in content and style? (The fact that Lowell refused to attend the Festival because of disagreement with administration foreign policy would have made it all the more representative of present-day artists.)

Perhaps, you might say, it's just as well. The President had his day and will now leave art alone for the other three hundred and sixty-four. Let him think he paid homage. The idea of being paid homage could be taken as insulting, but why bother? Let the President think he is encouraging art. The idea of being encouraged is condescending, but why bother? We expect politicians to be philistines. And if they satisfy their middle-class longings to culture by the most superficial and least demanding means, aren't we degrading ourselves by getting excited about it?

Yes, that's true. But with the increasing participation of the government in indirect subsidy of the theater and other arts, the attitude of the President—and consequently, of lower-level government—becomes more and more significant. It is no longer a matter of a President having to consult his wife when a newspaper asks him what his favorite symphony is (and his wife says it's Brahms' Fifth). It is no longer a matter for snickering. Not when the government, say, can provide the funds for the building of a major regional theater.

Then we have two choices. We can patronize the President. Let him have his Festival and think it consequential; show him we admire his taste, his finesse, his awareness of art, even while we are wincing at not only his vulgarity but that of his advisers and of the many artists who suddenly forget their contempt and go running down to Washington at the first scent of a White House invitation.

Or we can start acting. Involvement is the rallying cry of our time and people are beginning to do something about situations they deplore rather than wisecrack over martinis. Not all Congressmen are anti-intellectuals, and those who are enlightened would act more boldly if they had voters pushing them.

Should President Johnson be allowed to satisfy himself with that ridiculous festival? And should the cause of art be left to artists who are snowed by "Presidential recognition"? And must the rest of us be left to snickering? Snickering gets you nowhere.

Where Have All Our Heroes Gone? (*March 25, 1966*)

You would think that the playwright who had found his artistic identity would be in fairly good condition. An artistic identity—a style, a way of writing, a mode—is the most crucial goal. And once found, with the overall shape of his work determined, the playwright can then search for a direction, settle down to the full development of that identity, go ever deeper into his discovery, and range over whatever matters excite him. In short, with the language learned, he could turn to the problem of what to say.

Unfortunately, things do not always work out so comfortably. The playwright who has found his way is not always con-

WHAT IS CALLED A THINK PIECE

tent with it. Especially when he finds, halfway through his career, that his way has begun to look a little dated.

The reaction is natural. It is, in its own way, the symptom of middle age. Convinced that we will always be young, we are shocked, one day, to find that we are not.

But if youth carries with it the excitement of today's new truths, middle age allows the rewards of maturing yesterday's. A bright idea is only a beginning and it must be tested and made wise before it can move into the mainstream of progress. If youth is for promise, middle age is for fulfillment.

The playwrights who were young at the beginning of World War II were intent upon bringing realism to the theater and applying it to important contemporary, social, and psychological problems. Now they should be perfecting that realism, applying a mature style to a mature view of the world.

These playwrights, however, are reluctant to fulfill that responsibility. Their eyes have been caught by the flash of tomorrow's theater—the abstract plays, the theater-for-its-own-sake plays, the plays that use the full forces (music, dance, mime, ritual) of the theater. And they try to adapt to it, sacrificing the hard-won discovery of their artistic identity in the process.

All terribly deep, but what is the point?

The point is that the middle-aged American playwrights are in serious trouble and our theater is suffering because of it. Look to Broadway drama and you will see nothing—a retired Lillian Hellman, an uncertain Arthur Miller, a bewildered Tennessee Williams, a defeated William Inge. Forgetting the identity they found years ago, they are trying to catch the beat of the newcomers. Have you ever watched a middle-aged couple frug?

Miss Hellman had developed a fine, personal, intelligent style of realistic playwriting about realistic problems in such plays as *The Little Foxes, The Children's Hour, Toys in the Attic*. They marked clear progress along a definite road. Suddenly, Miss Hellman abandoned her identity to take off with the abstractionists, writing *My Mother, My Father and Me,* an Ionesco-based play as awkward as only the work of a postgraduate sophomore can be.

Miller began somewhat later than Hellman, and was accordingly more advanced. His plays, while still realistic and devoted to social comment, were less restricted to conventional time sequences. Flashback and interwoven scenes were used comfortably and language was somewhat more poetic than Hellman's older stage realism (as opposed to "real realism"). Miller found his artistic identity somewhere between the writing of *All My Sons* and *Death of a Salesman* and began a steady growth that ended abruptly with *A View from the Bridge.* He did not write another play for ten years, and when he did, it was in a totally different style. *After the Fall* is a great play—there is no doubt of it—but it is troubling. Its manner was not really Miller's, and his next play, *Incident at Vichy,* marked a return to the old. That would have been heartening except that it was awful.

Tennessee Williams hit his stride in 1945, with the production of *The Glass Menagerie.* This was still newer playwriting, more inclined to poetry than Miller's and moving away from group problems toward the personal. With *A Streetcar Named Desire,* he began developing deeply, within that stride.

Then he, like Miller and Hellman, saw Genet, Ionesco, Beckett, and the wave of new theater rising behind him. Abandoning himself, he turned to the abstract, writing *The Milk Train Doesn't Stop Here Anymore* and the recent *Slapstick Tragedy,* both awkward and, still worse, craftless.

Finally, William Inge, who was concerned with people and the things of the theater. Realizing himself with *Come Back, Little Sheba,* he moved along a straight line through *Picnic* to the much unappreciated *Natural Affection.* Then he too left his style and wrote the dreadful *Where's Daddy?*

Maturity is the key to personal progress, as necessary to over-

24

all advancement as is youth. We cannot do without either. The theater's future is dependent upon the young, but what good is the future if there is no present?

This Man Is Sick (*August 12, 1966*)

Lenny Bruce died on August 3 and that has nothing to do with the American theater. The trouble *is* that it had nothing to do with the American theater, because it *should* have. But since accepted culture in America is neatly insulated from any kind of reality, the terrible reality of Bruce's tragedy must be outside of it. The theater, like art and music and literature, is maintained by and for "nice" people who have their culture packaged and produced in neat little bundles that keep to the standards of what-to-say and how-to-say-it so as not to seriously arouse any kind of honest passions. Once those passions are aroused, American culture will very quickly show its true colors, resenting and destroying whoever dared to (heaven help him) be himself.

Lenny Bruce was a comedian who followed the wrong circuit. Starting where most comedians start—on the training grounds of the Catskill Mountains—he worked his natural comic sense along with such other beginners as Buddy Hackett and Alan King. But somehow, he didn't move with them, although the styles, material, and deliveries were not dissimilar. Hackett grew popular and developed himself as a self-deprecating little boy. King grew popular and worked out a standing theme of suburban monology. Bruce floundered.

At about that time (the late fifties), a group of comedians moved away from the pasty-faced, juvenile American style of wisecracks into areas that had some relationship to reality. They were called "sick comedians"—a typical American attitude—we call anything strange "sick," and nothing is stranger to America than a dose of the truth. Among them were Mort Sahl (dealing with politics), Shelley Berman (dealing with personal emotions), Jonathan Winters (dealing with the irrational and absurd).

Bruce decided that this was a good trend to latch on to and switched his material from the standard Hackett-King business to the matters of religion, literature, politics, and morals that occupied the intellectual comics. Unlike Sahl and Berman, he had never been an intellectual (self-styled or otherwise). He was show business and pure entertainer, just looking for a gimmick. And because of his straight-comic orientation, he was the most successful of all at combining serious material with humor. In fact, Bruce was hilarious, and really nowhere near as intellectual as many of his supporters would have you believe.

He moved ever more deeply into material concerning the church, sex, and justice. He bombarded official religion, phony heroism, superficial morality. American hypocrisy is at its most hateful in these areas, and the hypocrite will accept anything but revelation. Bruce, though hardly intelligent about such matters, was hysterically funny and deadly honest. He would not be put up with.

So America murdered him. The excuse was the accusation of narcotics addiction. I am not aware of whether or not Bruce was an addict and I really don't care. I don't intend to discuss that problem. But it seems to me that the massive deprival of his right to work was not justifiable for any reason. Bruce was arrested in at least five states, and nightclub owners became fearful of being closed by the police. Bruce was accused of using obscenity (in fact, when he was "obscene" it was usually in mimicry of small-time vulgarity. In personal attitude he was infinitely "cleaner" than most comedians on regular television). At his peak, in 1960, he earned $100,000 a year. Last year his income was $2,000.

He was found dead, "apparently" of an overdose of narcotics.

26

His friend blamed it on "an overdose of police." I don't know how much of my own humor is drawn from his. I don't know how many rich, wild, true laughs he has given me. I don't know how strongly my idea of the best theater comedy to come is based on his freewheeling, sure-entertainer sense of the ridiculous. And I don't know how I will ever be able to steal his material again.

The overdose may have been of narcotics. It certainly was of police and a vicious use of law. But more completely, it was an overdose of America—American untruth, immorality, hatred, and genuine obscenity of attitude. The shame is not that he was only forty years old but that his murder shows the kind of sickening soil in which American culture is supposed to grow. You cool it too, sweetie.

Ego Trip (February 10, 1967)

Time for soul-cleansing. I have made a number of factual errors in reviewing plays, and as they accumulate they disturb the sleep, jangle the nerves, and make life, if not impossible, difficult. So it is time to admit them, and if Freud is right, all will be well.

But before going any further, you should be warned that errors of judgment shall not be included. This is only because they do not exist. I never make errors of judgment, and as my father says, even when I do I don't. So do not expect me to say oh—my—God, *Sooner or Later* was really terrific and how could I have been so stupid? Will never happen. If I said *Sooner or Later* was terrible, it better well have been terrible.

The worst mistake I think I ever made was in admiring the pictures that Larry Rivers painted for the set of LeRoi Jones' *The Slave*. Mr. Rivers, of course, is a well-known artist, and I,

27

of course, think I know a good deal about art when in fact I know very little. So there was the set and there were the pictures and I thought they were fine and said so.

But the play was a bitter mockery of West Side New York white liberals, and Mr. Rivers' paintings—as he later explained —were the kinds of pictures that such people would hang. They were not in his style at all but were parodies of Franz Kline black-and-white abstractions.

Once Rivers said this, the point of the pictures was plain enough. A very race-conscious white liberal would naturally hang black-and-white abstractions to advertise his commitment to interracism. The joke was Rivers' and it went over my head. The point: If you don't know about something, don't talk about it.

Another mistake was made in reviewing *Man of La Mancha,* when I gave Robert Rounseville credit for his splendid baritone. Mr. Rounseville does indeed have a fine voice, only it isn't a baritone. It is a tenor. The strangest thing about this is that every time I have reviewed a Rounseville performance, I have complimented him on that excellent baritone. And with each compliment has come a correcting letter.

In any case, the *La Mancha* correction came in a bitchy letter from its author, and the thing that killed me was that while his script remained skimpy and pretentious, there he was, armed with my mistakes, irrelevant though they were. He could (and did) accuse me of having a "tin ear" and, obviously, he was right.

There was another error in that *La Mancha* review that its author gleefully leaped upon, and that was a misquoted line. As it happens, I really hadn't badly misquoted him and could have furnished him with a half dozen (well, maybe one or two) of my other reviews in which I had superbly botched a quote.

But those really shouldn't be considered errors. Certainly it is not a producer's problem to provide writing light for a scribbling critic, but if you prefer to avoid little flashlights in the dark, note-taking can be a perilous business. And too often there is that very criticlike dash into the office; the preparatory ritual (off with the jacket, roll up the sleeves, loosen the tie, roll in the paper, spread out the program, light the cigarette); and then the flipping open of the notebook to find absolutely illegible notes looking out like the crazed scrawlings of a backward chimpanzee on a very rainy night. Well, you've got to have a quote. Can't keep saying, oh, the jokes were ridiculous, oh, the lines were ridiculous. *Demonstrate.* So the notes are tilted, swiveled, held to the light until, my goodness, that's what it is. Only it isn't, as the playwright bitterly points out in an unprintable letter a couple of days later.

Okay, so much for misquotes. They're lucky if they get anything right? But what about saying that Jill Haworth (*Cabaret*) could barely manage the beginnings of an English accent and then going home to read the program and learn that she grew up in London? Rationalization time. Couldn't she grow up in London and have a bad-imitation English accent? Couldn't she have lost it? Afraid not.

Then, of course, there are the name mistakes. Running on for 70 inches about how great this performance was: really something to remember, extraordinary projection. And then crediting it to the wrong actor. Or even putting the star of last year's Broadway musical into this year's off-Broadway play. I must say, no kidding, that this is no fun for the actor whose review is fouled up. A review means a great deal to any performer, just as a personal, career thing, and it is nothing to be careless with.

Nor is a review anything to be careless with, in general. It is very easy to pass a glib opinion. Very easy. But it had better be substantiated; and if there are any mistakes, they had better be corrected. More than that, they had better not be made in the first place. The theater is a serious business, and criticism is (or should be) an important part of it. If a drama critic is sloppy enough to commit factual errors, he has no business writing criticism. An opinion is worthless if it is based on a foundation of misapprehensions, misquotes, and miscredits. It is easy to be cute about it, but don't let glibness disguise the truth. Standards for critical accuracy must be stringent and merciless, and without them the criticism collapses.

In the Cause of Trash *(February 17, 1967)*

Last weekend, for reasons too complicated and meaningless to explain, I saw the final preview instead of the opening night performance of a dreadful little comedy called *The Paisley Convertible* and was very much struck by the obvious enjoyment with which most of the audience received it. It is pertinent that this was a preview performance because the laughter could not be explained away as that of backers, relatives, friends, and hit-hungry first-nighters. No, the pleasure was legitimate.

Now my point is, if such theater is enjoyed by an appreciable number of people: (a) is it not genuine theater and (b) is there any reason why it should not exist?

To the first point, what is "genuine" theater? Is it only the artistic? Is it only whatever achieves what it attempts? Does it somehow rule out the productions that are strictly commerce-geared?

Or is it any theater at all—from the artful to the cheap? Is it anything that appears on a stage?

Let me make one thing clear. There is no discussing the value of *The Paisley Convertible*. It is a play only in the sense that it is based on a script, it is on a stage, it is set before scenery, and it uses actors. It is little different from *Love in E-Flat*, another paper bag that opened a couple of days later.

30

But aren't its stage, its scenery, its actors, its script, enough to qualify it as theater, genuine or otherwise? The limitation of "theater" to particular qualities, particular purposes, particular methods, particular kinds of productions, is an artificial one. *The Paisley Convertible* and *Love in E-Flat* are boring, foolish and wasteful, but they *are* plays.

Now, accepting that, what is to be done about it? Invariably, every critic jumps down on them for what they are (I suppose jumping down a little clumsily on what, after all, is a rather puny target). This is fair enough. More than that, necessary. A critic must always write from his own point of view, judging according to his own taste. And because there is a direct relationship between reviews and ticket demand, these plays almost always close (the exceptions come with a drawing card who appeals to people who do not ordinarily go to the theater—for example, Alan King in *The Impossible Years*. I might add that after King left, word of mouth kept it running to the presumable delight of other audiences).

But *should* they close? Think about all those people who would have enjoyed the plays just as the preview audiences had. This is theater for them. They aren't interested in the important, the artistic, the deeply exciting—they really aren't. Perhaps they never will be. But here is something that they would honestly enjoy. Why can't it exist for them?

The head of a major network once said, in an exceptionally honest outburst, that the vast majority of television programs may be pap as far as intellectuals are concerned but they are what most people in America like. Why shouldn't TV programming be geared to majority taste? I think that in a sense he was right—they are indeed what most people like and that is why most people watch them. Of course, this is dictatorship by the lowest public sensibility and the program level is doomed to be dragged ever downward. Nor is there anything produced for the fractional but still large numbers of educated people.

But in the theater the situation is quite different. There, the dictatorship is by middle-brow taste. If there is TV-level trash, it will be panned and will close.

Why shouldn't there be low-level theater too? I mean plain trash. I know this sounds as if I am arguing for the perseverance of the worthless and in a sense that is true, but I see no reason to deny *any* kind of theater the right to exist. Or the privilege of any audience to enjoy it.

If a theater critic has to be honest and the plays are terrible, and no customers come because of his review, what can be done about it? Obviously, nobody will read a bad review and conclude that he has worse taste than the critic. Moreover, most of the people who would enjoy these plays are not even review readers in the first place.

Well, getting the customer in is not my problem but the producer's. I think, though, that it is a problem he should try to solve as long as he is going to produce plays like *The Paisley Convertible, Love in E-Flat,* or whatever. Knowing as he does that these comedies regularly please summer-stock audiences before or after they open-close on Broadway, he should make it his business to hustle them in. Summer audiences *do* live in the city during the winter.

Too, there is a vast audience, in New York and across the country, that never gets anywhere *near* a theater. It just assumes that the theater is not its kind, putting it in the same class with concerts, ballet, museums, and opera. This audience would legitimately enjoy terrible plays, the worse the better.

But these plays close. And producers speak of "enlightening" the public. This is a terrible, smug, and basically unknowing condescension. Perhaps these people will one day be "enlightened," playground productions of *commedia dell' arte* notwithstanding, but meanwhile they are not even getting what they would *like*. At least TV gives them *something*.

My point, then, is that any kind of theater is genuine theater and that even the worst not only has the right to exist but is capable of providing real stage pleasure for many people. If TV offers only the worst, why should the theater offer (or at least presume to offer) only the best?

Straight and Crooked Plays (*March 3, 1967*)

Unbelievable as it may seem, there is not a single American play presently on Broadway. Under such circumstances, one cannot say that American drama under New York's commercial system is in trouble. American drama under New York's commercial system, as a point of fact, does not exist at all.

Being reasonable people, cultured, earnest, and concerned, we must ask two questions of this situation: Why has it occurred? What can be done about it?

The reason there is no American drama on Broadway today is as obvious as the last play that opened (and immediately closed) there—Arnold Sundgaard's *Of Love Remembered,* Mr. Sundgaard might well have written it thirty years ago. It is a story-play in the naturalist style, not very different from those Ibsen wrote in revolution against the artifice that dominated turn-of-the-century European theater. Its climaxes are basic melodrama (revelation, suicide) and its characters plot-following and bland. There isn't much point in elaborating on such a play, but its production on Broadway exemplifies the reactionary taste that has controlled and murdered American drama there.

Since producers and not directors select the productions for Broadway, the dominating taste is bound to be in the artistic right wing. New York's producers are still tied to realistic, story, message orientation, and it is such plays that they seek. But most younger playwrights have long since abandoned this style and there are ever fewer plays for such producers to consider. On the other side of the footlights (to use the Great White Way phrase), the audiences for such plays have almost entirely disappeared. Who is interested in dusty theater? Perhaps the hard core of post-middle-aged, but few others. The dynamic, restless, *necessary* theater audience—students, intellectuals, activators—has long since abandoned such plays for the more on-their-level medium of today's movies.

So between old-fashioned producers, disappearing playwrights, and uninterested audiences, how could there possibly be a continuation of such theater? There couldn't be and it is disappearing.

Yet plays are being written. A resident theater director told me the other night that if he were in a shack on the top of a mountain, 50 miles from the nearest neighbor, and were to open a window and whisper, "I am interested in new plays," a dozen scripts would arrive in the morning mail.

Grant, as he did, that most, if not all, of these scripts would be hopelessly amateur; it remains that they were written, and there are places for the best of them to be produced.

The American Place Theater is one of the most important producers for the new plays too modern for Broadway (one of its greatest successes, Robert Lowell's *Benito Cereno,* was rejected by every leading producer, from the Repertory Theater of Lincoln Center down—or up). Barr-Wilder-Albee have long struggled alone in the cause of modern American drama. Now the resident theaters across the country are expanding their outlook to include at least one new play within the program of classics. In almost every case, these theaters look for the advanced-taste plays that Broadway rejects.

American drama away from Broadway, then, is not dead. Today there is more to American theater than Shubert Alley. But it seems to me that playwrights have always been represented by their country's commercial theater, and should always be.

For thriving American drama, there must be thriving New

34

York, commercial, Broadway drama. New York is the country's cultural center of gravity, and the commercial, Broadway stage is the big-time, big-money, big-talent place for theater. No matter how desperately theater left-wingers fight it, Broadway theater is mainstream theater. It is what our theater is to the world and to history. And if there is no American drama on Broadway, then in a real, if not literal, sense there is no American drama at all.

What Broadway *must* do, if it is to survive as a place for American drama, is adjust its taste to reflect today. There is no sense in producing family, psychological, realistic dramas in a world that has grown to look at itself through modern, imaginative, knowing eyes. The world of art is moving rapidly through innovations, trends, and excitements. Composers are experimenting with various techniques and schemes. Writers of fiction have long since absorbed the discoveries of Proust and Joyce. Nonfiction is off on an adventure of its own. Movies are going in a dozen directions with geniuses like Bergman and Fellini leading the way. Here is a bold, very mod-pop film like Antonioni's *Blow-Up* exciting moviegoers across the country (although personally I found it impossible), and Broadway drama is still messing around with Sundgaard's *Of Love Remembered*.

Heaven knows, there are many who would be going to the theater if the theater were on their level. In the eighteen-to-twenty-five age group alone there are bright, knowledgeable people with interest and money enough to support Broadway plays. Sometimes you will even *find* them in a theater—at least when there is the occasional, modern work. At a *Marat/Sade*. At previews for a new Albee play. For something pertinent-sounding like *MacBird* or *Viet Rock*. At the off-off Broadway coffee shops, experimental theater clubs, and burgeoning church theaters. At something as new-styled as *America Hurrah* or Pinter's *The Homecoming*.

But too often they do not even hear about the very things that would excite them. *The Rimers of Eldritch,* an extremely

artistic and fresh approach to small-town America, is lan-
guishing at the Cherry Lane. Tom Sankey's *The Golden Screw*,
a devastating parody of the Bob Dylan career that viciously attacks slick America through folk-rock music, is probably going
to have to close at the Provincetown Playhouse.

The failure of such valuable plays is the price New York is
paying for its ultraconservatism. It is a price that has already
grown steep and will be exorbitant before some kind of modernity is finally bought.

I suppose it is possible that it will *never* be bought and that
reactionaries will drag Broadway theater down into chaos and
suicide. I don't think so. There is too much obvious ferment.
But the longer Broadway waits, the more unreachable its audiences will grow. New York's drama future is in a race against
time.

Sex Without Fear (*March 17, 1967*)

For all its dependence on sex for comedy, the theater is as se-
cretive about the reality of the subject as the rest of this country
seems to be. There is talk, talk, talk; joke, joke, joke. But just
as the American sex world around us, whether in books, on
bathroom walls, or in conversations, is only a nervous imitation
of the real thing, so our theater talks about sex, alludes to it,
even pretends to deal with it, when actually it is having absolutely nothing to do with it.

What reminds me of this strange and long-running situation
is the Robert Anderson quartet of one-act plays that opened
earlier this week under the overall title *I Can't Hear You
When the Water's Running*. As an evening of theater, Mr. Anderson's is quite good, even though it is rather old-fashioned,

but that is not my concern at the moment. My concern is with the general sexual attitude that Anderson's plays represent.

It is an attitude of easygoing romance. An attitude that resents sexual freedom as being a rationalization for promiscuity. An attitude that criticizes sexual education as sterilizing. An attitude that yearns for the Good Old Days when sex was just a little dirty and all brides were virgins and boys would masturbate in secrecy and there were no birth control pills.

Superficially, this attitude can be appealing, especially because Anderson presents it with theater coloration. In one playlet, a playwright-character who argues for sexual frankness on the stage blushes when four-letter words are used. In another, a mother who is eager to give her children a modern sexual education is treated as cold-blooded and destructive. Her willingness to understand a husband's infidelity is considered anti-love. In still another of the playlets, Anderson mocks the importance of sex in a vaudeville sketch about a senile couple.

But although these short plays seem to be wise, they are really only "wise"—fraudulent imitations of good sense, disguising a defense of Victorian values as naturalness. Sexual frankness on the stage is desired not, as Anderson says, by hypocritical playwrights but by adult ones. Modern sexual attitudes are not cold-blooded, as Anderson suggests, but intelligent. They do not sterilize romance but allow it.

It is perfectly true that some people are overeager to be liberal and that in their haste to educate they press to the point of harangue, overlooking the sexual joys that prompted the education in the first place. But their fault lies in excess and misuse, not in the idea of release from stupid taboos and ignorance.

Yet, for all its backwardness, the Anderson work is dealing with sex. Or is it? Where is the sex in these plays? In a cheap little joke about the size of a man's buttocks? ("You don't drive a spike with a tack hammer.") In discussions about sex education? In fact, Anderson is talking about sex in exactly the same style as it was talked about on fifties Broadway, when message theater had turned from social to moral reform. When plays like Anderson's own *Tea and Sympathy* lectured heavily on homosexuality (with the same simplistic point of view as his current one). When Tennessee Williams was preaching the virtues of honest lust (*The Rose Tattoo*).

But if such plays are old-fashioned, what has replaced them?

On occasion I have seen sex used freely on a stage. In a brilliant production of Genet's *The Balcony,* the Hartford Stage Company began the production by having the whore-altar boy strip to the waist and reveal her breasts. In a later scene, a self-castration was performed with shocking realism (within the play's extravagant style). These sequences were absolutely in keeping with the needs of the work and they were tremendously effective.

Nor was the Hartford audience offended. It was, as a matter of fact, conditioned to the artistic adventurousness of this very fine company and accepted the production on its true level. Nevertheless, a New York producer told me that he would not bring in the Hartford *Balcony* because it was "too dirty," and his is the ruling attitude in our presumably adult theater.

Other directors have also felt free to properly use sex in productions that called for it. But these situations are few. More often, a scene blacks out when eroticism is supposed to begin. We may be told that a couple is passionately in love but there is never a hand on a breast, a thigh, a belly, let alone real—or stylized—lovemaking. For all its bravado about sex, the theater is still so shy about it that there is all but an outright denial that it even exists. Only the usual cheap, leering flash of chorus girl bosoms, street-corner humor, and perhaps an opening scene with a couple in bed. But what happens in that bed? By the time we see it everything has either happened or never will.

So now off-off Broadway is having a stage party with all sorts of splashy sex effects while the rest of our theater is still giving well-meaning old lady sex lectures and pretending that lovers kiss when they get terribly excited. Something strange somewhere.

Art Is Off-Broadway (*March 24, 1967*)

There is talk of off-Broadway's rebirth and I am afraid that some people are beginning to believe it. I suppose there is no harm in believing it, but the sadness is that there is no truth in the talk. Off-Broadway died five years ago, and for all the successful productions there this season and last they are nearly all conservative, old-fashioned, and junior-Broadway. Remembering what off-Broadway once had been, it is very depressing.

What off-Broadway had been was a haven for theatergoers who were bored with the backwardness of uptown, were eager for a little adventure, and would put up with chilly theaters and simple scenery in exchange for adventure and a lower price scale.

It was a good combination, and through the late fifties and early sixties off-Broadway served an important function. It was the heyday of the original Circle in the Square with its brilliant productions of *The Iceman Cometh* and *Summer and Smoke*; the place for a thriving, classical art theater at the downtown Phoenix; the springboard for such talented actors as Geraldine Page and Jason Robards. The plays of Beckett, Ionesco, Genet, and Pinter were being introduced to New York. And there was a sense of excitement. Nor was any apology needed for its quality. The quality, in fact, was often first-rate, and even during the peak production years, with a hundred or so openings in a single season, the proportion of the worthwhile to the worthless was not bad at all.

Then the collapse came. Most off-Broadway producers blamed it on the unions, which had been raising their demands with the increasing success of these theaters. It was a debatable point. Even today, the off-Broadway actor is paid little more than the unemployment insurance rate. Just because acting isn't merely a job doesn't mean that an actor shouldn't receive reasonable pay. Moreover, the off-Broadway producers were not investing their money only for art's sake. They were in it for profit and their employees should have shared in it.

In any case, even with the rising union demands, the producers managed to cut corners. Some actors were asked to kick back part of their salaries. Some producers did not list all of their employees, saving money on Social Security and other contributory payments. Still the costs grew higher and plays that cost $7,500 to produce in 1959 were running close to $25,000 seven years later. With the financial investment greater and the risks riskier, the producers grew wary, avoiding the more extreme of styles and contents. Productions of the avant-gardists became less frequent. Except for a brief revival of *The Maids,* Genet hasn't been produced in New York in four years. None of Ionesco's newer plays has been done and, for that matter, none of the staples either, over the last few years. The Phoenix folded, a tragic death unpleasantly but successfully disguised as a merger with the APA (a "merger" that meant the Phoenix's complete dissolution).

Since then, off-Broadway has gone steadily downhill. The number of yearly productions has been sliced by more than half. More disastrously, the *kind* of play done there has grown fat and flabby. Avant-gardists are practically never produced. The improvisational revues have disappeared. In their places are realistic dramas, book musicals, and novelties, all devised in Broadway's right-wing style.

Just look at what is running now off-Broadway, presumably contributing to its renascence. The daddy hit is the generally clever *The Fantasticks,* an enormous seven-year success and a leftover from the Good Old Days. But long-running are such doilies as *Hogan's Goat,* the unbelievably melodramatic William Alfred play that could well have been written sixty years ago, and *The Pocket Watch,* a tacky little soap opera, and *The Mad Show,* a mildly amusing revue in the style of about a hundred others running in and out of the cafés. All right, that's last year.

But look what's happening *this year.* The biggest success is *You're a Good Man, Charlie Brown,* a coy, childlike thing following the "Peanuts" cartoon aspirations to the philosophical-sensitive. *Eh?* is an English import with not only the look but, unfortunately, also the content of mod thinking patterns. Both *Fortune and Men's Eyes* and *Hamp* are old-fashioned message plays, one pleading for prison reform, the other for military reform. *By Jupiter* and *Man with a Load of Mischief* are book musicals, the former a revival. They are all running strong.

But are they what should be off-Broadway? Well, that isn't so easy a question to answer. Off-Broadway isn't "for" anything, and theater is theater. Whatever the purposes, values, and satisfactions of these productions, they are stage works and it would be foolish to deny their right to exist. But there was something important that off-Broadway had been providing—something that the commercial pressures on Broadway forbade. And it is no longer there.

Well, just about. *America Hurrah* is indeed playing off-Broadway and it is one of the most exciting theater events in many seasons. *MacBird,* however silly, still represents a fighting minority point of view and that is a very important thing to have around.

By and large, though, the role that off-Broadway assumed five years ago is now being performed by off-off Broadway, and although those theaters are far more prolific than off-Broadway ever was they are also far more amateur. Whereas the theatergoer once had a fairly reasonable choice of either the superprofessionalism of Broadway or the reasonable polish of off-Broadway he now has only the coffee shop amateurs to turn to.

It is an unfair choice to demand, and there is a real theater need for more off-Broadway adventure. But being eager for it must not lead to seeing it where it doesn't exist. Off-Broadway is very active these days, and that is good, but it is also very conservative these days, and that is bad.

Now Starring (*January 19, 1968*)

Last summer at the Shakespearean Festival in Stratford, Ontario, I called Zoe Caldwell—then preparing to open in *Antony and Cleopatra*—and asked if she'd like to meet me for a drink. We had met once before when I had been sitting in on classes at the American Conservatory Theatre, and Miss Caldwell said sure, fine, she'd be right over. The next thing I knew, a pink Jeep with a pink-and-white striped canopy was tearing onto the motel's gravel driveway and came screeching up to my door with the whole car almost leaning backward while braking, the way they do in movie cartoons. Caldwell hopped out, rapped at the door, and then flopped into a chair with a glass of straight gin. For sheer vitality, personal charm, good humor, snappy intelligence, and general vivacity, I have never met any actress her equal.

The same may go for her acting ability. Certainly, Zoe Caldwell is one of the finest actresses I have ever seen anywhere, with perhaps only Rosemary Harris and Irene Worth her peers in the United States. And yet most of you probably never heard of her until the wonderful reviews she is just now getting for *The Prime of Miss Jean Brodie*. Those of you who knew about her before might have caught her as Anne Bancroft's replacement in *The Devils,* or two seasons ago in Tennessee Williams' short-lived *Slapstick Tragedy*.

But Miss Caldwell was a brilliant actress long before *The*

Devils. Not merely a potentially great actress and not merely one "almost ready." Her reputation ranked high among resident theater directors when she first joined the Minnesota Theatre Company, and her *Mother Courage* with Canada's Manitoba Theatre Centre remains legendary. When I first saw her, doing Brecht's *Caucasian Chalk Circle* in Minneapolis, I was stunned by her sensitivity, discipline, and stage power as the peasant Grusha. To find her the next day as the elegant Mistress Millament in Congreve's *Way of the World* was nothing less than staggering. In the space of a single day, Caldwell had gone from straw-bundle determination to lily-fingered finesse.

Even then, though formidably talented and with a healthy chunk of the theater's important female roles under her belt, Miss Caldwell was unknown. And by "unknown" I mean unknown to the general public. She was unknown because she had not played Broadway, and Broadway stardom is the only way to become a great actress in the strange theater America.

Now there is another curiosity here. "Great actress" in this famous-Broadway sense does not mean great actress in any meaningful sense. By the Broadway-fame standard, Geraldine Page is a great actress. And Kim Stanley is a great actress. And Anne Bancroft is a great actress. Of course, none of them is. None of them has ever been able to play anybody but herself. None of them has worked regularly with the theater literature. Zoe Caldwell was a great actress years ago. Now she is a great actress in this Broadway sense.

Now you might ask, "Who needs it?" Well, for a long time Caldwell didn't. She was content to go where the theater challenge was, whether a Midwestern resident company, a Bernard Shaw festival in Niagara Falls, or a chance to do Cleopatra to Christopher Plummer's Antony in Canada. There was no sense accepting a trashy role in a trashy play just for the sake of playing Broadway.

But Caldwell is human too, and why not a little fame, even a

43

little fortune? If American standards for acting greatness demand Broadway appearances and raves from the New York critics, well, then sooner or later an actress' idealism is going to be broken down. I'm not suggesting that *The Prime of Miss Jean Brodie* is commerical hackwork beneath Miss Caldwell's dignity. It is a play with faults, but it is quite serious and has some very nice writing. More to the point, it is as splendid a vehicle for a virtuoso actress as anything I have seen in a long, long time. It was a plum for Vanessa Redgrave when she played it in London and it is a plum for Caldwell now. As *Brodie* catapulted Redgrave to international stardom, so it may do for Caldwell.

But what, really, *would* that do for Caldwell? What, really, did it do for Redgrave? Now she is a Big Star and makes piles of money. But doing what? A big, gloppy, soggy, and nauseating movie like *Camelot*?

I doubt that this sort of thing could happen to Zoe Caldwell. Her commitment to serious theater has been over too long a period, and has demanded too much involvement and training and, that's right, sheer dedication, to be tossed away for plastic glory. Yet one could say the same for Christopher Plummer, and there he is doing *The Sound of Music,* complaining about it, and then signing up for other, equally obnoxious money jobs.

Well, all of this is terribly wrong. What can our theater be if its definition of acting greatness is pinned to the commercial theater and plays that demand very little genuine acting? How can anyone be impressed by an actress who is seen only occasionally and in roles that demand only her own personality? How can an actress become great, or even good, when her work is sporadic and she is not faced with the challenge of different characters, different styles, different methods? And why should an actress even *try* to become very, very good when she will remain unnoticed and underpaid? Anybody who acts needs attention and recognition. Dedication and seriousness will take you only so far. Zoe Caldwell went as far as anybody could go and remained virtually unknown until a Broadway opening night. She won a Tony award for that—not for her Brecht, her Shakespeare, her Molière, but for a *Tennessee Williams disaster*.

Now she is winning acclaim for *The Prime of Miss Jean Brodie*, and I concede the acclaim is deserved. The title role is not only long but it is really the entire play, since Jay Allen's script is a biographical study (of a fictitious character) with its supporting characters just scenery. It provides plenty of space for interpretation, and a comparison of the Redgrave and Caldwell characterizations shows just how much space. Redgrave played Brodie as a magnificent person, victimized by a world too real for her romance. Caldwell's Brodie is as ridiculous as she is wonderful, as destructive as she is inspiring. Two fine actresses, two fine performances. But if Caldwell doesn't go the way of Redgrave, will she ever return to the serious stage? And, more important, will our standards for acting recognition remain foolishly tied to a kind of theater that almost never challenges an actor? Caldwell deserves her applause, but I hope she doesn't forget what genuine theater and acting really are.

Albee

The Ballad of the Sad Café (October 31, 1963)

CARSON MC CULLERS' novella *The Ballad of the Sad Café* is a weird story of lovers and beloveds, the deformed and the miserable. It is both beautiful and grotesque, a small masterpiece exquisitely written in a mysterious and strange style.

Edward Albee's adaptation of the long story opened last night at the Martin Beck, enormously faithful to the book but oddly lacking in power or involvement. Nevertheless, it is intriguing and even fascinating, and was presented in a well near perfect production, studded with first-rate performances and perfectly directed.

The most serious question it poses, really, is just where Mr. Albee stands as an American dramatist. Prematurely eminent with a body of work that includes only one full-length play and several one-acters, Mr. Albee faced a real test with *Ballad*. We'll come back to that later.

The Ballad of the Sad Café is set in a tiny and dreary Southern town where the very masculine Amelia Evans has been running a successful general store. Aggressive and alone, she repels all friendship until Lymon, a dwarf, comes into town, claiming

49

to be her cousin. And shocking the town, she takes him into her home—in an emotional sense he becomes her lover. And she gives him the love she never had given before.

The dwarf, taking this love, changes from a miserable and lonely grotesque to a cocky and happy little rooster. And then Miss Evans' husband returns. Here is the third side of the triangle. Amelia had married Marvin Macy only to reject him. They stayed together just ten days, never consummating the marriage, and with his love scorned he deserted her, becoming a criminal and winding up in prison.

With Marvin's return, the dwarf finds someone to give *his* love to. And so there they are—three people giving themselves only to find themselves rejected. Each grotesque in his own way —the woman defeminized, the husband emasculated, and the dwarf deformed. Or, if you like, the dominating woman, the dominated man, and their offspring, the love-cripple. A trio you will find in almost any Albee play.

The climax of this two-hour, one-act play is a fight between Amelia and Marvin over Lymon—a fight that, in its preparation, brings the play to the very brink of excitement. But here it falls down—the physical culmination of the emotional fury is not the hysterical and sexual tour de force it should have been. And it is representative of the play, which, simply, is not especially theatrical.

You may be able to blame director Alan Schneider for mishandling that big fight, but responsibility for the general episode's untheatricality rests at the feet of Mr. Albee. As for his actors, Colleen Dewhurst is superb as Amelia—although her essential femininity kept shining through despite the short hair, the hunting boots, and the jeans. Lou Antonio was strong as Marvin Macy. But it was Michael Dunn, as Cousin Lymon, who created as fantastic a character as you're going to see on the New York stage all season long.

Mr. Dunn, who is somewhere between three and four feet high, hops and swings about like a crazy little lovebird, screaming and yelping, parading and preening. And in his scenes with Mr. Antonio he brought a sorely needed electricity to the Martin Beck stage.

Mr. Albee has written this role—and remember, the original novella had minimal dialogue—with an enormous sympathy, a sudden understanding. Marvin Macy, too, was obviously felt. But not Amelia. As in all of his plays, Mr. Albee shows a complete unawareness of the female personality.

Returning to his status as an American dramatist, one must wonder just how much he added to Mrs. McCullers' book in this adaptation. Its fidelity—except for the loss of a believable Amelia—makes you wonder just how much of an artist he is. His dialogue is commonplace—his reputation must be held in abeyance.

As for the play, it is an interesting, provocative, and most unusual thing, exquisitely performed. If it is not especially moving, or especially theatrical—well, that is its very serious flaw.

Tiny Alice (*December 30, 1964*)

Edward Albee's *Tiny Alice* is at once extraordinary and ridiculous. The new play that opened last night at the Billy Rose Theatre wriggled and slipped through an assortment of philosophical pretensions as disorganized as a student notebook. But despite the befuddled profundity and because of the strange drive of Mr. Albee, *Tiny Alice* is a play of exhilarating theatricality.

It is about, first of all, Woman, the arch-villain of every Albee play, and in this case, nothing short of the Virgin Mary, as transposed into the world's richest woman. If you like, you can also read the Virgin Mary as Mother Church—in either case the seducer of the innocent, the murderess of the pure.

On the simple plot level, "Miss Alice" has decided to grant the Catholic Church $100,000,000 a year for twenty years (in a rather supercilious aside, it is mentioned that similar grants are also being given "Protestants, Jews, universities, orchestras, revolutions here and there"). The price for this grant, it is subsequently divulged, is Julian, a cardinal's secretary, who is a lay brother, sworn to celibacy but not committed to the priesthood. It is a foolish premise. The play, basically, is the murderous seduction of Julian by Alice, abetted by her sinister conspirators, a lawyer and a butler. It is, in short, a symbolic crucifixion, with Julian acting as both God (the lover of Mary) and Jesus.

Before getting on, notice the standard Albee figures. The dominating woman (Alice), the weak, subjugated man (combined in the cardinal, the butler, and the lawyer), and the pathetic, loveless, sacrificial offspring (of course, Julian). It is Albee, once more blaming vicious womankind for murdering the tenderness of men. And in this case, even more than in *Virginia Woolf* and *Ballad of the Sad Café,* tenderness of man is equated with homosexuality. Once again, an Albee play is all about homosexuality without once actually alluding to it.

Tiny Alice is also involved with the favorite plaything of the intellectual pretender—reality as opposed to illusion. The massive and stunning library set that William Ritman designed is dominated by a large-scale model of the palace in which the library is.

In a variation on a standard illusion, Albee tells us that the model is an exact replica, inside and out, of the palace, and in the library of the model there is a replica of the model.

It is an old idea that sounds a great deal more profound than it is. In this case it is used as a symbol for the reality problem that is being related to the faith problem. Julian has never been sure of his faith, and at one time committed himself to a mental institution for six years to ponder the question. He came away believing, "My faith—my sanity—they are one and the same," not knowing whether he had either. He also did not know whether he had had relations with a woman who believed herself to be the Virgin Mary or whether he imagined it. (The woman later died of cancer of the womb, which implies all sorts of sexual things too genuinely neurotic to go into.) In one way or another, all of this is attempted to tie in with Alice and her sexual-philosophic villainy, demanding that Julian accept on faith what he cannot justify in reality.

Between the martyrdom of Julian and the reality-illusion obfuscations, Albee finally advises that mankind must be humble in the face of mysteries. It is not a conclusion of shattering depth.

There are two very serious problems in *Tiny Alice* that all of this elaboration has attempted to clarify. On the one hand, it is a hopelessly mixed-up bag of confused intellectual preciosity and sexual justification. On the other hand, its High English is self-conscious and irritatingly inconsistent, ranging from inflated epic prose to annoying colloquialisms ("Are you playing it straight with him?").

Nevertheless, there is so great a strength to Albee's beliefs, and so pure a rush of dramatic excitement, that the faults must be overlooked. Besides, that lingual inconsistency is not nearly so offensive as the intellectual hogwash, and Albee really has written the bulk of his play in an English that is far superior to anything in recent American drama (not counting some of Tennessee Williams' beautiful poetry because it isn't really comparable).

The performances are superb, every one, and John Gielgud's Julian is masterful, building a fearfully human being through candor and sheer goodness into a dreadfully innocent victim. Irene Worth makes Alice as feminine as possible, considering that Albee still cannot write a believable female characterization. John Heffernan is a playfully sinister butler, but William Hutt tends to overdo his lawyer's villainy—something which he can easily correct. Eric Berry played the cardinal as arrogant and hopelessly materialistic—a peculiar characterization for a peculiarly written role.

Alan Schneider directed all of them with a terrifying sense of horror that all but sent the theater into thumping heartbeats of doom (and unfortunately, he actually used amplified heart thumps for a melodramatic ending that the play could have nicely managed on its own). All of this, set in Mr. Ritman's gigantic sets, has a weird look of gigantic microscopy that made it all unreal and, at once, real.

What is left, then, is what was begun with—an extraordinary and ridiculous play. But it is frighteningly rich theater, electrically alive theater, exquisitely performed theater—that, my friend, is a genuine prize.

A Question (*January 14, 1966*)

With each of his plays since *Who's Afraid of Virginia Woolf?* the question of how Edward Albee would develop arose and remained unanswered. *Malcolm,* which opened on Tuesday and is closing tomorrow night, presents a change in pattern. The new play does not even raise the question.

This is because *Malcolm* is not a play and Mr. Albee is not its author. True, it was he who removed some of the pages of James Purdy's novel and snipped out a passage here and there. And it was he who chose to ignore the descriptions of characters' physical characteristics. But the great bulk of the *Malcolm* script was not written by Albee. It is word-for-word reproduction of the book.

It is not, therefore, a play, but a stage reading of an abridged novel. And it is as clear an example as possible of the difference between literature and drama. Basically, a book is directed toward the mind, happening there, and a play is directed for the eye—it is physically seen. But there is more to an art form than this. Every medium has its disciplines, both structural and thematic, and for a work to succeed within it these disciplines must be observed. Nor are they necessarily abstract. For example, a painting must be restricted to its canvas—paint just does not adhere to air. That seems absurdly obvious, but in transferring Purdy's novel to the stage, Albee ignored some just-as-obvious dramatic restrictions.

For example, stage dialogue must be written to be spoken and it must be constructed within the dramatic scheme of a play. Book dialogue must be written to be read. The novelist has infinitely greater freedom in writing conversation than does the playwright because he is working inside a reader's mind. The playwright's dialogue is being spoken and the spectator is hearing it, watching characters say it. This dialogue must be speakable, must be plausible. That does not mean that it has to be ordinary, but it does have to be conversational within the idea of the play. For example, a playwright like Ionesco can have his characters speaking in endlessly repeated clichés and it will be dramatically reasonable because everything that is happening in the play is also caricatured, in that style, and it is stage-oriented. The work was conceived to be played by actors. *Malcolm* was conceived to be read.

So this is no play. And it would be foolish to attempt to fit it into Albee's works. The fact that some of its thematic material —its homosexuality, for example—seems common to the other Albee literature has significance only in that the playwright would naturally be attracted to works that appeal to his own intellectual inclinations.

But the homosexuality in *Malcolm,* if you look even superficially, is not at all like that in all of Albee's plays. First of all, it is very close to the surface, whereas Albee generally is more dishonest about it, sliding it in as an underlay. Second, it is not involved with dominating mother-images. The man-eater in

Malcolm is no mother but a young nymphomaniac. Third, Malcolm himself is what once was termed in smart sets AC-DC. And he is clearly described as being somewhat of a star at heterosexual lovemaking. No Albee hero would be so versatile.

But it would be unfair to discuss Albee's work in solely sexual terms—he really is an artist and is considerably deeper than this, even if his depth is prompted by the weird premise that homosexuality is the key to martyred purity. And before proceeding to his outer, splendid talents, that premise must be recognized as not only the consistent subtheme in his plays but the key to his artistic identity. If, as he says, he has an aesthetic, that is the only one it would seem to be.

What is evident about that in *Malcolm*—and what brings this discussion back to Albee's development as a playwright—is that an aesthetic alone is not enough to create a play. Furthermore, while Purdy's novel partly agrees with Albee's premise, it was not treated to Albee's professional playwriting abilities. And as transcribed to the stage, it does not have his native assets of fire and stage literacy.

This was exactly the problem with Albee's first attempt at adaptation, Carson McCullers' *The Ballad of the Sad Café*. Like *Malcolm*, this novella had a kinship to Albee's continuing premise. Like the adaptation of *Malcolm*, hyperfidelity was observed to the detriment of stage needs (although in the *Sad Café* case Albee was more than an editor, writing dialogue for a practically dialogueless book). And like Malcolm, it was theatrically sterile.

This leaves Albee in precisely the same position as he was at this time last year, just after *Tiny Alice*. He is still a playwright who should be writing original plays instead of adaptations. He is still the playwright who was prematurely hailed on much too slim a body of work. He is still the playwright whose genuine talent and intelligence are marred by preciosity, pretension, and an inclination toward immature and effete inside jokes. He is still a playwright who has an exciting sense of bold, extravagant theater. And his development still remains a question mark.

Box-Mao-Box (*March 11, 1968*)

A new play by Edward Albee is being given its world premiere at the Studio Arena Theatre in Buffalo and I haven't seen more garbage since John Lindsay last asked Nelson Rockefeller for a favor. Either Mr. Albee is going to discipline his verbal flushing or the promise he showed so long ago is just not going to be kept.

The new play is called *Box-Mao-Box,* and as Albee concedes, the evening is made up of two "separate works . . . conceived at different though not distant moments." They make one play only in the sense that *Box* is performed before and after *Quotations from Chairman Mao Tse-tung,* with a little bleeding in of *Box* toward the end of *Mao.* And there are no intermissions. The question remains whether an unintended duet can be called controlled work, but its answer is even more perplexing: *Mao* indeed fits into *Box* as if they were written together, but only because *Box* is so hopelessly random and incoherent that anything would fit into it.

It is a free-association ramble through the insides of a brain, rattling in and out of the corners of that cell. William Ritman's set is a simple (and mathematically beautiful) cube skeleton, though it is not the solid box that Albee requests in his script. There is no stage action—not even a physical actor. Only the disembodied voice of Ruth White, reciting an aimless series of observations and awarenesses. The influence of Samuel Beckett is obvious. Unfortunately, Albee has none of Beckett's poetic and artistic genius. Or even finesse.

Aside from the Beckett concept, the play itself—that is, what Miss White recites—is Albee at his worst. Literary posing, wholesale self-indulgence, an astonishing lack of polish, philosophical pretension, and dashes-within-brackets-within-parentheses writing (for example, "Nature abhors, among so many, so much else . . . amongst so much, us, itself, they say, vacuum").

With the conclusion of *Box,* the set brightens to reveal a shipboard and four characters. A handsome lady and a minister are reclining on deck chairs. A tacky old woman is perched on a rise, eating out of a can. Mao Tse-tung, unmistakably, is leaning against a rail and he is to be the only character who moves during the play—from one part of the rail to another, or up and down the theater's aisles.

It begins with Chairman Mao reciting from his *Quotations* (that famous little red book). Albee has selected from the political remarks (rather than the more comically platitudinous inspirational ones), and all of this is verbatim from the Chairman. Likewise, the dialogue of the other two talking characters —the minister is silent throughout—is all of a piece. That is, their entire parts could be soliloquies, since nothing they say is relevant to what the others say. The old woman recites a long, sentimental, rhyming poem attributed to William Carpenter and called "Over the Hill to the Poorhouse." And the handsome woman (called "the long-winded lady" though she is no longer-winded than the author) tells a long, long narrative reminiscent in structure and manner to the dog story in *The Zoo Story.* As it turns out, it is second-class Dorothy Parker without her style but with Albee's ("I cupped my hands around his lovely scrotum").

The effect is suffocating—as theater, as writing, as thought. There is so little humor to it that the banality of Mao's quotations and the old woman's poem seems not silly but overbearing. The long-winded lady's story, because it is haphazardly written and without momentum, drowns out the few segments in it that are genuinely interesting and well written (and Albee is quite capable of such work, which makes his sloppiness all the more irritating).

According to the author's program notes, this play was constructed on a musical basis, though you'd never guess. I assume he meant to mix individual character themes on a fugal level, contrasting the long-winded lady's tragic inertia with the rote-emptiness of Mao's citations and the violation by the poem's cheap style of its unhappy content. I guess, too, that he meant to resolve the three themes in the sense that you resolve a chord progression. But it works in no musical sense. Parenthetically, the Judson Poets' Theatre recently set some of Mao's quotations to cornball vaudeville music and staging, mocking the simpleminded wisdom far more sophisticatedly, theatrically, and good-naturedly than Albee ever begins to do.

Alan Schneider staged the production with an apt sterility, relying on his long experience with Beckett. The performances were professional, though none was in the class of Miss White's reading of *Box,* which brought a mass of pain to its emptiness.

But what, then, of Albee? For all the inanity of this work, it would be nice to appreciate his return to the abstract and his willingness to experiment. His retreat into naturalism the past few years has been cheap. The truth is, though, that whatever the form, he seems as careless and as pompous as ever—perhaps too pompous to ever be true and perhaps too careless to ever finish his work.

The Unappreciated

Eating a Heart Out (*July 28, 1964*)

IT's much easier to say "everybody is entitled to his opinion" than it is to accept it. When a play carries you out on so great a wave of enthusiasm that you are too washed out to speak —and you wake up the next morning to find yourself not only in a minority but really all out on a limb by yourself—you begin to wonder whether the world is as straight as you thought it was.

Of course, it is altogether possible that the play struck a peculiarly personal place in you. And it is altogether possible that only you and perhaps a handful of others were struck just that way. For you the play was a phenomenal event in your life. For almost everybody else it was a bore, or was foolish or whatever.

So you talk and talk about it—get frustrated, aggravated. For God's sake, *see this!* you tell your friends. It is just tremendous! Some of them go. Some of them think it was marvelous. Some of them think it was terrible. It closes after one week and remains only with you, that handful, and the author. It adds itself to the endless list of private infuriations that have long since convinced you the whole world is crazy and if it just took your word for things it would become magnificently civilized.

63

The season that just passed seemed to have had more than its share of these aggravating failures. And there may be nothing more in reviving discussion than pure masochism. But as your tongue can't help but pry painfully into the touchiest cavities, the mind keeps returning to those productions that were so astonishing, apparently, for just you and nobody else, almost.

Anyone Can Whistle has been brought into this column often enough to make even the breeziest reader aware of the personal pain its failure brought. The Stephen Sondheim-Arthur Laurents sideshow was so musically brilliant, so original and witty, and so dazzlingly executed that the generally negative response to it must be called the shock of the year. Some people said that you couldn't whistle any of the tunes and others called it "sick." These comments can be dismissed as ignorant. Others wrote letters expressing astonishment that anyone could have enjoyed it. That is simple opinion—the sort that everyone is entitled to.

Bertolt Brecht's *Arturo Ui* ran for just one week in November. As has already begun to happen with *Anyone Can Whistle*, it is becoming one of those productions that gain enthusiasm too late from the very people who refused to support it (this happened to productions like *Candide* and *House of Flowers*). The Tony Richardson staging of the bitter allegory was electricity-charged. Christopher Plummer gave the performance of a lifetime. The excitement was palpable. Practically nobody, at least in print, thought much of it.

There were more. *Semi-Detached* was written by David Turner with so dazzling a blend of bitter satire and abstraction as to be almost a whole new genre in itself. It barreled along with a wild-eyed logic that mixed hilarity and social infuriation into a great ball, tumbling it down a rickety old mountain. It, too, closed prematurely.

George White's adaption of Yves Jamiaque's *A Murderer Among Us* was the most successful instance in memory of actually bringing the feel of another country to an American stage. Its provincial France was the real provincial France. Its philosophical playfulness and idealistic resignation was Gallic in the best sense and all of it was astonishingly Dufy-like in look. It was a perfect little gem. It closed after one perform-ance.

Bert Shevelove's rewriting of the William Gillette vehicle *Too Much Johnson* represented the most cockeyedly offbeat humor of the season. Its satire was so gilt-edged that the separation from what it was satirizing was infinitesimal. Perfect deadpan—so difficult to do, so rare to find. Mr. Shevelove seems to have a humor that only some people can sense (he showed it in the book he co-wrote with Larry Gelbart for *A Funny Thing Happened on the Way to the Forum,* and not many people sensed it there, either). The play received most unappreciative reviews and it ran three weeks.

There is no standard run for productions in the aggravation category. *Dynamite Tonight* opened and closed on the same night. A few of us are still running around raving about this wacky "comic opera for actors." We will talk about it, proba-bly, forever, proving to be pains in the neck to everybody, espe-cially to most of the others who also saw it. So what? We know better, right? *Dynamite Tonight* was brilliant, right? The whole world is mad, right?

And so off we go, the two of us, wandering into the drizzly night, mumbling to ourselves and cursing the world for not agreeing with us.

Dynamite Tonight (*December 12, 1966*)

Three years ago, an exciting, bitterly antiwar and very funny 'comic opera for actors" called *Dynamite Tonight* opened off-Broadway. Incredibly, the most powerful New York critic at

the time denounced it and the production closed after one performance (a combination of producer realism and chicken-
heartedness). The Yale School of Drama (in New Haven) has
shown the splendidly good sense to reproduce it, and the
Arnold Weinstein-William Bolcom work now seems, if anything, an even more successful theater piece than it was in that
original production.

Dynamite Tonight is a true opera, and its use of popular and
theater music styles should not confuse that. Opera is theater
that uses music for its overriding expression. Mr. Bolcom's
jazzy, vaudevillian, pop-dissonant score is serious and theatrical,
and its employment of tango, soft-shoe, and song-and-dance
figures (as well as mock grand opera) is utterly justifiable
within an operatic context.

To be sure, the music remains eclectic, and that cannot be
explained away as mimicry. There is much of Stravinsky's *Story
of a Soldier* and Milhaud's *Creation of the World* in it and certainly great helpings of Kurt Weill. But these are not the most
unrespectable of sources, and Bolcom has not restricted his
work to derivation. Much of his music is quite original, nearly
all of it is absolutely right for the pitch of the work, and it is extremely effective.

The libretto that Mr. Weinstein provided could not have
been more desirable for operatic setting. Its basic identity is
musical and its use of language is sympathetic with word
sounds, rhythmic movement, and general substantiation of the
ruling mood. That mood is one of giddy horseplay about cartooned soldiers before a background of a terribly real war.

Dynamite Tonight is set in an army bunker (marvelously designed by Paul Shortt to look like the insides of a battered
radio). The battling countries are bloodily make-believe, those
in the bunker wearing vaguely World War I uniforms and the
"enemy" in tattered operetta. As long as everybody remains in
this shelter of burlesqued tragedy, things are fun and dance
But whenever anyone enters or leaves through two doors ele-

vated at the rear, blasting, bombing war movies are roared across a great movie screen.

The story is intentionally fairy tale. A ludicrous captain with a military brainwash spends his time safely below while urging his men to go out there and fight. His assistant is a sergeant who fills bombs with dynamite powder that is rolled out of a tunnel in a mechanized cart, making the whole business look like an amusement park ride. A prisoner is taken and put in a chain cage, where he moans nonsense-language Wagnerian arias for his lost love Tlimpattia. She appears, first as a dream and then as a prisoner. Having come to announce the war's end, she is killed in genuine tragedy—which *Dynamite Tonight,* of course, is at its root. But this is all bitterly laminated with a ricky-tick vaudeville routine that celebrates peace even while nobody knows who won the war ("No news is good news").

The performances are superb. Although this was supposed to be the first Yale production to use students, the cast is primarily professional. Mr. Bolcom's more difficult coloratura composing was scaled down for Linda Lavin (Barbara Harris, who sang the original Tlimpattia, had the voice for it), but she was just fine. Gene Troobnick's Captain was deep in the Second City style that permeated the production and was correctly informal and nonsensical. Alvin Epstein was brilliant as the Sergeant, carrying sensitivity and humanity into physical movement; and George Gaynes made as tragically operettic a prisoner as he had in the first production.

Paul Sills directed without the Schweikian middle-Europe feeling that made the original seem so modeled on Brecht (although that influence is unshakable) and kept the word games and old-theater, old-movie horseplay completely in common with the running movement and tone. This version also seemed to have more music (including rock) than the original. And Carl Eberl's direction of the chamber orchestra interplayed perfectly with what was happening onstage.

What was happening onstage was modern theater deep in traditional theater modes; theatrically valid, politically relevant, and intellectually contemporary work that marvelously fulfills its primary obligation to be alive on a stage. How absurd for it to run only through December 20.

Peterpat *(January 7, 1965)*

Peterpat is the nicest love story I know. Because it is written straight—it is genuine and decent and can say things like "I think you stink" the way a good wife can. Because its fun is the kind of fun there is in a marriage and when somebody gets sore it is because there has been some hurting going on. Because it has a lady organist named Louise Rush sitting in a box playing "Tea for Two" roller-skating rink style. Because Joan Hackett is in it and she is wonderful and beautiful. And because when she says "I love you" to Dick Shawn just before the final curtain, it is really moving without making you feel as if you've been tricked into chilling.

The romantic comedy that turned up at a time when the romantic comedy was dead is called *Peterpat,* it was written by Enid Rudd, and it opened last night at the Longacre Theatre. It is about a vain, adolescent, helpless writer of trashy pocket books and the girl he marries, betrays, and returns to. It is around two and a quarter hours long and it will leave you amused and touched and that's a promise.

Read the title as *Peter/Pat.* They are the couple and the names are linked because, as in most marriages, they become an inseparable partnership. When Pat says, early in the play, that she doesn't believe in divorce, it is not because of a religious conviction so much as it is because marriages really can't be dissolved—at least, most of the time. Living together blends people.

68

Even so cockeyed a couple as this. Joan Hackett's Pat is bright and vulnerable, always saying exactly what she means with a grand overemphasis for sarcastic comedy. She calls her husband's mistress Sneaky Sandra, with the humor as bitter as her pain. And when she asks, "How could you leave me for another woman?" it is the simplest, saddest, straightest way for saying it. It is a hackneyed line that has suddenly become fresh. This is to the equal credit of Miss Hackett and Miss Rudd.

For it isn't that Miss Rudd hasn't heard these lines before. It's that she doesn't seem to have ever paid attention to anything stupid. That is how she managed to write a play that was sentimental and nice. That is how she can have Miss Hackett say that she can stand her husband loving another woman, kissing another woman, but not sleeping with another woman because that is disloyal and disloyal is the worst thing anybody can be. Could an argument be simpler? It couldn't. Could it be more ordinary? It couldn't. And it couldn't have sounded more original.

Dick Shawn begins the play by staring blankly out at the audience and then calmly tossing a paper plane at it. He is as helplessly at the command of the world as he could possibly be and spends the evening proving it. Mr. Shawn is funny when he expects Pat to do everything a wife should do and is funnier when he learns she is pregnant (he says he wishes it had been a tumor, hastily adding, not malignant—not malignant).

Later in the evening Shawn plays a series of physical mishaps that display him at a kind of comedy that is very difficult to play (too broad). He plays it comically and freshly—as indeed he plays the evening through. He is a very good Peter.

But, oh, Miss Hackett's Pat. She is skinny and her ankles are just slightly heavy. Her features are odd. Her hair is straggly. She is flat-chested. And she is extraordinarily beautiful, as much from a fantastically inside glow as from those perfectly imperfect features. Hackett is also a magnificent actress, vocally, physically, and spiritually.

The two of them were directed nearly perfectly by Joe Layton, from their offstage singing while the sets change to a complicated lights-on, lights-off scene toward the end. Remember, *Peterpat* is not a roaring laughter kind of thing. Just expect to spend a whole evening smiling, occasionally breaking out into a big laugh, and generally simmering in the good straightness of it all. It is a wonderfully warm comedy.

Inadmissible Evidence (*December 1, 1965*)

John Osborne's new play, which opened last night at the Belasco Theatre, bears once more his mark—the fiery hatred of the commonplace, the accepted, the mundane, and the ache to be a part of it. And if *Inadmissible Evidence* makes it quite clear that his *Luther* was an out-of-character incident in his playwrighting life, it also indicates a return to natural growth. The new play, then, is not nearly so "well made" as the last, but it burns fiercely with the earlier drive. I think that is more important.

Especially since that old drive is coupled with a basic dramatic sense and a marvelous knack for brilliant dialogue. *Inadmissible Evidence* is not nearly the profound analysis of modern man it is meant to be and it is not consistently interesting. As a dramatic structure it goes, really, nowhere at all. While Osborne intended for us to realize, at play's end, that the result was in the cards right from the start, we know it right from the start ourselves.

Nevertheless, the play is so frequently involving—as a mental-dramatic gymnastic—in a way rarely seen today, that whatever the lapses in philosophical construction and whatever the inconsistency of interest, it is by and large a very involving and very exciting theater piece.

The play begins with a trial of its protagonist for being a "wicked, bawdy and scandalous object," but it is soon apparent that the trial is imaginary and the charge is really being leveled *by* himself *against* himself. William Maitland, an attorney, has lived a life of self-indulgence, barricading himself against a world he knows to be stupid, doing a job he is not at all interested in, living a life he considers pointless.

In the meanwhile, the world—a world he has lost contact with—is deserting him: his wife, his momentary sexual conquests, his clients, his colleagues, his employees. And finally, his mistress. That they really do not want to leave him is of little matter. He drives them away with cruelties, indignities, insults, all the while trying desperately and futilely to keep them. He is an acute emotional nymphomaniac.

Somehow or other, Osborne was attempting to tie this in with the original, embarrassingly Kafkaesque trial and its point that "It is inhuman to be expected to be capable of giving a decent account of oneself." In a sense, the tie is made. Maitland is a bright and realistic man—he does not attempt to live up to an inhuman moral standard and is convinced that this cannot be considered "wrong." But he senses society's judgment of him by that standard anyhow.

But this tie-in is not satisfactory enough to make a complete connection. Besides, Osborne never answers the most obvious challenge to his premise—why doesn't Maitland attempt to live up to *any* moral standard?

Still, if plays were judged by their intellectual incisiveness, there wouldn't be many at all. The reason that *Inadmissible Evidence* is not a complete play is not its philosophical inadequacy but its dramatic flaws. Maitland may be a dazzling-bright character, but he never gets anywhere and even becomes, at least occasionally, a bore.

Anyone would if he were onstage every moment of a two-and-a-half-hour play, nearly always doing the talking. Osborne has written for him his most brittle dialogue since *Look Back in Anger,* and Maitland's billowing egotism flies up and down the stage and all around the theater in flash upon flash of wit, fury, despair, and eloquence. Especially wit, although not always relevant. Osborne has wonderfully funny and royally nasty things to say about most everything, and just about all of it is apt. But he is so eager to say it all that he drags it into the play on the slightest of pretexts until it sounds just bitchy.

Nicol Williamson's performance in the bravura central role is everything the word "virtuoso" means—the sweating, frightened, boastful, confident, hopelessly neurotic Everyman, unwanted by a world he wants. Supporting him is a generally splendid cast, especially Peter Sallis and Ted van Griethuysen in double roles. Anthony Page's staging is tense and very theatrical. So is the play, very often—it really doesn't work and yet it works so well.

Hooray! It's a Glorious Day (*March 10, 1966*)

Hooray! It's a Glorious Day . . . and All That is the funniest musical in years. And years. A knowledgeable, witty, and marvelously accurate parody of our not-so-modern musicals, laughing them to pieces much in the same way that Sandy Wilson's *The Boy Friend* did with twenties musicals.

What Maurice Teitelbaum and Charles Grodin have done was more or less combine the dime-a-dozen plots of *Guys and Dolls* and *How to Succeed in Business* and interlace them with the clichés of virtually every show-businessy musical of the forties and fifties. Aside from the fact that their book spins merrily along with barely a slip in tone (a remarkable improvement in itself over the books it is mocking), they managed—with Ethel Bieber's help—lyrics that perfectly match it, formula for formula. And Arthur Gordon's music goes right along for the ride, providing pseudo-stock ballads, inspirational chorus songs, production numbers, soft-shoes, and what have you.

What you have is a beautiful lesson in show business, for very clearly and very seriously beneath *Hooray!* is a sharp criticism of every last thing that is dusty, dead, and ready to be buried in old-fashioned Broadway musicals. Including the glaring awareness of everybody in those musicals that they are in a show as well as in a musical.

What I mean by that is your dead certainty, every time you're watching a musical, that the people onstage are interested, more than anything else, in the fact that they are onstage. So the villain looks annoyed every time the orchestra accompanies his entrance. So the hero advises us to wait for his ballad. So the cast, while doing their in-one number (in front of the front curtain) wonders whether the scenery behind has been changed yet.

The fun and games continue in the musical staging and dances, which manage to mimic every last tired Broadway habit. The serious ballet, the dance in the park (where the office scenery disappears to reveal benches and grass and nannies and cops and somebody wonders where the office went). And the endless, obvious song cues.

The plot is impure, adulterated, and alloyed musical theater nonsense. After a mocked, running, skipping, shouting opening number ("He's a Comin' ") by the chorus boy and girl office staff, the company president announces that he is in trouble and is summoning an expert from Chicago. Before switching there, we are introduced to the characters—Betty Plain (the Eve Arden secretary secretly in love with the boss), the old washerwoman who aches for her lost son (always keeping her door open for him, to later complain, "They're stealing me blind"). And the bright-eyed, eagle-spread chorus.

Now we're in Chicago with two gangsters who are going to have their sap buddy impersonate the expert. The sap sings his parrot song. Muggsy does his number, as he has been pleading to do. Carl Strong, the hero, is the one in the wild chalk stripes and black shirt (Sky Masterson out of *Guys and Dolls*). After some hotel room dialogue ("Awright, you guys, knock it off") they're to the office. But as soon as the eyes of Carl ("I knocked around for a while, at loose ends, not knowing what to do") meet the eyes of Kitty Sweetness ("That's a nice smile, Kitty—you should use it more often") there is nothing for them to do but sing a duet (see *West Side Story*) and provide a cue ("Kitty, I'm taking you out on the town tonight") for an irrelevant nightclub tap-dance act, where the dancer always assumes the same worried look to let us know that This Step is Tough. The act ends, as it must, with Kitty, her trenchcoat, her beret, her lamppost, and her reprise of "The Wonderland of Love" ("My dreams all ended at dawn/Until I met you").

The second act opens with an ingenious and hilarious sextet that, like most of Mr. Gordon's music, almost camouflages some good composing with laughter. And perhaps things are not quite so funny thereafter, but very nearly and that is funny enough.

Sandra Devlin's choreography was a show in itself, mixing a good deal of Michael Kidd with a chunk of Bob Fosse, a helping of Jerome Robbins, and a sure awareness of repetitious Broadway dance schemes. Mr. Grodin's direction was the controlling hand on all the humor, and the performances were letter-perfect, especially Ronald Holgate's as the hero, Joan Kroschell as Kitty, Louis Criscuolo as Muggsy, and the whole chorus. It is all theater-theater fun and very funny indeed.

To Bury a Cousin (May 17, 1967)

There is a very talented playwright in the house, and I mean a playwright. Gus Weill is a true writer—easy and poetic, natural and confident—and he knows what a play is supposed to be, how a stage can work. His drama is called *To Bury a Cousin*; it opened last night at the Bouwerie Lane Theatre, and for whatever its faults—there are some—it is positively wonderful.

Mr. Weill's play is about a man most people don't write about—a very ordinary, weak, confused man. The kind that most men are. He isn't a leader and he isn't a thinker. He doesn't do wild, exciting things and he gets pushed around. But he does suffer and his suffering is real. For whatever his troubles and whatever his mistakes, he did live. He did know his own grief. Now he has died, a suicide, and *To Bury a Cousin* is about why he died and whose fault it was.

It is written in the form of a dramatic inquest. Ben, a playwright and an original person, has come home to somewhere in the Deep South to bury his cousin Bert. He has also come to place the guilt for the suicide on the shoulders of Bert's parents, his wife, his circumstances. The interweaving flashbacks show guilt enough. Bert's parents were narrowminded, dominating people, very much responsible for their son's virtual impotence. More believably, his wife's prudery murdered whatever physical love might have been possible between them ("He waited for me and I waited for him"). The play's treatment of this subject alone—the relationships between marriage, love, and sex—is so wisely conceived that I think it in itself worth the work.

But there is much more. In gliding and flowing through a lifetime, with incidents of family, marriage, and discovery of sex through a wonderfully physical prostitute, *To Bury a Cousin* weaves a dramatic collage of delicate intensity. And Mr. Weill's use of naturalistic scenes in open-time sequence is proof enough that dramatic realism can be applied in modern ways.

The writing is lovely, sometimes even exquisite. In conceding his wasted marriage, Bert says, "We were the animals in the sea who never came ashore. We were never meant for the sea and we never came ashore." He then asks his cold wife to "just depart with your old suitcase and some newfound dignity," and swallows "all the pills for all the pain." And yet she is not entirely villainous. Mr. Weill knows his people too well to hate them entirely. Despite the casual, ignorant selfishness that makes this so destructive a family, he mixes sympathy with even the most earnest hatred. And in understanding their position as Jews in Gentile country, he puts a sensitive finger exactly on what this situation can do to people.

Sometimes he goes too far. The introduction of a superpatriot American Legionnaire is gratuitous, and the stupid business of Communist-hunting really has nothing to do with the play. Having a rabbi accused of being a Communist in the middle of a Passover ceremony is excess melodrama. Considering Mr. Weill's impressive dramatic ability, it is quite beneath him.

Philip Oesterman, Jr., staged the work with a great sensitivity to its changing moods and a choreographic attitude for its rapidly moving scenes (upon Douglas W. Schmidt's perfect, ever-growing, turntable sets). The performances are excellent, and John Scanlan is genuinely tragic as the self-ruined Bert. Rosalind Cash is lush and vital as his prostitute, Janet Dowd frightfully wifely as his Hilda, and Mary Boylan and Edwin Cooper deeply real as his parents. But it is Mr. Weill's evening, and its terrible eloquence is contained softly, even tearfully.

Saturday Night (February 26, 1968)

Jerome Kass' *Saturday Night* is a beautiful, beautiful play and it was just about perfectly presented last night at the Sheridan Square Theatre. I haven't seen anything so intelligently and well written, so filled with compassion and so theatrically balanced in some time, and although its naturalism is not exactly in the most modern mode it would be senseless to deny the simple grace of the play. It is serious and funny and painfully sensitive, written with the strength of confidence and filled with knowing sympathy.

It is set in a plain, Jewish, Bronx apartment, where a twenty-nine-year-old has given up her girlhood to care for an aging father. Her days are spent as a librarian, her evenings at home, where she listens to music, reads poetry, and dreams of culture, beauty, and art. On Saturday nights, when her father goes to the movies, she entertains a girlfriend, trying to share a beauty that has been sustaining her solitarily all week long.

On the Saturday night on which the play occurs, Rochelle Harris is as usual expecting her friend Ellie. As soon as her father leaves she excitedly changes into a splashy hostess gown and covers the drab furniture with bright-colored spreads, much as she has covered her life. Then she proceeds to share sexual and cultural fantasies with her friend while damning the world, her own in particular, for its crudeness, its insensitivity, its dreariness.

But Ellie is no Rochelle. She is a fat, gum-chewing, hair-teasing, thirty-two-year-old simple girl who wants no more than an Ira with a good job who will carry her away from Pelham Parkway to the Grand Concourse and—who knows?—maybe even Westchester. Ellie is beginning to resent Rochelle and is calling her on the fantasies. And soon, very soon, we realize just how troubled Rochelle really is. Mr. Kass may be mocking a type with her reverence for Camus and Sartre, and her rigid atheism, but he is not settling for easy humor.

Rochelle's mother was mad and she fears the same fate. Rochelle is not really a martyr to her father's needs. He needs her and does fear her abandonment, but she is also using him as an excuse for self-seclusion. She tells Ellie, finally, that her father "is my life—he and you and Saturday night."

But when her father is reported missing she goes into crisis. A family friend brings his buddy around to cheer up the girls, and for a moment she leaves her self-made tragedy in a cathartic gale of laughter (the buddy, a wonderful character, is a would-be comedian, short on education but long on reflexive understanding). Finally the father returns with a revelation about himself that ultimately shatters the glass lid that this poor girl has, in fright, placed over her life.

I don't think that this synopsis does Mr. Kass' play enough credit. The story is so real and so unmelodramatic—it is so measuredly told and its conversation is so artfully real—that is quite nearly mesmerizing. Every character is a definite person —not a caricature mechanized for stage devices but whole and personalized.

And every character is played that way. This production has been perfectly cast, and Zina Jasper's performance as Rochelle is awesomely complete, powerful, and artistic. Miss Jasper has taken this neurotic, frustrated, unhappy, highly verbal, and rather superior girl and moved right into her life. It is acting of the highest order.

Director Burt Brinckerhoff draws first-class performances from the other actors as well. Moving them continuously without being obvious about it and concentrating on definition, teamwork, perfect diction, and projection of character, he follows Mr. Kass' play in keeping the work realistic and yet filled with the one extra dimension that is art. Gina Collens' Ellie is rough without being too coarse and pushy without being too obtuse. She, unlike Rochelle, has a relief from tragedy. She, unlike Rochelle, can settle for what is possible. But then she, unlike Rochelle, is not the sensitive person blasted by circumstance. Lee Wallace is eager, uncomplicated, and human as the friend. Marvin Lichterman is entirely delightful as his comedian pal (Brinckerhoff directed his comic scene brilliantly, knowing that the jokes were usually awful but realizing how just such jokes, especially in just such circumstances, can get just such people giddy). Shimen Ruskin is at once oppressive and pathetic as the father, just as he should be. All excellent. All blending into a play. All translating a script, which, after all, is only words on paper, into a play, which is what Mr. Kass really wrote, *really* wrote. It is very, very good.

Jimmy Shine (*December 6, 1968*)

Jimmy Shine is a funny, lovely, painfully gentle play that manages—without being fake-sensitive or psychedelically souped-up—to understand just the thinking of today's young people. It opened last night at the Brooks Atkinson Theatre, and it shows Murray Schisgal stepping out into a playwriting beyond mannerism and into confidence, craft, a knowledge of what he wants to say and how he wants to say it.

In the past, Mr. Schisgal neatly combined a vaudeville sense of humor with a cartoon style, but was hung up mocking clichés, which he did well but compulsively. That hang-up is gone. In the past, too, he stumped for individualism—not the old anticonformity business but real originality of person. An originality that had no room for artiness, bohemianism, or any of the other advertisements people hang on themselves as proof of specialness. This is something that means a great deal to me, and so I am glad it is in *Jimmy Shine* again. Only everything (with but one exception and I'll mention it later and briefly because it is minor) fits together just right, and but for a few directing slips the production is just about perfect.

The play is about a starving young painter living in a Greenwich Village loft—sounds like another Schisgal mocked cliché but with a twist. The fact outline *is* cliché and it's a joke, but the painter himself is a lousy artist. More important, he is a particular and singular human being. He is the original Jimmy Shine.

He is immediately established as mildly freaky: beer chilling on top of an ice cube, a mat of hair pasted on his chest. He is also with a prostitute, a frequent enough satisfaction, it turns out, since he is "the only abstract painter in the Village who isn't getting laid."

The play then moves into a flashback structure, which Schisgal handles with consummate skill, moving back and forth from the present to Brooklyn high school days, a quick trip to San Francisco ("home of all that moves and grooves") and a painfully funny attempt at going straight working in a fish store.

There is also a love story, but don't let its corny sound put you off because (a) it is intentionally corny (again, Schisgal and clichés) and (b) it is also possible enough. It is as follows: Shine is superbuddies with a school classmate, as boys are prone to be superbuddies in high school. A born follower, he is talked into skipping college by his pal, the idea being to become Village painters. Though he has neither an interest in nor a talent for painting, his friend—the ultimate phony—convinces him that it is possible ("visualize, conceptualize"). So he goes off to paint while the buddy decides to go to college. As it turns out, need I say, the buddy never does become a painter. He goes into his father's real estate business and marries the girl Shine adored.

So the artist holes up in his loft, painting terrible pictures and dreaming about the girls he never gets while satisfying himself with a lovely and quite real prostitute. His vulnerability, his insecurity, his vague decency, his impatience with formal convictions, his uninterest in the straight world and its values—these are the hallmarks of today's young, and they are incorporated into this one character of especial reality. When the play ends, he is still nowhere—still painting though now relieved of taking himself seriously—and so at last capable of doing something. For Schisgal (and for me) the only thing that counts is what you do. Properly, the ending is neither sweet—though it may seem that way—nor sour. It is merely right, and the play, of course, is the story of an artist.

The only thing wrong the evening through is a tying-loose-ends-together scene where the old girlfriend leaves the old buddy and offers Shine his long-dreamed-of elopement. The kind of writing that went into this scene is not the kind of writing that went into the rest of the play, and the same goes for what happens in it.

But, as I said, it is a minor mistake and don't think much of it, especially when there is so much else. For example, the very body of the production, which inhales and exhales like a living thing as the cast contracts and expands from Shine's singular life of the present to his social life of the past.

Now here I have to wing it. Donald Driver is credited with the staging though it is common knowledge that he left the production some weeks ago. None of his flashy, pseudo-Peter Brook symptoms are there and that is good, but his ranging sense of stage action, choreography, and musicality is very much present and I am sure it is to his credit. On the other hand, there are some very cheap directing jokes that aren't his style at all and I suspect they are the work of his uncredited successor. As for the performances, Dustin Hoffman is entirely brilliant in the huge title role, sustaining his previous impression as a real and profound actor (despite his reflex performance in *The Graduate*). Rose Gregorio is touching as the prostitute, Cleavon Little terribly funny as a hippie. Other roles are relatively straightforward. Finally, the songs (musically staged) were by John Sebastian of The Lovin' Spoonful, one of the real composers in modern art-rock and the first of those tremendous talents to try the theater. It is the breakthrough of such music into the theater (don't let *Hair* and *Your Own Thing* fool you) and it is exhilarating. As very much is this special and sweepingly fresh play.

Joe Orton Died (*September 8, 1967*)

HAL: My father holds it as a cherished belief that a whore is no
fit companion for a man.
FAY: As a creed it has more to offer than most.

Loot, a play by Joe Orton

There is a special tragedy in the death of an artist. Such a
man, no matter what his creative motivation, shares his life—
and himself—with all the rest of us. And his death ends that
sharing, deprives us of what he would certainly have done had
he lived. Such a death is really an abortion of unborn works of
art. And as miserable as is the death of any person, that of an
artist—aside from plainly human matters—is, I think, especially brutal. It has no right to happen.

Last month, Joe Orton was apparently murdered by his
roommate, who just as apparently committed suicide. If the
whole thing weren't so horribly true, Orton himself would have
loved the incident, its ludicrous melodrama and the various,
lurid speculations reported in the newspapers (overdoses of
drugs, homosexuality, and so on). But it is true and Orton is
dead at thirty-four. You probably never heard of him.

He was an English playwright and had only three plays (two
full-length and a one-acter) produced. Of them, only *Entertaining Mr. Sloane* was seen in the United States, and upon receiving outrageously negative reviews from most of New York's
critics it closed a Broadway engagement after a two- or three-
week run. It was the best play of the 1965–1966 season.

That such a play is unappreciated in New York—at least,
upon first producton—comes as no surprise. Invariably, the ruling sensibilities are too constricted for the adventurous, the
original, and the especially bright. About half the best plays of

any season are doomed to quick closings because of this. And so although the fate of *Entertaining Mr. Sloane* was very upsetting, and remains so, Orton was young, productive, and in England, where theater conditions were healthy enough to assure his survival. Sooner or later, I thought, New York would be ready for him and in the meanwhile he would turn out a body of good plays. But he is dead.

Entertaining Mr. Sloane was a terribly serious and very comic play written with the surrealism that marks most modern drama. Its style was undeniably influenced by Harold Pinter's, dressing extravagant situations in perfectly ordinary clothing so that a perfectly wild premise could be followed to otherwise logical conclusions. But once this influence is conceded, Orton must be given full credit for personality (and I mean that in a very literal sense). His plays are his, and their tone, their values, their humor, and their theater devices are unarguably original.

Entertaining Mr. Sloane is set in a house located in the midst of a rubbish pile. The rubbish within the house is little different from that outside. It is that of humanity and its moral hypocrisy, greed, lying, and personal cruelty. Most of all, the rubbish is that of the family unit and its perversion of love for personal gratification. Yet, for all of this, Orton's play is wonderfully comic and even sunny in its appreciation of people and their weirdness.

The story is about the frighteningly amoral young Sloane, who is picked up and brought home by a sex-starved, children-starved, love-starved lady. He is immediately desired by her trivial and homosexual brother and soon is getting the best of both of them (the "best" meaning clothes and cars, since he is hopelessly without values). But their father recognizes him as a murderer, and although Sloane kills the old man, his guilt places him in the couple's power. Having begun as their master, he winds up their slave.

The play is written in dry, hyperformal dialogue, and because of this, the most outrageous things can be said with absolute relaxation. For example:

KATH: When did they [his parents] die?
SLOANE: I was eight. They passed away together.
KATH: How shocking.
SLOANE: I've an idea that they had a suicide pact. Couldn't prove it, of course.
KATH: Of course not. With a nice lad like you to take care of you'd think they'd've postponed it.

Kath herself is a magnificent combination of the touching and the ridiculous. Despite her obvious, tacky looseness she will say, "I'd the upbringing a nun would envy and that's the truth. Until I was fifteen I was more familiar with Africa than with my own body." And yet when her brother threatens to take Sloane from her she is heartbreaking ("If you send him away I shall cry like the time you took my real baby").

Loot, Orton's second play, was well received and is still running in London. It is even funnier than *Sloane*, though it is not as diverse and is often silly. Again, Orton uses symbols easily and sparingly. In *Sloane* it was the garbage piles of humanity and in *Loot* it is a bank robbery committed by tunneling in through a funeral parlor. People are so concerned with trivia they will even use—and entirely fail to comprehend—death to achieve it. And perhaps this is their salvation. Its fun and silliness makes life bearable and even enjoyable. So for all the playing with corpses and coffins in *Loot*, and for all its hatred of the police, the play has grand fun with mock melodrama and incidental put-downs of anything from the church to the British royal family. A comic footnote to it is a change demanded by the Lord Chamberlain—England's censoring office—changing the name of a brothel from Consummatum Est to Kingdom Come, which is, of course, even funnier.

The Beatles' "A Day in the Life" was played at Orton's funeral. It was perfect for several reasons. He had been working

84

on a script for them. More than that, the magnificent lyric ("I read the news today oh boy/About a lucky man who made the grade/And though the news was rather sad/Well I just had to laugh . . ." *) captured not just his sensibility but that of today's dignified and mystically elated young people. His plays, plus a third, completed just before his death, remain. But that is all there will be. And I think it is rotten that he died.

Entertaining Mr. Sloane (October 13, 1965)

Entertaining Mr. Sloane is an abstract play in a conventional setting and the effect is startling—a combination of the bizarre and the near-true. It is a form that is almost entirely new to New York theater (the only comparable work was *Semi-Detached,* a fine play that ran briefly a couple of years ago). The kind of theater that it produces is strangely frightening, weirdly comic and so odd, so new-focused, that taking it in is like seeing the whole world different.

Joe Orton's play (which opened last night at the Lyceum) is set in a consummately vulgar lower-class home that is right in the middle of a junk dump. The significance of this is properly obvious—no point messing around with obscurity. His people, in their odd-end exaggeration, are the messy shadows that lurk in family relationships. Their story is a contest between degeneracy and depravity.

This all sounds perfectly pretentious, I know, but what Mr. Orton has done that avoids pretension is to mate his sordid scheme with freshly straight-faced and not-so-straight-faced comedy. The mixture between the perverse and the ridiculous is coolly stirred and it comes bubbling up as arch, pointed, and, yes, sensitive theater.

85

The lady of the house is a flabby, half-mad, and completely stupid forty-one-year-old, living with her senile father (called Dadda). She picks up a strange-looking young man and brings him home as a roomer. To say he is strange-looking hardly describes the look of Dudley Sutton. His Mr. Sloane appears to be an albino, very lanky and with the widest, sneakiest, phoniest-innocent eyes I have ever seen a normal-eyed actor manage. (The performance is frigidly superb.) Within moments, the lady is broadly and absurdly seducing him. Orton blends her virginal insistence with an overpowering maternalism and comes up with a sorrowfully pathetic lady.

Her brother is another matter. A businessman who conceals his commonness with flashy clothes, he is sadistic and condescending to his sister and hasn't been spoken to by Dadda in twenty years. He is also a homosexual.

For the first half of the play, the strange Mr. Sloane is in charge of everybody. As emotionally and sexually colorless as an albino's pigmentation, he is free to use himself as animal bait. He becomes whatever people want him to become—a muscular, athletic youth for the brother, a son and lover for the sister. With these weapons, Mr. Sloane gets himself bed, board, a chauffeur's uniform, and plenty of spending money.

For a while things are cold-bloodedly marvelous for him, but his own nonhumanity puts him at his twin-lovers' disposal. At the play's end he is the subject of a contract, drawn to share his sexual comfort. He represents a child as the victim of parental sexual needs.

A story outline, however, does little justice to Orton's darkly clever play. The way these characters are written, in their primary-color exaggeration, they are midway between comic strip and photograph. The sister, magnificently played by Sheila Hancock, speaks as if her mouth were a pinhole (she pronounces "Sloane" as "Slewn")—her accent is a hodgepodge of affectations and Cockneyisms. Her need for a baby is overwhelming ("Mama worries for you") and her love is tearworthy.

The brother, who is Orton's father image for this strange family, is depraved. His decision to take Mr. Sloane for a young lover is cool and emotionless. But he is a homosexual and so he is somebody, which is a great deal more than Sloane is. Lee Montague is perfect at blandly spinning Orton's forthrightly ridiculous lines ("Four boys—a borrowed car—what did you need a woman for?").

Alan Schneider's direction took this very difficult material and evidently knew exactly what to do with it. His characters take turns reciting clichés and burning black holes, and Schneider kept them perfectly balanced. This balance extended throughout the play, matching comedy against oddity against pathos inside William Ritman's very right set. Furthermore, and most splendidly, this direction moved the play slowly, then quicker until it whirled into the third act like a cracked top, finally stopping to sit comfortably in its chilly conclusion.

I must concede that not everything about this play is perfect. From time to time Orton steps too far for comedy and gives in to a too-obvious joke. And his whole point about family relationships, granting the exaggeration for drama's sake, is a bit hard to swallow. But its point really isn't the point—Orton probably didn't consider it the main thingness of his play anyhow. The point is really the play and its character, and the play is remarkable.

Rave Review
(The Overrated)

Luv (*November 11, 1964*)

I̲T must have pained Mike Nichols to direct a full-length play covering a piece of territory that he and Elaine May used to polish off in a quick ten minutes. Murray Schisgal's *Luv*, opening last night at the Booth, is a bright enough little cartoon that goes on and on as if a half-dozen duplicate reels were spliced together. And by the time you've pretty well got the idea, it just doesn't seem so bright anymore. Mr. Schisgal's snickering at "the general American conception of love" begins to seem but a half step superior to the subject. It is a cliché itself.

The author's sense of superiority, aside from its becoming tiresome, begins to get offensive. His target is so small and his weapon so large. His tone is so smug and his attack so crude. His invitation to the audience to come and share a laugh at the expense of everyone except itself becomes very uninviting.

Not that the laugh is undeserved. Mr. Schisgal's target is moon-croon love, *McCall's* magazine love, do-you-love-me love, popular music love. It is fool's love. But it is not nearly so prevalent as Schisgal thinks. It is what we see in movies but it is not what most of us honestly believe. We are all pretty silly in many ways, but this just doesn't happen to be one of them.

The love Schisgal is snickering at, really, is the love that exists for popular romance and people who criticize popular romance. Because it is basically irrelevant to all of us, it can't possibly be commentary.

Luv is funny, from time to time, especially when Eli Wallach is showing Alan Arkin and Anne Jackson exactly how caricature should be played. Mr. Wallach is a line sketch of the materialist—the man who is doing things the American Way. By day he is a stockbroker, by night he sells "bric-a-brac and personal accessories." "All I want," he says, "is you and the opportunity to be incredibly rich some day." His cliché is money and success.

The "you" is the wife he gets rid of in the first act and tries to win back in the second. She is a Dr. Joyce Brothers type— right down to the encyclopedic knowledge of sports, reported quiz-program style. She is modern, she is efficient, she is the educated housewife—*her* cliché is the slick-magazine home life with the husband home from work, newspaper under the arm, asking, "What's for dinner, hon?"

Alan Arkin is Schisgal's third caricature—the bohemian. At school he studied Greek and premedicine. He tells the old "sensitive" story about the dog laughing at him. He plays the guitar (flamenco), writes poetry, and walks around wondering what life is. The play begins as he is about to leap from a bridge. Wallach rescues him so that he can palm off a wife and marry the "girl he loves."

From that point forward, Mr. Schisgal attempts to write a play of continuous mockery. The phrases of popular love gush from everyone's lips ("Where there is no trust there can be no love," "Her eyes, her lips," "Give love a chance," and so on). Popular love songs are sung seriously. Jackson leans against a lamppost, mocking the classic prostitute. Much of this, especially early in the play, is very funny. But never again are those original conceptions—the silly materialist, the silly poet, ever repeated. They get mixed up and lost in the torrent of mocked clichés that pour all over the out-of-left-field slapstick direction that Mr. Nichols threw in to get laughs.

The sweating for comedy becomes desperate. The clichés aren't working—they've become abused (although Schisgal must be granted a superlative ear for them). Water is splashed, vaudeville routines are worked in, weak jokes are pressed ("I don't care if she belches Beethoven"), and all the while those mimicked clichés continue—"You don't mean?"—"Yes. . . . Yes!"

Wallach is marvelous—he becomes exactly the animated cartoon, seeming to go from frame to frame almost in stop action. Anne Jackson turns her parody too cold, making it almost bitter when it should be just four-color and unreal. She isn't funny even when she is whipping out a portable graph that charts her husband's depressed sexual desires (according to Schisgal, the American Marriage is sexless—a comment that is hackneyed and senseless).

Alan Arkin is completely undisciplined and generally impossible as the poet, relying completely on Second City mannerisms and betraying a virtually amateur command of stage sense.

Man of La Mancha (*December 23, 1965*)

Although there are a number of interesting things about *Man of La Mancha,* there is nothing very interesting *in* it. Which is pretty remarkable considering that in any musical, between the book and the music and the dancing, there usually is *something* that manages to catch the sense of theater. The only theatrical thing in *Man of La Mancha* is a tremendous stairway attached to the ceiling that comes dipping down like a doomsday passage.

That stairway is about the only thing that moves in *Man of*

La Mancha, if you want a picture of the kind of activity smashing around the ANTA-Washington Square Theatre last night. Director Albert Marre must have spent rehearsals nailing his cast's toes to the chalk lines. And there they stayed, unless you want to call Jack Cole's oddities choreography. Mr. Cole has a really extraordinary knack for getting *The Thief of Baghdad* into anything he does, and it is a game in itself figuring out just how he is going to sneak a belly dancer and some turbaned floor-slappers into the unlikeliest places. The marvelous thing about this is that it fools you every time—Cole never sneaks *anything* in. Just when a musical has absolutely nothing to do with turbans and belly dancers, there they come.

To be fair with Cole, there was another brief dance earlier in the musical's only act, but then that wasn't being fair with us. Something about a girl being raped by a bunch of guys with whips and stuff like that. Pretty weird.

If Dale Wasserman's book wasn't quite that weird, it was odd enough in its attempt to combine episodes from *Don Quixote* with the life of its author. Beginning with Cervantes' imprisonment for trying to collect taxes from the church, Wasserman has his cellmates try him for being an idealist, a bad poet, and an honest man. To identify this as ten-cent depth and the flimsiest of dramatic structure is to be excessively kind. At any rate, it now enables Cervantes to play out his book.

Some episodes proceed, gratefully interrupted now and again by some very good music and some very bad lyrics. Because of the relentlessly unchanging mood of the storytelling and because of Mr. Marre's inability to coax any variations of tempo, vocal dynamics, or characterization from his cast, it all settles into a pretty soggy rut. Which is rather a shame because there is no reason why a musical can't be relatively quiet. Nor is there any reason why a musical can't be relatively serious. But there is a difference between quietness and stupor, a difference between seriousness and talk about "this glorious quest" to "dream the undreamable dream."

94

The most interesting thing about *Man of La Mancha* is that it is the first musical to my knowledge that has been attempted in the ANTA-Washington Square sort of theater. That is, a rounded, deep-dish house that surrounds a boldly thrusting stage on three sides.

There are many problems that such a theater poses for a musical—scenery is virtually ruled out, and so is absolute realism. Choreography must be in patterns viewable from all angles. And most seriously, the structure of the book must be designed so that the drama is played for depth rather than width. The greatest problem is that there is no tradition from which to have learned. It is all new ground.

The fact is that *Man of La Mancha,* while suffering from the handicaps of such a theater, took no advantages of its intimacy or its allowance for three-dimensional theater. Instead, it looked terribly bare, as if it had been designed for gobs of since-removed scenery. And its poor actors squirmed out there in the midst of the audience with little to do and less reason to be there.

Nevertheless, Mitch Leigh wrote a very fine Spanishy score and was lucky to have oboe, bassoon, flamenco guitar, and all sorts of nice things orchestrated into it by Neil Warner. Someday there will be a terrific Spanish musical. But please without Joe Darion's amateur lyrics, which have nothing to do with the characters' situations or vocabularies and run to lines like: "Still I yell to the sky/Though I can't tell you why/That I like him."

As for the performances, Richard Kiley was his usual professional self in the title role. Joan Diener, between bosom flashings, managed to make the oddest faces while straining for soprano under the wildest head of hair since Sparkle Plenty. Robert Rounseville's beautiful baritone was wasted in a small role, the significance of which I have yet to understand. Irving Jacobson brought his Sancho Panza down from the Yiddish theater, which was about as apt as the Cole belly dancers. And to cap it all off, the small singing chorus managed to be off pitch right down to the last belting beep.

So what else is new?

Rosencrantz and Guildenstern Are Dead
(*October 17, 1967*)

Rosencrantz and Guildenstern have long represented one of the great jokes in drama. Supernumeraries in Hamlet's majestic tragedy, they exist only to fumble their trivial tasks, to be constantly ridiculed, to be confused, and finally to die the only offstage deaths in the play. Even their deaths are unimportant to Shakespeare, just as their lives are unimportant to Hamlet.

Tom Stoppard has taken these two characters and built an entire play around them. Or rather, he has added another side, indeed a backside, to *Hamlet*. His play, *Rosencrantz and Guildenstern Are Dead,* exists only in tandem with *Hamlet,* just as the characters exist only because that prince exists. And as a play, it cannot be considered without the Shakespeare beside it (or at its front). This itself makes it unusual in conception, and as a matter of fact, the entire play is extraordinary. Whether it is effective as a stage piece is quite another question and the answer is: generally but not always. It is comic, yes, and terribly bright. It is very literate, occasionally moving, and very eclectic. It is also confused at times because of the excessive trickiness of its concept, and it hammers at a philosophical point of view that is never developed beyond the basic statement. Its existentialism is shallow and its debt to Samuel Beckett extreme. Mr. Stoppard is clever but his play is not profound, as he meant it, so much as it is a theatrical flamboyance.

The play, which opened last night at the Alvin Theatre, speculates on what Rosencrantz and Guildenstern were doing all the while that the Hamlet tragedy was transpiring. And what it concludes is exactly what might have been concluded had it never been written—that Rosencrantz and Guildenstern were doing absolutely nothing. Just waiting. Waiting for something to happen. Waiting for some explanation for their presence. Watching events—and time—go by. This is *Waiting for Godot* paraphrased, in point and even in style. The events have meaning for others, perhaps great significance and high tragedy. For Rosencrantz and Guildenstern they have no meaning at all. Their lives are ticking by on a clock marked in moments, and they have only the present to go by. Neither remembers any past and neither can imagine a future. Except for certain death.

Their deaths are certain for various reasons. Mr. Stoppard's most important reason is that everybody must die and it is this Kafkaesque fatality that is presented as the play's theme. But this is never developed beyond the simple statement of it. The real reason for their death is that *Hamlet* has already been written and that Rosencrantz and Guildenstern die in it. Now the play is in the land of Pirandello, and its relationship to *Six Characters in Search of an Author* is also obvious. The story of their lives, as of those six characters, is written and concluded. It can be lived no other way.

Conceding these thematic and theatrical debts, *Rosencrantz and Guildenstern Are Dead* must still be taken for a genuine theatrical tour de force. The contrast between Stoppard's clean and intelligent English for the two messengers and Shakespeare's blank verse spells the great difference between what one's life looks like and what it really is. The uncertainty of their purpose and the irrelevance of Claudius' court to their own lives grasps the futility of individual existence compared to the sweep of history. And even the absurdity of that history. Rosencrantz and Guildenstern "drift down time clutching at straws," not knowing what they are supposed to do and unable to simply relax and respond to life.

The playwright's clear-minded understanding of *Hamlet* is awesome, and his use of the few Rosencrantz and Guildenstern scenes from the play is marvelously merged with his inventions for them. It is strange that he omitted their one moment of insight (we are "the indifferent children of the earth") but his conception of them as victims is deeply sensitive and his play nearly always manages to elude the trap of sounding like a collegiate burlesque (which it basically is). Derek Goldby's direction, though sometimes overdone, is vividly theatrical, though I don't see why he made the actual *Hamlet* scenes so foolish (everybody is played as though by tacky, melodramatic actors). Brian Murray and Charles Wood are pricelessly funny, hopelessly pathetic, and altogether brilliant as the interchangeable title characters. And all is generally handsome. As a theater experience, this is striking and funny. As philosophy and even as a play, it is not quite so sure of itself.

Your Own Thing (*January 28, 1968*)

After all these years of silly and wasteful condescension, the theater is at last recognizing the existence of rock 'n' roll music, though as might have been predicted, by the time it did, pop music had already moved off into still newer, more sophisticated styles. In any case, *Your Own Thing* is the second off-Broadway show this season to use the music, and you can expect more. I hope that as the music becomes more theatrically familiar, the authors will be able to apply it to subjects other than the music scene. For now it seems that shows using rock music are going to be *about* rock music.

This one, which opened Friday night at the Orpheum Theatre, has adapted Shakespeare's *Twelfth Night* to that milieu (it also happens to be the second musical within a single week to

98

be based on the comedy, which must be chalked up to coincidence rather than imitation). Count Orsino has become the manager of a rock group called The Apocalypse, of which Sebastian is a member. Donald Driver, the director-librettist, has managed to neatly preserve the plot outline without doing disservice to either the source or the new work. His is the writing of a man obviously relaxed with Shakespeare and in occasionally interpolating genuine *Twelfth Night* speeches he both proves the relationship of the two plays and provides humor through contrast.

I wish I could say many other good things about this production, but the fact is that Mr. Driver's cleverness and imagination have got the best of him and the work is both overwritten and overdirected. There are far too many things in it, and although a number of them are admirable they become overwhelmingly complicated. In its separate parts, *Your Own Thing* is fascinating, comic, and theatrical, but as a whole it is long-winded and tiresome.

Its overall conception is in mixed media. Robert Guerra has designed a pale, cardboard-cutout set to provide a good number of planes for the projection of movies, slides, and lightwork effects. Visuals by Des Pro Studios are almost always flashing upon them, sometimes for pop purposes (presumable comments on the proceedings by Everett Dirksen, John Wayne, Humphrey Bogart), sometimes just for abstract effect.

These are far more fascinating than the book itself, which is relatively conventional in style, even with its capitalization on the obvious homosexual implications in the Shakespeare original. After all, wasn't Count Orsino attracted to Viola in her male disguise? Now called Orson, he is still attracted, only he feels guilty about it. Finally deciding hell's bells, if he likes him he likes him, Orson discovers that it is not only a girl but that she is displeased to have been liked as a boy. It is a neat twist based on an accurate perception of the play, and I wish the rest of Driver's book had been as neat. It isn't.

As for the Hal Hester-Danny Apolinar score, it ranges from up-to-date rock to near-Broadway trash, spending most of its time in the middle area of heavy-beat monotony. It was difficult to tell whether the musicians were somewhere backstage or on tape, but in either case their sound was too distant for balance. I wish the Hester-Apolinar lyrics ("All that glass/All that chrome/Can I ever call this place home?") had been even more distant, but the stage mikes, astonishing for a small theater, made that all too unlikely. I will say, though, that they sometimes managed to flow into dialogue with a liquidity that is beyond most Broadway lyricists.

Unfortunately, there was very little choreography, which is kind of crazy considering how tightly the new music is wound up with dance, but what there was was excellent, and since no other credit is given I assume it was the work of Mr. Driver. As for the performances, they were what is usually called "energetic" and the voices were good, if of the show-biz-brass school. Especially admirable was the Viola of Leland Palmer, comic, physical, and professional.

There is some good work here, and further proof—if anybody needed it—that all the new uses of music and sound and light are workable in the theater and can be disciplined. Nearly all of it is better than the embarrassing title. But facts are facts, and *Your Own Thing*, for whatever its ingredients, has come out of the oven half-baked.

The Price (*February 8, 1968*)

Despite the noisy resentment of his master status, Arthur Miller has still been enjoying international reputation and a general (if increasingly vague) American respect as the country's reigning dramatist. It has now been some time since he earned that reputation—and reputations must be constantly earned. His new play, *The Price,* opened last night at the Morosco Theatre, and it did little to prove continuing accomplishment for him. There is still a strength, still an ease with the language, still a dedication to reason, still an ability to create striking characters, and while these are not the most fashionable of abilities they are true to the stage. But they are not enough to make an evening of theater. *The Price* is an old-fashioned drama, and a carelessly written one, displaying Mr. Miller as a slackening artist.

As a story, it is about a point, that is, there is no real story at all but a situation designed to be a discussion table. Like Miller's most recent plays, the discussion is about the responsibility of one human being to another, and like virtually all of them, the human beings involved are members of a family that includes a mistrustful father, a martyred mother, and two brothers, one successful and one not.

The stage is set (and wonderfully by Boris Aronson) in the attic of a condemned house, where the accumulated furniture (the past) of the Franz family is to be sold (expurgated). Two brothers, who have not seen each other since their father's death eighteen years earlier, are reuniting for the sale. The reason for their estrangement is that Walter, the older one, refused to lend his brother $500 to finish school, forcing Victor to sacrifice his future to support their impoverished father. Victor, a policeman and a confessed failure, now finds himself middle-aged, eligible for retirement, and without purpose in life.

He enters with his wife, Esther, an aggressive woman who still hopes to make something of him. They are soon joined by Solomon, a remarkable appraiser and a splendid character, who proceeds into a comic routine that almost excuses the talkiness that went before him. He is delightful, claiming, in thick Jewish accents, that he is eighty-nine years old, was formerly in the British Navy, and was once part of an acrobat team ("They should rest in peace, I worked at the bottom"). Miller's comedy writing is wonderful—rich, relaxed, and extremely funny—and it is strange that he never let loose with it before. But it becomes a self-indulgence, not entirely relevant to the play, which cannot proceed until Walter arrives. When he does, *The Price* takes on straight melodramatic characteristics, relying entirely on revelation—the dead father had actually turned down Walter's offer to help; he hadn't ʳeally needed to be supported, having some money of his own; the younger son suspected this and perhaps even wanted to fail.

But the backs and forths of these revelations grow ludicrous and complicated, and Miller's point finally gets lost among the alternate hedgings and assertions. Clearly, the point originally intended was that for whatever mistakes and whatever motives, the younger son thought his father was helpless and so had to fulfill his responsibility. But Miller overcomplicates this point for the wrong reasons and oversimplifies its genuine subtleties. Put more simply, the author has taken a fairly obvious problem in living (as a pop psychologist might put it) and talked it to death while missing its essence. In a real way, *The Price* is a failure in logic.

Yet there was some genuinely metaphorical material established, if misused. The condemned house is a good symbol for a dead family, and the old appraiser, who is afraid to buy the whole lot for fear of not living long enough to sell it, is wonderfully representative of the need for a purpose in life. It is a need that the son Victor cries with. Despite the foolishness of symbolic names (Solomon, Victor, Esther), there is a basic breadth of meaning that these people and their situation represent in the abstract. But Miller was never a playwright for the abstract—was always a playwright dedicated to discussion. It is discussion that kills this play—too much of it saying too little.

The performances by Kate Reid (Esther) and Harold Gregory (Solomon) are superb, those by Pat Hingle (Victor) and Arthur Kennedy (Walter) bland. The difference is the difference between backgrounds in character acting and backgrounds in post-Stanislavskian realism. Miller's own static direction did not help. The play has its moments, but it may very well be, sadly, that the playwright has had his day.

Hair (May 10, 1968)

When *Hair* first opened at the Public Theatre, it was as middle-class a vision of hippies, and as tame a production, as its corny subtitle (*The American Tribal-Love Rock Musical*) forewarned. The book was a really dumb teen-age love story with long hair, and the lyrics reflected it. Whatever value lay in *Hair* was in its use of middle-range rock music, and there's no denying it was the first musical to do so.

Now it is on Broadway, having moved to the Biltmore Theatre, and it is considerably different from the original, not as bad, though not much better. Gerome Ragni and James Rado have just about eliminated their book (not entirely and what remains is as idiotic as ever) and Galt MacDermot has written a great many more songs while dropping a few of the old ones. This was necessary because *Hair* has become a succession of songs and dances, with no libretto to absorb any of the time. So there are now thirty different numbers and I haven't heard so many in a Broadway show since *The Most Happy Fella*.

But *Hair* is unique on Broadway for more reasons than that. In fact, it has absolutely nothing in common with the Broadway musicals, whose formula has been slavishly followed for so long that with only few exceptions they remain old-time song-and-dance shows. Considering the pop music phenomenon now in progress, the uniqueness of *Hair* proves just how backward Broadway really is.

It is set on a stage that has been stripped bare. There is a striking proscenium of lighting equipment and occasionally a screen (except for some strobe stuff there are no lightworks at all). Otherwise, the props are utilitarian. The company is all hippies, most of them looking pretty authentic. The band is off on one side and the original rock quartet has been expanded to include some brass and an electronic sound producer. This has given the music added depth, and Mr. MacDermot used the opportunity to update some of his music, especially in the beginning, giving his score at least some relationship to the creative sophistication of today's pop. However, the house amplification system is as outmoded as those of most Broadway theaters and cannot take the volume, creating a great deal of sound distortion.

As for the show itself, it only occasionally shows the excitement which the new music and dance promised and projects the sloppiest and silliest of hippie thinking. As a theater production it is virtually amateur and is as un-Broadway in this respect as it is in its modernity. Tom O'Horgan, a prolific and creative off-off Broadway director, has replaced Gerald Freedman as director, and what he gained in openness he lost in finesse. *Hair* is messy enough to reassure its Broadway audiences that anything related to hippies is disorganized and immature, and that, perhaps, is the saddest thing about it.

The performances are as untied-together as the direction. It is difficult to determine what was staged by Mr. O'Horgan and what was choreographed by Julie Arenal since there are few dances as such. One can imagine just what a professional choreographer with a taste for the frug and the knowledge to turn it into theater dance might have done with this opportunity. But in casting for authentic hippiness, either O'Horgan or Miss Arenal overlooked the need for trained dancers. Enthusiasm can be very effective at, say Café La Mama, but on a wide stage and in a musical theater context, it can't pass for dance.

Finally, the book problem. Without a doubt, the libretto is the bane of the Broadway musical and the idea of it will have to be revolutionized before any further progress can be made.

But the answer doesn't lie in no book at all. There must be something to give music and dance the added dimension for theater. The sheer chaos of *Hair* must be blamed on its book-lessness as much as its direction. The bits and pieces of dialogue are only frantic corks for production gaps, and the widely publicized nudity is ridiculous, having nothing to do with anything. As a matter of fact, neither does the rampant obscenity, though I suppose an argument could be made for its liberalizing effect. Liberalization, of course, is the point of *Hair,* but what good is so admirable a purpose when the work is so sloppy?

Dames at Sea (*December 3, 1968*)

Dames at Sea claims to be a "new thirties musical," rather than a parody of one, because parodies are passé. But disclaimers notwithstanding, the show at the Bouwerie Lane Theatre is indeed a parody, generally a broad one, nearly always unfunny and labored. And, yes, parodies are passé.

As such productions go, *Dames at Sea* is fairly accurate in its mockery of thirties show tunes, lyrics, and books, but the idea is so tired that it all comes off as a fifties varsity show and is produced with what looks like the budget of one. George Haimsohn and Robin Miller have written a book that mixes a "42d Street" backstage movie with a *Hit the Deck* musical. Jim Wise's music mimics and sometimes paraphrases the songs of Kern, Youmans, and Porter, and the Haimsohn-Miller lyrics go along with the joke ("It isn't Leslie Howard/Or even Noel Coward/It's you, it's you, it's you").

But these are already too broadly done to be called reproduction rather than parody, and the beguine number is practically stolen from another parody, Sheldon Harnick's "Boston Beguine." Director Neal Kenyon hammers down the broad stage gestures and tap-dance routines until only the cloistered could miss the point and finally the King Kong joke ("It would be like Fay Wray saying no to King Kong"). I have had it with King Kong, with old comic books and radio programs, and with twenties, thirties, forties, and fifties things, not to mention sixties, which must be due.

The *Dames at Sea* company must be congratulated for going through the thing as if it were the latest word in camp. Bernadette Peters has the voice, the face, and the tip-tapping toes for the kid who becomes a star, but not the body. David Christmas played her sailor like a counterman from Mother Hubbard, and Steve Elmore spent the night (vainly) trying to do Paul Lynde in his dual role of ship captain and director. Tamara Long overdid the big-star business.

With the producer too cheap or careless to provide well-painted scenery, press the costumes, or even replace torn stockings, the production looked pretty chintzy. Even the good work in reproducing the music and lyrics, the better work of Sally Stark as a gum-chewing, straight-shooting, wisecracking chorine, or the superior vocal arrangements by Richard J. Leonard —not any of these could save the old and overdone idea. In brief(s), it is a middle-class fag show, tidier than most but still so hackneyed it is itself a camp.

1776 *(March 17, 1969)*

What Broadway needed was a patriotic musical, right? I don't think so. *1776* has thrown in two lines (maybe three) about "commitment," as if they referred the show to the current revolutionary movements, but the new musical at the 46th Street Theatre has as much to do with present rebellion as a watermelon at a race riot. *1776* is pure patriotic documentary, right down to the Liberty Bell ringing at the finale, and its only surprise is no American flag with every program.

It's really kind of difficult to believe that Peter Stone actually set out to write a musical about the decision of the Continental Congress to declare American independent. Yet there it is, complete with a calendar ticking off (I believe the expression is) the days until the Fourth of July. Nor is that the only peculiar thing about this show.

It begins with at least ten solid minutes of music—music that seems written, if you can imagine, for an operetta by Mozart, complete with recitative and harpsichord. Need I say, this is soon enough abandoned for show-time patriotism, but then again, music is almost abandoned entirely. There are endless stretches without any songs at all, and not a single dance (well, a suggested minuet and that's it). Then, suddenly, there is a burst of long and rather involved song. It is rather a strange production, even aside from the fact that it has no intermission at all, stretching its two hours and twenty minutes from the endless to the eternal.

But strangest of all is its story. Mr. Stone has followed the series of patriotic clichés that was drilled into all of us in the days before anyone complained about history textbooks. Thomas Jefferson being terribly idealistic, Benjamin Franklin being terribly wise, John Adams being terribly dour. To liven this up, Stone has given Jefferson the added quality of being hot for his sorely missed bride, and for a frivolity has her imported by a thoughtful Franklin for a touch of inspiration. Once out of bed, Jefferson rips off the Declaration of Independence. So much for humor. Franklin is made out to be earthy and Adams is given a touch of New England conservative romance (the best kind). This does not stop any of them from being cardboard characters from summer historical pageants, and the whole business is rather bizarre when you think of the American image that was so long sustained by just this sort of thing. It is an image that has become, practically, a national neurosis.

This story is staged, before Jo Mielziner's extremely simple set (only one basic change, no flies, no trolleys, no curtains), with barely a trace of movement—which isn't exactly what musicals are about. Though much of Sherman Edwards' music is complicated in structure, it is hard to say how much of that was his doing. Ed Sauter's orchestrations were so beautifully understated, with such clear inner voices and interesting harmonies, that he has to get major credit for the handsome sound. Brasses muted, woodwinds rich, and lots of strings.

Working with this was just about the best-rehearsed singing I've heard on Broadway. Peter Howard provided handsome vocal arrangements and the voices were all good and strong. Unfortunately, they were also all male (virtually—two women made brief, and quite unnecessary, appearances).

But all this credit detail should tell that there is little else to talk about. Certainly, Mr. Edwards' lyrics are nothing to speak of. The prosody is sometimes atrocious ("par-ti-*ci*-ple," "de-pen-*den*-cy," "sex-u-*al*"), and he is not above tossing in an extra word to fill out a beat. His lines run from the trite ("I live like a nun in a cloister") to the banal ("Because I have crossed the Rubicon/Let the bridges be burned behind me").

Peter Hunt's staging left everything to be desired, and then some. His big ending is to leave the signers of the Declaration in a tableau exactly like the famous painting, but since they were more or less glued to those spots all night, it was hardly a feat. Anyhow, I wouldn't have believed I would ever see such a tableau in any theater. Mr. Hunt is inclined to running jokes (a soldier clonking cross-stage, or repeated remarks by the same character), and that tactic more or less sums up his finesse. The individual performances were examples of professionals on their own—Howard Da Silva (Franklin), William Daniels (Adams). They earned all the praise that such professionalism deserves. That's more than I can say for their vehicle—a wooden replica of souvenir-shop patriotism.

The Broadway Musical

Anyone Can Whistle *(April 6, 1964)*

I T's not simply that *Anyone Can Whistle* is a brilliantly inventive musical. It's that the bursting vitality and adult originality of the new Stephen Sondheim-Arthur Laurents show are proof of the very point the production made at the Majestic Saturday night. And that point is that life is a miracle and the living of it is miraculous for those who are really alive. It is a ringingly bright shout for individuality, and because it is so individual itself, it is whole, it is fresh, it is new, and it is perfectly wonderful.

Thank heavens that there still are adults in the theater. And that they are willing to assume that their audience is adult too. Mr. Laurents has written a book that fairly glitters with fey wit and mature insight (although it is occasionally confused). His humor does not condescend with cheap broadness, his characters do not insult with nice-guy, sweet-girl superficiality. He has not written a simple story geared for handy songs and dances. Nor has Mr. Sondheim provided simpleminded music for it. Here are songs that combine musical sophistication with theatrical flair. At once melodic and interesting, they easily represent the finest Broadway composing in years.

The wildly abstract story is set in a small broken-down town, run with a hand in the till by a slinking, brassy mayoress and her band of salivating yesmen. The only going concern is the local mental hospital, which has been nicknamed the Cookie Jar and its inmates "cookies."

Anxious to find a new source of revenue for the foundering village, the administration creates a miracle—water spouts from a rock (left over from an earlier Peer Gynt Festival) and tourism begins. But the hospital's head nurse demands that her 49 patients be allowed a visit, hoping to discredit the commercial shrine. The mayoress, who also realizes that the curative waters will never work on the patients, takes off after the nurse. It is at this point that the new psychiatrist arrives, dancing the samba while he analyzes, and throwing the whole show into high gear. From that point onward, it's everybody for himself—the big Majestic stage explodes into glorious life, time after time, while the fireworks of wit flash giddily.

This show has jokes wherever you look, and sometimes where you don't—dance jokes, musical jokes, intellectual jokes. You catch a quick, acid parody of a *West Side Story* dance and turn around to find a conversational cliché being mocked. Although the general attitude is that you can, indeed you *must*, fight "city hall," the musical shouts it by being alive with endless asides, caricatures, and mockeries.

Think of a mayoress who struts like the young Bette Davis and think of her as a high-kicking, negligee-trailing Angela Lansbury, flanked by four bellhop-chorus boys swiped from a nightclub floor. Think of a marvelously individual psychiatrist —who turns out to be patient number 50—hilariously separating the pilgrims from the cookies (there's no difference, of course). And think of him wonderfully vital and genuinely acted by Harry Guardino. This is a mesmerizing performance.

Think of the idealistic nurse, who flees from the corruptors, only to return in red wig and feathers, disguised as the Lady from Lourdes, coming to investigate the new shrine. A sudden burst of music (the old song "Lady in Red") and you are off laughing again. The lady is played by Lee Remick, who is all legs, dazzle, and magnificence—Miss Remick is a marvel. And think, finally, of series after series of Herbert Ross' exciting and witty ballets.

This is—you must know by now—a real original, and that is just what it is asking us to be if we want to be alive at all. It never falters until its very end, when it inexplicably lets itself be halted by a love ballad and a quiet finale. But that is too late to rob this sprite of its spirit. *Anyone Can Whistle* is as alive as it is telling everybody to be, and that makes it both important and exciting. [Following antagonistic reviews, the show closed within a week, and would have been included in the chapter called "The Unappreciated" if it weren't so significant among the musicals of the sixties.]

Fiddler on the Roof (*September 23, 1964*)

Fiddler on the Roof is a musical of such consummate artistry that it seems lightly vulgar to call it "wonderful," but it *is* wonderful, *just* wonderful, and the word will have to do, at least for the moment. There is much to be said about it.

What Jerome Robbins has done is to create a time, a feeling, a warmth, and an enormous excitement that bristles through between emotion strong enough to put permanent lumps in mass throats. He has done it with time, with swirling color, with rhythm, with rushing sweeps of changing moods. He has done it with movement that for sheer beauty and relevance is paralleled only by his own *West Side Story*. He has also done it with a Jerry Bock score so lovely, so original, so rightly apt as to establish the composer securely in Broadway's first rank.

And he couldn't have done it without Zero Mostel. Mr. Mostel's praises have been sung to the skies, but it is time to sing them to the heavens. To see him dance is to see an angel in underwear, to listen in on his conversations with God is to be privy to the secret of life. Watch him as the curtain rises. A fiddler is on a roof ("Every one of us is a fiddler on a roof, trying to scrape out a living, even if we fall and break our necks"). Mostel is below, and soon he is lifting his feet, just this much, and then he is shaking his belly—*slowly*. There is nobody else in this world who can shake a belly slowly.

Soon his fingers are jabbing at the air, high above his head. Jabbing, poking, dancing. The key to Tevye—to the Jew—to humanity—is in that shake, that poke, that dance. It is the finger stuck in the pie of human confusion.

Joseph Stein has based his book on Sholom Aleichem's stories, mostly those of *Tevye and His Daughters*. Set in the orthodox Jewish community of a provincial town in turn-of-the-century Russia, it has as a broad pattern the need and the heartbreak of changing traditions. Small traditions—the tradition of paternal matchmaking, the tradition of male-female segregation. And large traditions—intermarriage, political systems, homelands. The small breaks come easily. The large breaks, when they are necessary, leave shattered remnants, sometimes. New lives, sometimes. Whatever happens, life goes on and there still is hope, especially as long as Tevye has God as a friend.

God must surely be Mostel's friend, he talks with Him so easily. God is not so easy to talk to on a Broadway stage. He can become awkward, embarrassing to an audience. Mostel is His friend. He can berate God, apologetically; he can gossip with God, confidentially; he can complain to Him, prayerfully.

While Mostel is dealing with God, Mr. Robbins has set a stage to moving—in great hora circles, on stomping Russian pinpoints. He has the great watercolored washes of Boris Aronson to set things off before a brilliant background in bright, imaginative colors. He has a masterfully trained, superbly talented cast to do his work.

And he has the Jerry Bock score. Mr. Bock has already shown his originality in setting music perfectly to a time and a place. He has already displayed his marvelous talent for melody. He has never done either so well before. He has composed a score that uses swelling harmonies, bursting rhythms. Sheldon Harnick's lyrics still tend to be rather too simple, but they are improving and are beginning to show traces of effective character depth.

The cast backing Mostel is superb. Maria Karnilova is a gallant wife. Julia Migenes is a daughter with a glorious voice. Bert Convy is youth itself as her radical love, and Beatrice Arthur is a comical matchmaker.

It is all of these elements, joined in a surging, mellow, vastly professional entirety, that make *Fiddler on the Roof* a classic creation. It is a rich, sunbursting, magnificent show.

Oh What a Lovely War (October 1, 1964)

Oh What a Lovely War is an abject failure. It is a failure at being the bitter entertainment it wishes to be. It is a failure at being the ironic teacher it wishes to be. It is a failure at being the cynical observer it wishes to be. In fact, it only succeeds at being the naïvely collegiate, pretentiously supermoralistic one-way tract it really is. Whatever were the reasons for its general success in London, they are not readily evident. It opened last night at the Broadhurst under the joint auspices of David Merrick and Gerry Raffles.

Joan Littlewood's attempt to re-create the madness of World War I in terms of its own absurdities is a victim of its material as well as its form. The very first sketches reveal the attitude that is to be hammered the evening through. It is the elementary observation that war is ludicrous, per se. From that point,

Miss Littlewood proceeds to go absolutely nowhere with period songs of ironic gaiety paralleled against cold-blooded statistics. The songs are what one might cull from a cursory examination of wartime patriotism ("Pack Up Your Troubles," "If the Sergeant Steals Your Rum," and so on). The statistics are the truth.

The production's point of view is basically that this was terrible—hardly to be disputed, but neither is a condemnation of child beating.

More irritating still, *Oh What a Lovely War* bribes both itself and its audience by cuddling all concerned with the assurance that they are wonderful and intelligent people gathered together to celebrate their mutual sensitivity. Not only is Miss Littlewood disgusted with war. So are her cast, the orchestra, the audience, the ushers—everybody. We are all humanists, we can all laugh ruefully at the killers' madness. We are all terrific.

Well, that is an awfully easy kind of laughter. And it is awfully easy to snicker at the last of the adventure wars. And it is awfully easy to imply, ominously, that the final war is just around the corner. But it is also awfully easy to forget that World War I wasn't the last world war. That there was another useful war fought for an important reason. And that the next world war, if it comes, is evolving from a set of circumstances a great deal more complicated than the assassination of an archduke at Sarajevo.

Don't remind Miss Littlewood of that. It makes it too difficult to be humanistic. Besides, bitterness is so fashionable it would be a shame to make it difficult by demanding perception.

As for the form of this production, it fails there too. In its self-conscious and unsuccessful theatricality, it ignores every fundamental of the professional stage. And provides none of its own.

The stage is bare except for monolithic entrance and exit forms on either side. At the rear is an electric sign that flashes raw war data. From time to time a screen is dropped and rear-

116

projection slides show maps or casualty photographs. All is black and white, as are the satin clown costumes worn by the cast. This is trivial and ineffectual theatricality.

The structure of the entertainment is slapdash, a string of sketches, usually in the music-hall style and occasionally Brechtian in a mild way. The humor used is elementary irony, invariably heavy-handed and occasionally coarse.

The songs are played and sung straightforwardly (and sometimes badly) with virtually no use of musical technique to reinforce attitudes. Dance and movement in general are almost totally ignored. The performers are capable, although often unsure of themselves, and practically all of them wear the same expression of smug morality as does the production. The sole exception was Victor Spinetti's versatile ringmaster. Miss Littlewood's direction is of the most undisciplined sort.

In brief, *Oh What a Lovely War* is neither amusing nor bitter, neither pointed nor dramatic. It is small-time humanism.

Kelly Green (*February 19, 1965*)

Did anyone here love *Kelly?*

The idea of dropping $650,000 in one night would fascinate anybody, but the closing of the musical *Kelly* after a single, premiere performance a couple of weeks ago has prompted an especial amount of curiosity as well as the old question, "How could the producers have been unaware of something that was so obvious to everybody else?"

That question is asked after every Broadway disaster and the answer is usually that the producer was too close to it, or the director was too close to it, or something like that. This is a valid answer when a production has an intangible problem, which was hardly the case with *Kelly*. It is literally incredible that so many people did not see disaster ahead and I don't believe it—they *did* know, at least those who knew enough to know.

And in that sentence lies the cause of the *Kelly* debacle. The people at the very top of the production—the producers—did not know enough to know how bad it was. When *Kelly* played its single, fateful performance at the Broadhurst Theatre, the word "panic" was smeared across every scene, every song.

The producers were "David Susskind and Daniel Melnick in association with Joseph E. Levine." Mr. Levine, the movie tycoon, had invested $250,000 in the show and chose to keep away from creative aspects. This left Susskind and Melnick, who contributed $150,000 between them, with the remaining capital provided by a record company and private investors. (It was reported that *Kelly* cost $650,000, but it didn't look it and these things tend to be exaggerated because of some weird prestige in losing a fantastic sum. Let's say it lost a half million, a tidy enough amount.)

At any rate, Susskind and Melnick were pretty much in charge of the production from the very beginning, when it should have been perfectly clear to an experienced operator that Eddie Lawrence's book was in hot water. Nobody will ever know the details of the first final draft, but it obviously had only one essential action—the leap of the title character from the Brooklyn Bridge—and that action was impossible to physically portray on a stage. What that meant was that the remainder of the story would have to be pure artifice, with a nonessential ingenue, a superfluous subplot, a pasted-in secondary romance, and cues for chorus numbers and dances. More seriously, because the story was really just that leap, the production numbers could not follow naturally because there was no natural story to follow from.

Nevertheless, the production proceeded. Fully professional people were hired for all creative capacities. Herbert Ross, a marvelously original choreographer, would also handle the

118

direction (at which he turned out to be marvelously unoriginal). Hershy Kay would do the orchestrations (and did them surprisingly badly, making Moose Charlap's mediocre score sound awful). Oliver Smith would design the sets (and designed them nicely). Everything about *Kelly* was to be professional.

Notice the word "professional." Although there have been worse musicals than *Kelly* (*Sophie* and *Café Crown* are just two), they have usually been the work of rank amateurs. Because practically everybody involved with this one was a pro, the failure seemed shocking. But the reason for that failure was amateurism nonetheless—producing amateurism. (Susskind has had a little theater experience, but his background is in television, as is Melnick's.)

The show's hopelessness became apparent once it was mounted and began tryouts. The producers' naïveté multiplied the problems—they didn't know where to look for help, where to begin to correct. Television writers with little theater background were frantically called in, and the rewriting upon rewriting made the production a pile of inappropriate safety pins. Revisions had nothing to do with a basic conception because there *was* no basic conception. Characters were written in, written out, and combined, with fear the only driving force. The Boston engagement was cut short and the Broadway premiere was pushed *up*—which is completely unheard of when a show is in trouble. Confidence makes you anxious for more time to rework.

There is a clichéd question that is usually asked at this point: What can be learned from the *Kelly* failure? The answer, of course, is nothing. Professional people have long since learned the lesson and amateurs will always make the same mistake. People still dream of making a fortune rather than making a good show, and that dream keeps them going—on the wrong track—through all the revisions, all the bad out-of-town notices, all the sheer fright. It never works.

Broadway is no place for beginners, and beginners are no place for a half-million dollars.

The Customers at Lindy's Know (*March 5, 1965*)

When *Baker Street* opened a few weeks ago, the very gala premiere audience included Jerry Bock and Sheldon Harnick, which wouldn't be anything out of the ordinary. Bock and Harnick are presently on top of Broadway and are in a perfect position to be living the Beautiful Life. What would be out of the ordinary about their being in the *Baker Street* opening night audience?

Not much, except that they had written at least one of the *Baker Street* songs even though the program clearly credited the score to Marian Grudeff and Raymond Jessel. Theater regulars would notice either Bock or Harnick and smile knowingly to each other, whispering the not-so-inside information.

There is something very wrong here—wrong because it involves deception but even more seriously wrong because that deception has come to be cynically accepted as just another fact of Broadway life. What if a manufacturer printed a completely erroneous list of materials on the label of his product? He wouldn't dare—the government would pounce on him faster than you could say "Federal Trade Commission." He wouldn't for another reason—the small matter of ethics.

Yet, there is *Baker Street,* making it quite clear that Grudeff and Jessel had written the songs. And there was *Kelly,* giving Eddie Lawrence and Moose Charlap credit for all the music, while an extra song had been contributed by Carolyn Leigh and Jack Segal. *Something More,* ostensibly composed by Sammy Fain and Marilyn and Alan Bergman, had a song by Jule Styne. The list is endless, and there is no record of it because when a composer sells a song he sells it completely, including the copyright. Generally, whoever has bought the song has bought not only program credit but legal credit. He gets the royalties; he, for all intents and purposes, wrote the song. And never, never, never will the real composer please stand up. The pact is made in heaven, the conspiracy is near-total. Most musicals keep their secrets very well. An enormous percentage of them have songs by outsiders.

Such outright deception is not limited to music. In reviewing *Kelly*, I criticized Hershy Kay for falling from his usually high standards of orchestration. Why shouldn't I blame him—he provided the orchestrations, didn't he? That's how the producers' credits ran: "Orchestrations by Hershy Kay." How much clearer would you want it? Clearer than that, it turns out. Kay's work was thrown out in Philadelphia and other—substandard —orchestrations were used. Kay's credit remained.

Golden Boy provides an example of misleading credit for dancers. The producer credits the choreography to Donald McKayle, adding that Jaime Rogers was his assistant. The musical has very inconsistent dances—it opens and closes with phenomenally exciting and original prizefighting sequences while the in-between choreography is hackneyed and second rate. McKayle received the critical credit for the good and the bad, but which did he do and which did Rogers do? And which was done by Herbert Ross, who was called in to do the emergency choreography and whose name is nowhere to be found in the *Golden Boy* credits?

What about directors? *Funny Girl* played things fairly straight (amazingly straight for Broadway). Garson Kanin had begun staging it when Jerome Robbins was called in to stem the mounting tide of trouble. The program reads: "Production Supervised by Jerome Robbins, Directed by Garson Kanin." Anyone would be confused, but at least he was being told, albeit vaguely, that Robbins had had a hand in *Funny Girl*.

This is a little clearer than the *High Spirits* situation, which had Noel Coward listed as the director with no mention of Gower Champion, who had been called in during the out-of-town emergencies.

As far as credit for the book is concerned, it would be foolish to even begin giving examples of misinformation. If there ever were a Broadway musical that opened without a line being written by an outsider it would be hard to find. But minor doctoring would not make a production misrepresentational. It is the wholesale, uncredited revision that is offensive.

A theatergoer has the right to be told exactly who has done what he has paid to see. When he reads a theater program, he should be able to believe the producer's word. He is not a sucker to be insulted by outright and outrageous misrepresentation. A professional production has the obligation to be aboveboard in all respects, certainly about its credits. It should be as bound by simple ethics as any business operation. There is absolutely no excuse for the false credits that continue on a massive scale.

When did I become a reformer?

Richard Rodgers, Incorporated (*March 26, 1965*)

There was something seriously wrong with *Do I Hear a Waltz?* and it wasn't simply that it was an unhappy production. For one thing, it wasn't all that bad—mediocre, yes, but terrible, no. What was wrong was wronger than that because while a terrible musical is nothing worse than either a lapse or an absence of talent, *Do I Hear a Waltz?* displayed the ugly face of cynicism—the conscious degradation of proven talents: Arthur Laurents, Stephen Sondheim, and perhaps most incorrigibly, Richard Rodgers.

Keep in mind that being Richard Rodgers at this point is

being a man who not only has made a fortune but has made so enormous a public reputation as to be nearly critic-proof. Because Rodgers keeps that in mind, and because of that fortune, he is in a position to produce his own shows as well as to control all of the subsidiary financial situations—original cast recordings, movie sales, touring companies, and so on. He is a corporate enterprise.

The result of such theater-as-a-business is a musical like *Do I Hear a Waltz?* which is so unfailingly commercial in conception that it makes the rest of Broadway look the very soul of artistic purity. In fact, for all of the Broadway interest in money, there is rarely a production that is without any personal concern on the part of its producers or creators. *Do I Hear a Waltz?* is extraordinary—it advertises, in all of its hollowness, its blandness, its sterility, the absolute callowness of its creators. Considering that Rodgers' success was built on genuinely creative contributions, it is ironic to see him condescending to the theater—and the public—that gave him his reputation in the first place.

And even more ironic to watch him hiring other talents to prostitute themselves in his assistance. Mr. Laurents' *Time of the Cuckoo* was hardly classic theater, but it was a very nice play, written by somebody who believed in it and cared about its people. It has been made shallow, butchered by its own maker. Mr. Sondheim is a seasoned lyricist who has shown himself altogether capable of real sophistication. The lyrics he wrote for Rodgers will embarrass him whenever he is reminded of them—they seem written solely to satisfy the misplaced demands of a producer seeking only a return on an investment.

Worst of all, Rodgers himself. More than just a tunesmith, his magnificent talent for melody is backed by a full command of compositional technique. He is trained for and is capable of a real musical maturity. While the Broadway musical was advancing, there was no reason for it to pass him by. It was not as if he were incapable of writing extended musical sequences cor-

123

relating song with dance and drama. It was not as if he did not have the training to go beyond the pop tune and into the excitement of new developments. It was simply that he was no longer interested in new developments. He no longer cared.

But nobody cared about *Do I Hear a Waltz?* They were mere hirelings. John Dexter's listless direction allowed the whole production to slide into lackadaisicality. Beni Montresor's washy designs were born of rich ideas, unfulfilled, and they were blighted with shabby and perfunctory side sets. His costumes made everybody, especially pretty Julienne Marie, look ridiculous. Sergio Franchi and Elizabeth Allen displayed fine voices, but both needed direction badly, and because Dexter was so spiritless, Franchi's acting was poor and Allen's was obviously modeled on Katharine Hepburn's in the same role (in the film *Summertime*).

So Laurents cynically chopped his play into clichés, cheap jokes, and boredom. So Sondheim wrote the corniest, most simpleminded, unmusical lyrics of his career. So Rodgers wrote a series of formula tunes that might as well have been composed twenty years ago.

And so Herbert Ross' emergency choreography, which was the only part of the production that showed interest by someone, stood out as weirdly out-of-place art and showed the whole shoddy enterprise up. Funny—the music for this was bright and original, but to whose credit was it—Rodgers' or the dance music arranger's (Richard de Benedictis)?

The development of the modern musical is the single most important accomplishment of contemporary American theater. In no instance has it been furthered by a calculated commercial enterprise (although its best examples usually make lots of money). But how often can a talent like Sondheim's be compromised without being destroyed? How often can Arthur Laurents degrade himself without becoming permanently stooped? And how large a fortune must Rodgers amass before facing himself with the fact of a stature that was stunted, an ability

that was stifled, and a legacy of degrading the very musical theater that he himself had helped bring to the brink of greatness?

The Total Musical (*December 9, 1966*)

Even though none of them has entirely worked, three of the
four musicals that opened this season have tried for something
separately inventive and that is very encouraging. The vitality
of Broadway musical theater should hardly come as a shock at
this point, but things have been depressing in recent years. The
exciting movement that *West Side Story* started toward the intertwining of story, dance, and music elements has been sty-
mied. Since *Fiddler on the Roof* there has been no example of
it, and that was more than two years ago.

Now, in the few months that this season has progressed, there
are three examples of originality and seriousness of artistic purpose. And even more encouraging, they represent not only a
continuation of the new movement but a striking out for separate directions *within* that movement.

The Apple Tree comes closest to the general direction that
the trend has been following. This Bock and Harnick musical
is made up of three one-act works. The first (*The Diary of
Adam and Eve*) and the last (*Passionella*) are constructed
along the standard, old-fashioned Broadway lines of a story that
is artificially hooked for song and dance cues. Neither of them
is essentially musical.

But *The Lady and the Tiger* is built as a continuous dancing, musical organism, its music interweaving with the story
and the choreography. Once begun it cannot be stopped. Its
tone of voice is mockery, the object of the mockery being flamboyant, overproduced, exotica theater. Bock's music hauls out
pounding drums and gaudy superbrass while the staging never

quite stops being dance movement. In this case, it is difficult to say who was responsible for it. Mike Nichols is credited with the overall direction, but obviously he could not have staged this since there is practically no nondance work. Lee Theodore is listed as "choreographer," but Herbert Ross is credited with "additional musical staging." Programs are a confusing business, intentionally and improperly. I would place my money on Ross for this entire sequence. He has worked with such new theater styles before.

Bock's comic music was composed away from ordinary song patterns and moved through the production on long constructive lines; between it and the fluid movement and the entirely musical conception of the piece, *The Lady and the Tiger* is well into the new direction of musical theater. It manages to neatly evade (if not solve) the problem of what a "book" should be by keeping dialogue to basics.

Cabaret was hurt by this problem of how to write a book, and spoiled its enormous ingenuity by falling back on the standard scheme of the foreshortened play. As a result, it has one foot in the old musicals and one in the new. It tears right down the middle.

In its musical terms, *Cabaret* is brilliant. This was in great measure due to choreographer Ronald Field, who created a fantastic, expressionistic grotesquerie of prewar German degeneracy for the cabaret scenes that intercept each cardboard scene of the play's other half—the story half. The darkened stage is backed by a large, distorting mirror that twistingly reflects the auditorium, just as the garish cabaret reflects the Germany that spawned Nazism. John Kander was forced by the story end of things to compose several standard ballads, but he reveled in the cabaret moments and the musical style of thirties Germany, twisting and scratching his way through bitterly melodic, extremely singable songs.

In these sequences, which make up a full half of the show,

here is no need for dialogue, reliance being on the situation of a cabaret show. So everything falls into Mr. Field's hands and he builds a nightmared nightclub world around an extraordinary performance by Joel Gray as a carnival-bizarre master of ceremonies. With a weird female band onstage and a jumping line of unreal performers, a whole world comes alive in black neon.

I Do, I Do! could be no more different. Its hymn to the joys of marriage is saccharine-sweet and its look is all antique charm, polished as only designer Oliver Smith can polish. But structurally, it is trying many of the same things as its dark opposite, *Cabaret.* Harvey Schmidt is after continuous music, as is any modern theater composer, and his partner, Tom Jones, designed the preface to be entirely musical. There is no dialogue for those first ten minutes as Mary Martin and Robert Preston weave song into song with never-ending, deceptively simple-looking musical staging and dance.

But although a story (a generally soggy one, I'm afraid) does begin and work through the play, it is held to extremely simple and infrequent dialogue. Mr. Jones was making one of the few serious attempts to cope with the problem of the book part of the new musical form. I think that minimizing it as "story" is certainly part of the answer, as is the abandonment of any attempt to write a play *as* a play. Jones is going in a reasonable direction. However, the excellence of *I Do, I Do!* is generally rooted in Gower Champion's masterful direction and his continued interest in establishing a particular *style* for a musical and absolutely maintaining it. While this is not as obvious an innovation as this two-character show's elimination of dancing choruses and scenic changes, it is of vastly greater significance.

Compare such originality and modernity (as well as that of *The Lady and the Tiger* and *Cabaret*) with the empty, formulatic, archaic style of *Walking Happy,* with its sketchy story and pop tunes, and you can see why this season's beginning is so encouraging. American musical theater remains exciting and vital, the only thriving stage form in our country's otherwise stagnant Broadway mainstream milieu.

What Do You Mean, "Commercialism"?
(*August 4, 1967*)

David Merrick's decision to present an all-Negro *Hello, Dolly!* in Washington this fall is appalling, offensive, ridiculous, and unimaginably reactionary in both a theatrical and an ethical sense. That he is doing this after so many people have grown sensitive at last to the details of racial insult makes it all the more shocking. That it comes after a month of sickening riots, brought on by frustrations born of just such backwardness, suggests that Mr. Merrick is insensitive to even the most obvious tempers and problems of his own country and its people.

The all-Negro show, naturally, is a theater phenomenon created by white people. Its basic attraction is in the presumably exotic appeal of Negroes. (What could be more degrading?) It was designed for audiences as white as its performers were black, and of course, it began at a time when there were virtually no Negroes in any theater audiences. Such a show, a freak show, really, was part of the American tradition of bigotry.

And such theatrical presentations were popular so long as that tradition was allowed to continue. Shame enough that it continued so long. If *The Hot Mikado* was comfortably long ago, *Carmen Jones* wasn't.

Still, we have got out of that bag. Nobody would have dared produce a black anything in the last seven-eight years. Nobody would have been crude enough. White audiences, at last at the beginning of a racial education, would have rejected it.

Mr. Merrick realizes this, no doubt. His black *Dolly* is something else. Washington, D.C., is more than half Negro, and Merrick's *Dolly* is not designed to give white audiences a Negro show. It is crudely designed to give *Negro* audiences a Negro show. [Giving *white* audiences a black show was saved for New York.] It is simple business. It is based on simple commercialism, simple racism. And it is disgusting.

It is also antagonistic to any serious conception of theater. When the look of a production is being decided by the race of its audience and not by the needs of the particular work, then vulgarity can go no further. And commercialism can go no further. You might as well look for an audience's cheapest instincts and go satisfy them. They like religious abuse? Give it to them. They want exhibitions of deformity? Why not?

Hello, Dolly! is not the greatest musical that ever happened, its ecstatic reviews notwithstanding. It is, however, a very stylish musical that was assembled by the ultraprofessional Gower Champion. It was executed with exquisite taste, even with its camp accents, and managed a likable kind of cartooned elegance. It had, need I say, absolutely nothing to do with Negroes.

This is not to say that Negro performers should not be in it. The plight of the Negro actor in America has been extensively and properly deplored. While matters have improved, they have improved only slightly. It is still very difficult for a Negro to get a role that is not specifically designed to be "Negro." That is rotten and stupid. There are plenty of roles in plenty of plays that could be quite reasonably played by Negro actors— major roles and obviously not maids or waiters or baseball players. The point is not to hire (or reject) an actor on the basis of his race, unless a racial difference would so crucially affect the story of a play as to upset it. The hiring of an actor *because* he is Negro is as offensive as the rejection of him for the same reason.

But Mr. Merrick's *Dolly* goes further than just hiring Negroes because of their race. He is hiring *only* Negroes. He is making his show "Negro." It is a *race* show. It has nothing to do with *Dolly* and it has nothing to do with the theater. It has to do with a box office, and a box office so red-necked that it has not even the least awareness of either personal or theater ethics.

It is also upsetting that Mr. Merrick has been able to *get* Negro actors for this production, considering that some of them have turned down roles in revivals because of dated, moronic attitudes (APA had trouble casting a shuffling-Negro role in its *You Can't Take It with You*). I sympathize enormously with the out-of-work Negro actor, but I cannot go along with his taking such a job. Nothing is worth humiliation.

Yet Pearl Bailey accepted the lead in Mr. Merrick's production. Now Miss Bailey has had trouble enough with racial mistreatment. And Miss Bailey is regularly employed. She doesn't need the insult and she doesn't need the money. Yet she refuses to see any problem in working this production. I suppose it isn't for me to point out to Miss Bailey that she is participating in a large, commercial abuse of her race. And that Merrick mightn't have hired her for a *Dolly* that *wasn't* all-Negro.

Frederick O'Neal, the president of Actors' Equity (and a Negro himself), was more aware of the production's implications. He said: "We are sacrificing our principles for a few bucks." That's exactly right. A few bucks for the cast. A few more bucks for Miss Bailey. And a few bucks for Mr. Merrick.

I have no doubt that Merrick will smugly desposit his profits after carefully publicizing his production in Washington's Negro sections. His rationalization will be that he is a businessman and that an all-Negro *Dolly* is still theater. The pity is precisely his insensitive, narrowminded smugness and the appeal that it has to bigots. The pity is that Merrick really *isn't* bigoted. Apparently he has an interest in neither liberalism nor reaction when it comes to finance. The pity, I am afraid, is that this is exactly how too much of this country feels.

Zorbá (November 18, 1968)

Harold Prince is one of the few theater people who sense just how far the musical has come and where it can go. Like them, he is now confronting the crucial problem of modern musicals —the battle of the book: how to replace the idea of a story (or find a new way to tell it). Mr. Prince and a couple of other people know all about blending dance with music and song. The question is how to tie it all together, and Prince's new show, Zorbá (at the Imperial Theatre), gives no answer. Moreover, it doesn't manage to camouflage the problem with a sheer wholeness of conception, as was done in some of the other shows he has produced or directed. Conception is the big word here—it is what is coming to replace the idea of a "book"—but the concept of Zorbá has not been completely thought out and as a result it is a mixed-up musical whose parts are not consistent with its idea. It is a show of great interest from a theoretical point of view, but of vague vitality as theater.

Zorbá, of course, is based on the Nikos Kazantzakis novel Zorbá, the Greek, which meant trouble from the start because there is a detailed story to follow and musicals simply don't have the time for plot detail. Consequently, librettist Joseph Stein was engaged to write a shorthand version of the novel's plot and it is as follows: Nikos, an uptight intellectual, runs into the earthy Zorbá on the way to Crete and is talked into taking him along.

This becomes the story of a conversion. Zorbá represents the basic joys of life (wine, women, et cetera) that Nikos is missing in his life of the mind. Frankly, I find anti-intellectualism from an intellectual as obnoxious as I find primitivism from the civilized, but blame that on Kazantzakis if you want to. In any case, they get to Crete, where Zorbá meets, woos, and moves in with an old French cabaret singer. Nikos (played well by John Cunningham despite a shortchanged part) squints behind his wire-framed glasses until Zorbá drags him out of his shell and into a romance with a local widow. Both ladies die, but the men survive into vitality, proving, I guess, that women exist only for male pleasure.

That is the story, as this show leaves room for it, and there is even less room than in the usual musical because Prince's concept, and his emphasis on music, dance, and a look-feel, apparently won out on every question about cutting. Evidently afraid to wipe out the book entirely (which will have to be done sooner or later), he left it in shreds—an outline of an outline.

But what was that concept? *Zorbá* opens with the whole company, main characters included, onstage in a Greek café, facing the audience. They sing and clap and dance and play musical instruments and are altogether delightful, beginning the show powerfully. Then they start to tell the *Zorbá* story and the production slips back into conventionality, with sets sliding in, down, up, and out and events rushing in upon other events' heels.

Every so often, members of the company intercede to prod the characters into action, or comment on their behavior. Small groups arrange themselves along a horizon line—even up front —singing and watching. This quasi-Greek chorus use of the company, always on steps or platforms, was doubtless Prince's basic image of the show—an image in which he delighted and I can't blame him—but it is impossible to tell just what he meant it to be, and like his vision for *Cabaret*, it splits the show between the story and the conception.

Now the problem is that Prince was inspired by Jerome Robbins, who is most responsible for his new kind of musical, and I

wish more directors would follow his lead. But Prince is no
Robbins. You really do need a choreographer-director for it,
and while Prince has become unusually good in blending
music-with-dance-with-plot, his ideas are way ahead of his capabilities. New-style musicals must be directors' musicals, that's
true, but those directors must be (like Robbins) masters of
music and dance as well as of basic theater. I suspect that
Prince gave his composer (John Kander), lyricist (Fred Ebb),
and librettist imprecise instructions.

The actual playing-out of *Zorbá* is curiously heartless, as if
the show never got out of the theory stage. The company is im-
pressively orchestrated and moves well during the musical numbers, though the straight-play sequences are almost unstaged
and uniformly dreary. Sequence from talk to song is almost always smooth. Ronald Field's dances for the lovely small chorus
of real-people types move beautifully within the production
whole, but the *Fiddler on the Roof* influence is embarrassingly
obvious, and Field, like Prince, is no Jerome Robbins. Kander's
music was beyond song but not quite into continuous music,
and though its technique was impressive it was all craft, without melodic inspiration. It was neat of him, though, to tailor
French music for the French lady's songs while leaving everything else Greek. Kander composes to suit a show's location and
period, as a good theater composer should (and few do), but
his music is too mental. Since there were no credits for the
dance music, I assume he wrote it, and it was very good. Some
of this is due to Don Walker's orchestrations, which were
among the finest I've ever heard in a Broadway theater. As for
Ebb's lyrics, they were not up to his usual standards (which are
high), simply, I hope, because he had trouble grasping the production sense. That was clearly the problem with Boris Aronson's handsome, artful, but oddly moodless sets.

Herschel Bernardi's performance in the title part was,
frankly, terrible. The role of Zorbá demands an actor-performer
of great charisma, and Bernardi, hidden beneath six ridiculous

pounds of makeup and wigs, looked and sounded as if he were wearing a rubber mask on both his face and his presence. He had none of the animal magnetism that is Zorbá's nature. And his dancing, crucial to the role, had the relaxed freedom of Lyndon Johnson at the Electric Circus.

Maria Karnilova was his infinite superior as the lovelorn French lady, though I wonder why she, as he, made no attempt at dialect. But, especially in a twenties cabaret number, she was delightful. These two headed the *Fiddler* cast (after Zero Mostel left) and are part of the show's unfortunate attempt to be a Greek version of that masterpiece. As Mr. Prince undoubtedly learned, it isn't so easy to make ouzo from schnapps.

Attention Must Be Paid (*November 29, 1968*)

On Sunday night Burt Bacharach's first Broadway musical will open at the Shubert Theatre. The fact that it is Bacharach's makes it more than just another musical, because he is a composer and Broadway's musicals are usually written by "composers" in only the most limited sense. They are piano players —they are what used to be called tunesmiths, writing simple songs in simple arrangements. And just how much of those songs they really write, when you think of how music actually sounds in a show, is debatable.

Theater music is team-written. Once the "composer" has written the dozen or so songs for the show, then the real musical work begins and the team of real musicians enters the picture: orchestrators, dance music composers, vocal arrangers, and of course, the musical director. It is *these* people who put the music together. Remember, a Broadway show has more music than you hear on an original cast album. There is underscoring, continuity, and the overtures for both acts. The man who is credited with writing the score is seldom the man who writes the music as you hear it in the theater. He writes only the melodies, sometimes suggests the harmonies, but has little to do with the way the songs are played, how they are sung, or the show's musical structure.

Occasionally, though, composers have had a hand in this—the handful of genuinely trained musicians who have written for the stage. Kurt Weill, Leonard Bernstein, Stephen Sondheim, and even Heitor Villa-Lobos. When such men compose for the stage they can truly be credited with the music. Bacharach is such a composer, fully trained, and his music shows it.

He is best known for very popular songs like "Alfie" and "Wives and Lovers," written with his lyricist, Hal David. But these and all of Bacharach's songs—especially after he began hitting his stride a couple of years ago—are more than just tunes. The titles alone indicate the tricky rhythms if you just pronounce them—"What's New, Pussycat?" "Do You Know the Way to San Jose?". Moreover, Bacharach brings a full knowledge of musical theory to bolster his increasingly original structures and has, beyond that, the one thing most essential to a song composer—a talent for original melody. Song after song of his is catchy, tuneful, and, for special satisfaction, musically clever.

However, Bacharach has written more than songs. His scores for movies (*Casino Royale, After the Fox, What's New, Pussycat?*) are playful, extended, and bright—far more so than the films themselves. Also, and unlike most Hollywood composers, he does not rely on two or three tunes, with elaborate variations on them, to fill out the rest of the time. A Bacharach movie score is full. And it is always orchestrated by him, as are his songs when sung by Dionne Warwick. The sound is Bacharach's, from original composition to final performance.

The question is: Will he be able to have as complete a say with his Broadway music? In most cases, Broadway's musicals are machine-made. They all have the *show-tune* sound—a

sound produced by songwriters collaborating with orchestrators, none of whom can imagine any different kind of music for
a show.

In a way, these orchestrators are the chief villains because,
unlike the songwriters, they can't fall back on the excuse of musical ignorance. You can't be an orchestrator without being a
musician. Broadway orchestrators are a strange crew. A few of
them have virtually all the business sewn up and they grind out
the orchestra parts with a cynicism I have never seen matched.
Knowledgeable musicians, they are convinced that Broadway
composers are hacks (which is generally true) and that no good
music will ever be written for a show (which is not true, no
thanks to them). They produce the hack arrangements for the
awful music they are handed, knocking off the same brassy,
small-string-section arrangements year after year. The rut is
ruinous.

Bacharach said that for *Promises, Promises* he would try to
write his own orchestrations and dance music. He should have
—he alone knows exactly how to make his music sound the way
he wants it to and he would have had a chance for inventive
composing with the dance score.

But whatever the reason (probably lack of time), this didn't
work out. Anticipating that possibility, Bacharach said that if
he couldn't write all of this, he would make sure to hire people
who would do as he wished. "My music for the theater will
sound like my music anywhere else," he said.

Well, we'll see Sunday night, but I wonder whether he will
have convinced his producer and co-workers that all theater
music needn't sound the same. I wonder how he will cope with
Broadway economics which limit a pit orchestra to a fraction of
the size he is accustomed to in recording studios. I wonder how
he will like working without sophisticated audio equipment
and its advantages for dubbing, sound-mixing, and reverbera-
tion. I wonder whether he will be able to use the electric instruments he is accustomed to.

No doubt he will be frustrated by other practical limitations of the theater, but of course, limitations are a challenge to any artist's ability. The trouble comes when limitations turn into obstacles. And the importance of *Promises, Promises*—I'm talking strictly about its music—lies in its ability to beat those obstacles, mainly the one of Broadway tradition. Audiences love that Broadway show sound so much they have stopped listening. Now they will be faced with a real musician, and whether the show is good, whether Bacharach's score works for it or not, the music must be listened to. As any music must be listened to. We have insulted music—even the tacky theater music—by letting it grind past us. Here is a chance with a composer and he must be heard.

Promises, Promises (*December 2, 1968*)

If its music had been written by your ordinary hack, *Promises, Promises* would be a perfectly entertaining musical—even a little more than that—though as a matter of fact, it is put together in a style that ordinarily prompts the usual Broadway brass. But the musical that opened last night at the Shubert has a score by Burt Bacharach, and that has turned it into something very special. There are songs and more songs and more songs, one better than the other—tricky rhythm songs, funny songs (not just funny lyrics but funny *music*), fresh harmony songs, lovely little guitar songs. One coming after the other, and it is the first music I've heard on Broadway since I don't know when (I've heard songs, I haven't heard music). Between the Bacharach score, with its neat, tricky lyrics by Hal David, and the more than good enough Neil Simon book, with its regular spurts of giddy comedy, *Promises, Promises* is easily the most satisfying and successful musical in a very long time.

It is based on the Billy Wilder-I. A. L. Diamond movie *The Apartment,* which I only vaguely remember—and I think comparisons in such cases are pointless anyhow. As such, it is a story musical and a conventional one. Mr. Simon's book outlines the plot, providing regular hooks for songs. There is little relevance between the staging of the story parts and the staging of the musical parts, and there is just about no dancing at all, though when there is dancing things are just fine. A couple of times, Michael Bennett sneaked some quick little dances into incidental scenes and that suggested what might have been, but the program doesn't even credit a choreographer (Bennett is listed as stager of musical numbers), and that ought to indicate the emphasis placed on dance.

The emphasis of a musical is ordinarily determined by whoever has the most power. That is unfortunate of course. Although musicals appear to be team efforts, they must be set at one angle by one person. Ideally, it is a choreographer-director. But the powers for *Promises, Promises* were obviously Mr. Simon and Mr. Bacharach, and the show is theirs—it is either book or songs, one alternating with the other, and evidently Robert Moore, the director, followed their lead.

Well, it is good enough. I hope Bacharach someday has the chance to really write music, not just in the song form, and has a theater person pushing him beyond his "sound." He is capable of all kinds of things. But this score is swell enough, and a real breakthrough for Broadway. Not only has orchestrator Jonathan Tunick been faithful to Bacharach rather than the show-tune cliché, but the whole archaic system of show biz has been shattered by the use of an amplified orchestra and electric instruments (organ, bass fiddle, guitar). Loudspeakers run up the sides of the theater, right to the second balcony, and an honest-to-God recording engineer is in the house. There is a four-girl group, yet, in the orchestra pit. Now all of this isn't working up to full potential, but it can and it will. For the moment, Bacharach has proved that modern sound can be put live in a theater—not just his class rock but the qualities made possible by modern electronics.

The show follows the story of a kind-of-dumb, kind-of-nice insurance company guy whose bachelor apartment suddenly becomes the desire of all the philandering executives. In an obvious variation on *How to Succeed in Business Without Really Trying* (and this show undeniably has that one's look), the single guy works his way up the corporate ladder by making his apartment available to the right people. He becomes disgusted only when he finds the girl he loves (from afar, from afar) a near-suicide in his own bed. The message was supposed to be about American corporate ethics and moral hypocrisy, but the hands of Simon are not those of Wilder-Diamond, and in the show it boils down to some nice Jewish-mother, family-doctor, chicken-soup wisdom. This is the usual Simon message and I always find it a letdown, as I do his suckerhood for easy gags, because Simon can be tremendously funny in a wacked-out way. But again, the qualms are minor.

The performers aren't major but they're good, especially Jerry Orbach as the hero-nebbish. The book has been written so that he and the audience are on one side, with the rest of the world on the other. After an awkward beginning with too much narration, this begins to work, with Orbach regularly confiding and establishing a personal relationship. Orbach finally found himself in last year's *Scuba Duba* and is no longer trying to be John Raitt. Now he is human, warm, and making Bacharach's endlessly tricky songs sound easy.

Unfortunately, Jill O'Hara is not such a pro and needed the strong direction that Mr. Moore was not providing. She has a far better voice than Orbach, especially for Bacharach music, but she was pretty well lost when it came to acting and movement, and it is Moore's fault. Some other professionals in the company—A. Larry Haines and Marian Mercer—were lovely and grand in some wonderful set pieces, though they were delivered in and out of the show like sandwiches. So there are weak points to talk about. There is also a sleek (okay, sometimes too sleek) production to enjoy and some wonderful music. That should do.

The Resident Theaters

**The Story of a Director Who Had Trouble
with the Authorities: Act One**
(February 24, 1967)

THE dismissal by Philadelphia's Theatre of the Living Arts
of Andre Gregory, its artistic director, seemed to come as
the final straw in an all too predictable pattern of stupid behavior by resident theater boards of trustees. The expelling of
Mr. Gregory was the third such resident theater act of violence
in the past month.

The first director to go in the recent spurt was John Hancock
of the Pittsburgh Playhouse, and the circumstances were the
most upsetting, even though the Pittsburgh theater was the like-
liest place for such a thing to happen. This was a situation
that showed just how dangerous a board of local businessmen,
bankers, and nontheater people can be in a theater situation.
The Playhouse had long catered to Pittsburgh's lowest theater
tastes, and when it decided to follow the national trend and "go
artistic," it hired the country's finest director and its most accomplished resident company—William Ball and his American
Conservatory Theatre.

Mr. Ball's experience with the Pittsburgh Playhouse is now legendary—the conflict between his artistic drive and its television mentality prompted a divorce within six months. The Playhouse, though it didn't know it, had lost a brilliant company because of its bland tastes and the bland-taste audiences that it had always courted.

Still feeling the need to be artistic (and still dominated by antiart forces), the Playhouse hired Mr. Hancock away from the San Francisco Actor's Workshop, which he had joined when Blau and Irving moved to Lincoln Center.

Hancock proceeded to schedule a season of serious, valuable plays to be produced with the creative, modern imagination that typifies the best of our resident theater directors. Prominent in his program was a highly experimental *Midsummer Night's Dream* and Brecht's seldom-produced *Saint Joan of the Stockyards*.

Midway through the season it became apparent that Hancock was not attracting the younger-minded, intellectual audiences that he needed. The Playhouse had traditionally drawn Pittsburgh's middle-classers (financially and mentally), and this was hardly the audience that Hancock was appealing to. But instead of updating its subscription methods, instead of courting the city's more educated adults, instead of reorienting its audiences as it had been reorienting its theater, the board turned on Hancock. It forced him to alter the season's program and create what is probably the most shameful moment in America's brief resident theater history. Hancock had to publicly announce that he would try to program plays that would appeal to everybody (meaning, of course, the commercial, the broad, and the cheap). It was a terrible statement and Hancock should have resigned before making it.

You might say that this is easier for me to say than for the guy who needs the job, but I don't think so, and neither, I suspect, does Hancock. In any case, the subsequent developments could have been anticipated. An art-motivated director can never justify his own prostitution and Hancock was finally fired.

Herbert Blau's experience with the Repertory Theater of Lincoln Center was not much different. Certainly his record with Julius Irving was unimpressive. During one and a half seasons, they presented some of the finest plays in the international dramatic literature—exactly the plays that a resident theater ought to produce. But every one was botched, some beyond recognition, and it was obvious that Blau did not and would never have the ability to direct productions.

But the insistence by Lincoln Center that its company succeed financially, artistically, critically, and immediately was ridiculous. There is no company, anywhere, that was born brilliant. Because the Blau-Irving attitude was so right, and their artistic capabilities so weak, they should have been producers, using other directors; and they seemed to realize this. For the first time in its short history, the Repertory Theater of Lincoln Center presented an artistic play (*Yerma*) with real ability (even though, as a whole, it did not work). But such subtleties of progress were lost on the marble interests there. Blau "resigned" and several outright-commercial productions were booked into the Vivian Beaumont Theater for next seasons.

Now on the surface, it might seem that the same thing had happened to Mr. Gregory in Philadelphia. There, its occurrence seemed all the more shocking. In the few years that the Theatre of the Living Arts has existed, it has acquired a formidable reputation. It wasn't that this theater merely had an especially accomplished director and company, and chose interesting, diversified plays. If it were just that, Philadelphia would have been lucky enough, though no more so than Washington, Hartford, Houston, Cincinnati, and the other cities with first-class resident theaters. But the Theatre of the Living Arts is more than that—it is a theater with a special drive, a special quality, a spe-

145

cial attitude that gives it a unique personality. It produced a striking version of Anouilh's *Poor Bitos,* an *End Game* of especial reputation, a quality *Time of Your Life.* And in doing a new play, Rochelle Owens' *Beclch,* it displayed all the flamboyance, the originality, and, yes, even the silliness, of very new, young America. *Beclch* was a stupid play, but in doing it, and in the *way* it did it, the Theatre of the Living Arts proved its tremendous importance.

All of this specialness was born of Andre Gregory. The Theatre of the Living Arts *is* Gregory, and in him this theater, and Philadelphia, had one of America's most valuable directors. Not because of his technical skill, which is good but not great. Not because of his theater intelligence, although it is real enough. But because of his unique artistic personality.

But as a matter of fact, the firing of Gregory this week was *not* due to a stupid board of trustees. The board at Philadelphia presents the problems that all boards will present, but it was not consistently antagonistic to Gregory and appreciated his theater values. Gregory was fired in an emotionally heated situation that really had nothing to do with his theater policies. What happened was that David Lunney, the company's executive director, was refused a contract, took this as a vote of nonconfidence, and resigned. Gregory liked Lunney and had worked well with him. Hoping to get Lunney back, he suspended activities as artistic director. The board then fired him. But Gregory did not mean to quit and did not want to. The Theatre of the Living Arts is as much him as he is it. And as long as it will take Philadelphia to find a special person for its theater, that is how long it will take Gregory to find a special theater for himself.

Things are bad enough in New York and Pittsburgh. It would be lunacy for Philadelphia to let the same thing happen when the stimulus is not a downright trustees-director conflict but an emotional, senseless misunderstanding.

America Turns to Culture: Intermission (*May 19, 1967*)

When President Johnson and Congress agreed to the creation of the National Council on the Arts, the American intellectual and cultural community heaved a great sigh of relief to the effect of at-last-this-country-is-going-to-subsidize-art. The community also quivered with the stock fears of government censorship. But what has really happened?

What really happened was that the government's knowledge of the arts in general and the theater in particular was abysmally limited to only the most well-known, most well-publicized, most commercial artists and art areas. And the chairmanship of the Council was handed over to Roger Stevens, a Broadway producer with a heavily commercial record (sprinkled, I grant, with a few serious plays). Perhaps only coincidentally, Mr. Stevens had been a loyal supporter of the Democratic Party.

In any case, the people whom he chose for the Council reflected his show-business orientation. Among them: Elizabeth Ashley (the actress), Gregory Peck (the actor), and Meredith Willson (the composer). It is difficult to imagine three people less familiar with the deeper, more serious, artistic developments and natures of their fields. It is less than ludicrous to think of Mr. Willson—a composer whose cornball tunes reflect his Corn Belt sentiments—discussing composers with any sophistication.

The record of the National Council, then, was predictably a joke. For example, a plan called Project Discovery (the kind of title you might anticipate) was to provide mammoth grants in conjunction with the Humanities Division of the Department of Health, Education, and Welfare. Fine. There is nothing as lovely as a mammoth grant for a resident theater. Only these were grants that no independent, professional, artistic director would touch. And why? Because there were upsetting stipulations, the most upsetting being that most performances had to be played for student audiences.

Now I am all in favor of exposing young people to the theater. It is something one really can't be against. And they *are* the audiences of the future, cliché though that may be. But the artistic drive and professional standards of a resident theater can only be hurt when performances are not being constantly played to paying, adult customers. Moreover, playing for students means getting mixed up with boards of education, and that means having plays being approved by teachers, and *that* means Shakespeare and schoolroom classics and little else. Professional educators in general are almost as official, as mundane, as fretful, and as artistically conservative as politicians.

Two theaters were chosen for the first Project Discovery grants. One was the Trinity Square Repertory Company in Providence, Rhode Island. I might add that Senator Claiborne Pell, again coincidentally, of that same state, was largely responsible for getting the National Council's appropriation through the Senate. In defense of Trinity Square, its play selections have not been reprehensible at all and it had been actively working with schools long before the grant was given. But on the other hand, the second recipient—the Repertory Theater of New Orleans—was actually *created* for Project Discovery. And despite the amount of money involved, its directorship was rejected by many talented and hungry men—William Ball and Ellis Rabb among them. Finally, Stuart Vaughan, who happened to be out of a job at the time, accepted. He scheduled *Charley's Aunt, Romeo and Juliet, Our Town,* and *The Rivals.* Can you think of four plays less likely to upset a board of education? Can you think of four plays less likely to excite a contemporary student? Can you think of four plays less stimulating

148

to an acting company? By the way, New Orleans' acting company has been described as "Greg's boys" (the Greg being Peck).

Finally, Andre Gregory accepted another Project Discovery grant for the race-troubled Watts area in Los Angeles (will do-gooder clumsiness ever come as a surprise?). This is an especial pity because Gregory had created one of America's most exciting resident theaters in Philadelphia before he left over a stupid misunderstanding. He is the last director in the world who should be involved with governmental-educational thinking. A man committed to adventure and radicalism, he *must* be left alone. It would be tragic to think of Gregory on a Project Discovery program if it weren't so funny that he of all people would be on one in the first place.

Other National Council work has been equally awkward. Grants of $25,000 were arranged for theaters producing new plays, but only when those plays were approved by a Council-chosen committee (which approved archaic, silly plays like *Does a Tiger Wear a Necktie?*). Jerome Robbins was given a sizable grant for a musical theater laboratory, and that, as a matter of fact, was marvelous. Except I wish that Stevens hadn't been Robbins' producer on *Oh, Dad* and *West Side Story*.

Always the suspicious connections, always the money with strings, always the political influences, always the heavy footsteps of government machinery and Broadway-Hollywood thinking. How foolish for anyone to worry about political censorship of the arts. The government and its officialism are too unsophisticated for that.

Act Two (*November 10, 1967*)

About two months ago, the Inner City Repertory Company in Los Angeles opened its first season. As you remember, at that time I expressed excitement, well wishes, and extreme apprehension over the company's future. This was because its artistic director was Andre Gregory, one of America's most talented, creative, and radical directors; because Los Angeles is not exactly paradise for the nonconservative; and because Inner City was very tied in with federal and local bureaucracies and the Los Angeles Board of Education. Considering Mr. Gregory's political, moral, and theatrical liberalism, conflict between him and the authorities seemed inevitable.

Several weeks ago, Gregory resigned as Inner City's artistic director after being confronted with pressure, censorship, and meddling so excessive as to be almost unbelievable. He had not lasted through the scheduled six-week run of his first production.

When Gregory had first accepted the Inner City job, I wrote an article about the improbability of the connection. I also expressed doubt about the possibility of any kind of adult, innovative theater related to government and educational powers. In response, he wrote to me about his plans, incidentally expressing curiosity whether he "would last beyond that first production." He added:

> Like it or not, and there's no reason not to like it, unless government subsidy does prove a fiasco, there will be three government subsidized theatres [the others are in Providence, R.I., and New Orleans] whose purpose will be to bring free theatre to a young audience. If we take it for granted ahead of time that there will be censorship, that productions given these restrictions must be dull, that it is impossible for talented people to function openly and honestly in such an environment. If the more talented people give up on these programs before the programs are even tested, then there's no hope of anything positive ever being achieved. How do I know what I can do here or what anyone else can do unless I try.

Well, God knows Gregory tried to give Los Angeles fresh-thinking, contemporary theater. His first and only production was Molière's *Tartuffe*, reset in a Southwestern locale. (I did not see the production and whether or not it worked is irrelevant.) The shift was not whimsical. In Los Angeles, minority groups include Mexicans and Negroes. By putting *Tartuffe* close to the Mexican border, he could relate the play visually and musically to both. He could also apply Molière's disgust with religious hypocrisy not merely to the religious hypocrisy in America but to racial matters generally.

To implement this point of view Gregory opened his production with a series of slides relating Molière, the religious wrongs of his time, and the religious art of his time to present-day America. He illustrated the censorship of *Tartuffe* itself at the time of its writing and related it to American censorship of art in the name of morality (*Ulysses* in particular). He demonstrated the censorship of paintings. He showed vulgar commercialization of religion in America—neon crosses and that kind of thing.

Then the play began, with the role of *Tartuffe* played by a Negro. There was some rump-patting but not much in the way of the sexual broadness that would have been altogether proper for the play. And there was a momentary, affectionate kiss by Tartuffe of a white lady.

As soon as the Los Angeles Board of Education got wind of these evil, morally undermining ideas its demands to change the production began. As far as it was concerned, the slides would have to be deleted from the five student performances each week (though they could be retained in the three adult ones). Fifteen-year-old high school students could not be confronted with a Modigliani nude. Neon crosses might offend their parents. And the kiss of a white lady by a Negro man?

Gregory complied with all of this, figuring that it was more important for high school students to see integrated theater. Though I really can't agree with any bowing to censorship, I do understand the practical problems and comparative importances. But he complied with more. The second production was supposed to be the Bertolt Brecht masterpiece *The Caucasian Chalk Circle,* and as soon as the Board of Education got a whiff of Brecht's occasional rough language the scissors were whipped out. Gregory accepted that. He even accepted the subsequent demand that the play be dropped entirely when somebody informed the Board that Brecht had been a Communist and it just wouldn't do to produce a work by a playwright with such political beliefs. Okay, now we're well into the ridiculous, so it won't seem much more ridiculous that the Board approved *The Flies,* whose author, Jean-Paul Sartre, happened—you might say—to have political views of a somewhat similar orientation.

As a substitute for the Brecht, the Board suggested (imagine, plays being dictated to a professional theater by a Board of Education!) a choice of either *The Glass Menagerie* or *Raisin in the Sun* (the latter being the nice, inoffensive kind of racial play it had in mind for minority group theater). Gregory selected *The Glass Menagerie* and promptly cast a Negro as the Gentleman Caller.

According to the Board of Education, if a Negro were to play the character (and now we leave the absurd for the fantastic) then he would have to wear a blond wig, blue contact lenses, and white makeup. I won't even comment on this. It is an idea that would even stagger Governor Wallace. With no support from his major board of trustees powers, Gregory Peck and Dr. J. Alfred Cannon (a Negro psychiatrist!), Gregory resigned. Ironically, he had also received no support from his executive director, David Lunney, over whose dismissal he had left his original source of reputation, Philadelphia's Theatre of the Living Arts.

The Inner City Cultural Center will continue—it has almost a million dollars in federal funds. Presumably, its purpose will remain the same, "dedicated to the presentation of artists and works of special interests to the residents of a minority community." Considering its outlandish beginning, Inner City's existence as a theater may be only a theoretical matter. What good is that million dollars? And what service will be given to that "minority community"? What abuses will be showered on the idea of theater and art? What kind of theater will those high school students find? They will find a theater reflective of the very ideas that have alienated them in the first place. They will find a theater representative of the stifling nature of official culture and board of education anti-intellectualism. How much more can a government do for its people?

The Chinese Wall *(April 28, 1966)*

Center Stage here in Baltimore is presenting a flamboyant, vividly theatrical, and really extraordinary Eastern premiere of Max Frisch's *The Chinese Wall*. It is a perfect example of the kind of direction that is beginning to surge across modern American resident theaters—the direction that is creative itself, adding a new stage dimension with the various excitements of the theater: music, dance, movement, power.

The Chinese Wall is just right for it. Mr. Frisch's play was written in 1946, with the atom bomb a new shock. It was born of pessimism for humanity's future; its attitude toward tyranny is that it is eternal; it expected nothing from intellectuals.

The script is subtitled "a farce," but the farce to which it alludes is life itself and eternal stupidity. In fact, the play is a vaudeville in 24 scenes, enormously influenced by Bertolt Brecht, and we might as well get that out of the way at once. Frisch was a disciple of Brecht's, and this was an early play. As a result, the master's style is closely followed—the purpose of the drama is the message; the structure is episodic, the tone ironic; the medium is the parable; the method is theoretically alienating, that is, the audience is never supposed to believe anything that is happening. So the Chinese princess looks out to the audience and says, "I am not a Chinese girl. . . . You think I don't know that I am disguised, in costume? . . . Everything here is nothing but theater." And Frisch has her add (in nearly a paraphrase of Brecht's *Arturo Ui*), "But you sit and look at one another . . . and you are silent—and no one comes forward and says what it really is, and no one dares and is a man!"

The Chinese Wall is set in 221 B.C., at the inauguration of the wall, which was designed to hold back time. Frisch then treats time as meaningless in an atomic age, making the central figure a modern man and introducing various anachronistic figures—Napoleon, Brutus, Pontius Pilate, Columbus, Cleopatra, and so on. They encircle a central story about a tyrannical emperor ("he who is always in the right") and his daughter, the princess. She is perpetually fixed up with princes who are killed in battle, as good princes should be. Finally one survives, managing to escape by sacrificing 30,000 soldiers. But the princess is sick of his traditional violence, as well as his style ("What's the good of all that Chinese nonsense? . . . I didn't believe in princes any more.")

The subsidiary story is about the emperor's search for a man called the Voice of the People, who has been a subversive irritant and now is the last enemy (the world having been conquered). At a parade, a boy stands uncheering, and the emperor decides that this must be the traitor, ordering torture to produce a confession. The boy is a mute.

These are the effective elements in the play. Frisch's arguments about the bomb are the drag, and they are what director Douglas Seale has tried to minimize. The threat of nuclear destruction is the story of modern life, but harangues about it are inevitably self-righteous, superficial, and childish. Frisch's, even worse, are mixed up with elementary physics and hot air. When they come, Seale can do only so much with them.

He has done much more with everything else. The stage juts

deeply into the audience and is set as a peppermint-striped circus with go-go cages. There is a great deal of calliope and rock 'n' roll music. The Master of the Revels looks like Hitler. Romeo and Juliet are acrobats, Columbus is an Italian peddler, Cleopatra a Brooklyn stripper, Don Juan a Mexican bandit (the dialects, contrary to the American rule, are excellent). A world of purple irony springs alive with gaudy lighting, gaudy dance, gaudy stage life. The jokes fly fast ("Tomorrow the world." "What else is new?"). And Seale managed to update the script with minimal changes ("The Great Order" becomes "The Great Society").

All of this makes *The Chinese Wall* a tremendously theatrical and very funny show, despite its severe problems. The choppy structure has been smoothed by directorial linkages and the performances are splendid, especially Ellen Darrel Tovatt's as the serenely idealistic princess. John Schuck was very good as the emperor, and Donald Symington acceptable as the Contemporary (a speechmaking character representing the modern intellectual and a role nearly impossible to do well). Mr. Seale is the hero, however. It is craft and imagination that make a production like this possible. He has both.

William Ball's American Conservatory Theatre
(*June 3, 1966*)

It seems absurd to me that the American Conservatory Theatre, one of the greatest adventures in the recent resident theater boom, should be wandering the country with neither a home nor a specific future. Especially absurd because it is at a time when American Subsidy is flowing like mud over every little Shaw-producing company in the country.

Yet this trained company, headed by William Ball—the

finest director in America—has no plans later than September 18. Presently in the midst of a four-week season at the Westport Country Playhouse, it will move to Stanford, California, for three weeks of repertory and then back to Chicago's Ravinia Festival for three and a half. That is it.

Mr. Ball formed ACT little more than a year ago after having established a formidable reputation for himself in not much more than a few years of active directing. His work ranged from grand opera to Pirandello in London and Dylan Thomas off-Broadway. But in every single thing he did, the combination of technique and imagination showed him to be the leader of the modern staging movement in this country.

This movement is basically involved with a return to fundamentals so far as technique is concerned (diction, control, character acting), an interest in serious and classical dramatic literature, and most of all, a conception of the director as a creative artist. Not content to merely stage a play as written, the new director is moving on to his own vision of it, much as a conductor would do his own Brahms, his own Mozart.

In these aspects, Ball is unsurpassed. He will go directly to the core of a play's meaning and explode it. In directing Edward Albee's *Tiny Alice,* he saw it in an entirely new way, conjuring up great stage sensations and marvelous pictures. With the script referring to a fire in Alice's castle, he threw open a couple of giant doors to have smoke come billowing into the great hall, while sharp, brilliant light streaked through.

It is with such staging that Ball adds a strange and personal ingredient to the new staging trend. He is willing to try the broadly, the vividly theatrical—the grand-operatic. Too inhibited as most directors are for flamboyant, fearing corniness, Ball will come driving in with crazy, gravy-dripping extravagance.

He will also draw inspiration from anything he sees. Watching the Bunraku Puppets at the City Center this winter, he was struck by the puppets' being at center stage while the music and narration came from the side. And by the clocking, knocking noises. It led him to conceive of separate sources of sound and vision for drama. If you ask me what he would do with just that, I quote Edward Teller, the physicist. Professor Teller once explained flying saucers as miracles. When asked whether the miracles were "theirs or ours," Professor Teller replied, "They are miracles. How do I know whose miracles?"

If you asked me just how Ball would translate his idea of separate sound and vision, I have to answer, it is in his imagination. How do I know how he would translate it?

Perhaps Ball himself doesn't know. It makes no difference. He is swinging through stage space, mad to create, mad to juggle actors and splash lighting broadly about them.

But the company has nowhere to go after September 18.

When ACT began, it was invited into two theaters in Pittsburgh. There, last spring and summer, it presented a repertory that ranged from Goldoni's *A Servant of Two Masters* to Miller's *Death of a Salesman*. It did *The Rose Tattoo, Six Characters in Search of an Author, Uncle Vanya*. Great for Pittsburgh, right?

Wrong. After the summer the company had to leave under a cloud of vagueness.

So ACT began its wanderings. The American Theatre Wing donated New York facilities to keep the classes going. The company studied movement, scansion, Alexander Technique (a patent medicine body training method that Ball himself calls "crackpot" but which somehow works great things for body sense).

Now the company has almost a dozen plays in its repertoire. It is adding *Charley's Aunt* and *Misalliance* this summer. The sets are built and ready to be used. There are two complete casts for nearly every production. ACT is, I might add, the only major winter theater in the country that performs in repertory (while many companies call themselves "repertory theater," in fact they are not; they do one play for four or five weeks and then another. True repertory demands the nightly change of bill). All of this was ready—aching to operate. And all there was to do was work, rehearse, and work while Ball went looking for a new home.

During this time, the company grew in technique, in comprehension of Ball's attitudes, and most essentially, in fanatic devotion to Ball himself. I say essentially because I do not think much of conservatory systems. There is a great deal that must be taught to actors, but little of it can be learned in a classroom —diction, physical control, perhaps grace. Even these can be taught in rehearsal by a dominating director. As for acting itself, it seems to me that it is one of those things that can only be learned in the doing.

As for the devotion, it is difficult to describe the absolute belief the ACT people have in Ball. They are religious. He knows and they know he knows. And I'll tell you something else. I know he knows too. To watch him work is to see sheer genius.

Ironically, it is his genius that sometimes gets in the way of hardheaded thinking. He is so carried away with his vision that it is a wrench for him to come back to reality. Life to him is a series of stage sequences, vaudeville routines, and extravaganzas. Such an emotional structure is sensational for stage work. But when it comes to managing the business of ACT and straightening out its wandering stability, it makes things difficult. Especially difficult since all Ball really wants to do is be left alone to give some city the priceless gift of theater greatness.

Yet the company was stranded, practically like a shady producer's bus-and-truck company. And since he acts as his own business manager (a responsibility of which he should be relieved) he had to find a home.

So he had to keep away from his company while he criss-crossed the country looking for a city with brains enough to take in, no strings attached (as he correctly demands), what is bound to be one of the absolutely finest resident theaters in the

country. If not the finest. Why this company is not the Repertory Theater of Lincoln Center—even though Ball says he
hates New York—is beyond me, I believe the expression is.

Was Ball stupid to build a hundred-man organization with
no financial basis of his own? Of course he was. Was he foolish
to depend on American Subsidy—the foundations, the government, and the rest? Of course he was. Will any institution take
ACT in and really let Ball do exactly what he wants to do? I
doubt it. But now the company is formed. Now its important
work is in progress. Now what does it do?

A Director Performs (*March 28, 1968*)

In one splashy swoop the other night William Ball demonstrated the drive, the theory, and the personal inspiration that
have made him our best director and his San Francisco-based
American Conservatory Theatre our most exciting resident
company.

It all happened at a chicken-and-ice-cream dinner meeting of
some 175 West Coast psychiatrists and their wives at which Mr.
Ball had been asked to speak on nonverbal communication.
The actor and his audience could not have been better
matched: psychiatrists are professional observers, and Ball is a
congenital performer.

There also could not have been more of a challenge: psychiatrists are geared to analyze what they're seeing and hearing,
while Ball is intent on dazzling your perceptions with sheer
theatrical energy. Sure, he meant to speak on the subject—if
you'd asked him he would have said so. But for him and his
company, performance is all—always. And here was performance.

The place was buzzing—silverware clacking, glasses clinking.

Ball was introduced and hobbled to the dais on crutches. The crutches were there because of a twisted knee, but they were used as a prop since Ball's way of existence is to live all of life as theater.

So he swung and looped his way to the front of the house, teeth flashing and the black caballero hat tied around his throat and hanging down behind his neck. The houselights might as well have darkened, it was that much of a theater situation. And Ball proceeded to talk about nonverbal communication. He was to describe the whole stage attitude behind his directing—to demonstrate it, to involve his audience in it, to show just how restricting ordinary conversation can be. And just how expressive is the laugh, the grunt, the jabbed finger, the whistle, and the jam thrust (as he puts it).

Most of this material was drawn from an ACT class that is called "connotations." What does a snapped finger mean when it is done this way? (It means what-is-it; what's-his-name.) And this way? (It means I've got it!) and this way; and this way?

What do hands on hips mean this way; and this way? What does John Wayne's walk mean this way; but what would it mean this way? (It would mean I swear to God, sweetheart, I've just got to get that wagon train to Texas.)

Then Ball got his psychiatrists to do speaking exercises, count aloud, run out of breath. That, he said, is how to feel rage, scorn, superiority. Look it—get the physical manifestation of it—then you'll be it.

This is the basis of Ball's acting approach—"Do the act and the feeling will follow." He doesn't want his actors to think. How does this character feel? He wants them to *look* it. The audience doesn't know what the actor is thinking. The audience only knows how the actor looks. It doesn't matter to the audience—or the theater—whether or not the actor believes what his character is doing. It only matters how the actor looks. And

160

if the actor's belief will make the performance better, then any-how, "Do the act, and the feeling will follow."

The whole point is that the performer's inner analysis isn't enough for the stage. There everything must be overt and wholesale. "The top plus one is the place to go—and the courage to go there."

This is what Ball was demonstrating that night. Showing the difference between television acting, where the screen's size for-bids grand gestures and moving heads, and his kind of stage act-ing, where space invites sweep and flamboyance.

Now a lot of this is not good news to playwrights. The kind of directing that Ball represents is creative—it takes a script and then builds the stage production. It does not simply trans-late from the page to the stage. It adds theater. You can see it in the work of Peter Brook with the Royal Shakespeare Company, of Judith Malina with the Living Theatre, of Joseph Chaiken with the Open Theatre. When Ball gets his hands on even the most verbal of plays (like Albee's *Tiny Alice*), they become operatic, balletic, mimetic, musical, multicolored.

Playwrights don't appreciate this—Harold Pinter says his plays should be performed exactly as written and that he would not allow otherwise. It is sometimes debatable whether the play that Ball directs is the play that the presumed author wrote.

But whoever it is, it is of the theater. And it represents an expressive, uninhibited kind of acting that Stanislavski almost murdered with this inner-beingness. Ball is after the foot stamped in rage, the voice raised in anger, the arms waved in fury, the speaking up and out, the walking and trotting and running and skipping.

And there at the microphone, laughing, confiding, rambling, chiding, demonstrating, mugging, waving the microphone, he represented it all. When it was over—and the scheduled half hour had stretched to two hours—he bobbed off on his crutches to the applause, across the room, past his table, down the stairs, and presumably out into the night.

An outrageously stagy, melodramatic, and wonderful exit. Ball has the guts to do, this because it is his way of life. Afterward, when they bunched around him to express gratitude, they thought they were psychiatrists relating human behavior to the theater. They were really stage-door fans. Ball is all theater, and they had had themselves a performance.

The Great White Hope (*December 14, 1967*)

Howard Sackler has written an extraordinary play, an outright artwork, and has done it the only way possible: by combining a piece that can work entirely as pure theater with a point of view that is frightfully perceptive about a specific contemporary problem and about mankind in general. Moreover, Arena Stage here [in Washington] has given it a tremendous production, both spectacular and sensitive. *The Great White Hope* is probably the most important new American play ever to come out of any resident theater and is certainly the most impressive one that I have seen anywhere in a very long time.

It is based (with admitted looseness) on the career of Jack Johnson, who in 1908 became the first Negro heavyweight champion of the world. Calling his prizefighter Jack Jefferson, Mr. Sackler begins the play with Jefferson due for a crack at the title. The boxing world, the press, and the United States are outraged at the likelihood and convince the retired champion to reenter the ring to prevent it. Despite the rampant bigotry, Jefferson is easygoing about the prospective fight ("Been a whole lot of mean talk around here but I'm glad it came down to a plain old scuffle") and resents the Negro community's insistence that a victory will give the race self-respect ("If you ain't there already, all the boxing in the world ain't gonna do it for you").

He does win the title and is immediately vilified by a frightened country. The boxing world and the press immediately set out in search for a "great white hope"—any man who can defeat Jefferson. But he is too powerful a fighter. Meanwhile, the residents and government of Chicago resent his high living and the café he has opened there. Finally, his open romance with a white woman provokes emotional hatred. With the government ("We cannot allow the image of this man to inspire Negroes"), the bigots ("an outrage to every respectable Caucasian in America") and Uncle Tomming Negroes ("The majority of Negroes do not approve of this man") joining forces, Jefferson is picked up on a Mann Act violation in the midst of one of the most romantic, most tender love scenes I have ever seen on any stage. He jumps bail and flees to England, where there is enough prejudice to send him running once more. On the European mainland, he wanders from country to country, bewildered by his situation as a world-famous, outcast Negro and frustrated by lack of work. He is finally reduced to playing tug-of-war with a Keystone Kop band of German soldiers and then working in an "Uncle Tom's Cabin" circus act. Still struggling for self-respect, he refuses American offers of a lightened sentence, made by a country that cannot forget that Jefferson is still champion. Now suffering from brain damage, he moves weakly to Mexico and trains in a shabby barn, still loved, probably as no man was ever loved, by his white woman. Furious with this fate, he unbottles his rage against her while sitting next door to America like "a boil on the whole country's ass."

When she commits suicide after being expelled, he at last capitulates and returns to fight the latest white hope and both emerge defeated. The final scene, one of many unbearably powerful ones, has the white boxer—all white, white face, white robe, white trunks—carried about the stage with his face a mass of blood.

It is an astonishing story, easily enough for the theater with-out any other references. But of course, the references are wholesale. Mr. Sackler has tossed upon the stage the whole American racial mess—yesterday, today, and as it may very well be tomorrow. Jefferson, as even the most militant black nation-alist, is the captive of white America, unable to leave the scene of his pain. The Negro may win public recognition here, but like Jefferson's championship belt, the recognition is "just a piece of junky hardware turning green on me and I'm stuck with it." The threat and doom of Stokely Carmichael and H. Rap Brown are there too, and the fate of Muhammud Ali. And beyond all of that, the grim capture of any man caught in too-powerful circumstances, aching only to live his own life with some privacy and just a little joy.

The play's episodic structure is as unfortunate as it is neces-sary. It causes unavoidable moments of blackness, during which momentum is lost. Yet there are so many scenes, all necessary, in this long (three and a half hours) epic work that a director could hardly avoid them. Edwin Sherin, doing a generally mag-nificent staging job, sometimes could bridge them with music or drumbeats, but the gaps remained gaps.

As for Sackler's writing, it is regularly magnificent, ranging from perfect dialects of all kinds to heroism or romance, and is practically always poetry. And it is stage writing, written not for literature but for the theater. The humor is high, some-times giddy, sometimes mocking, and the use of vaudeville tech-niques by both playwright and director ties the whole thing to-gether with a special sense of high-stepping tragedy.

Sherin handled the enormous cast (60 actors playing more than 200 roles) with astonishing control and gave James Earl Jones whatever assistance he needed to make Jefferson a figure both heroic and personal, an awesome task. In this perform-ance, Jones passed over the line from being a very good actor to being a great one. Though there are no actual boxing scenes, his training ones were powerful. Shaving his mannerisms as he

164

did his head, and in phenomenal physical shape, he worked with every acting tool under inspired control—vocal technique, physical sense, intellectual understanding. Bravura actors are almost extinct in America, and now there is Jones. Jane Alexander played his white love as a woman of heartbreak and strength with no small amount of technique of her own. Norma Donaldson was flashy and bitchy as his discarded Negro girlfriend, and Lou Gilbert made his manager real without passing into Jewish vaudeville over it. Especially with a cast this size, it is impossible to give detailed credits. It kept consistently to the character of the production and worked in smooth ensemble, marvelous considering its size. Douglas Schmidt solved apparently impossible designing problems with great invention and, again, a deep awareness of the whole production's character.

So the result was great theater despite whatever weaknesses there are in it. They are minor, and considering my space and the overwhelming strengths, I have not gone into them. This production had better be brought to New York.

Enrico IV (February 28, 1967)

Enrico IV, though written about and discussed with a respect that borders on awe, is so rarely produced that it seems to substantiate the impression that lip service to "art" only disguises a general distrust of it as exciting theater. Such an attitude too regularly deprives audiences and theaters of the richest plays, and the Hartford Stage Company's production of the Pirandello proves its wrongness. *Enrico IV* is a bold and complex work, projecting an eerie mood and entwining itself with fascinating philosophical questions and puzzles.

It is about an Italian aristocrat whose sanity is shaken when his horse rears, throws him, and kicks him during a pageant. At

165

the time he is costumed as Enrico IV, the eleventh-century emperor of the Holy Roman Empire, and for the next twenty years he believes that he is in fact Enrico IV. To humor this delusion, his friends create a "throne room" in his suburban Roman villa and hire amateur actors to "attend" him. On their occasional visits, they wear costumes and play out the charade of Holy Roman history. The play begins with such a visit, only a psychiatrist has been brought along to try and shock Enrico out of his hallucination.

The shock which the stupid psychiatrist has in mind is involved with a life-sized portrait of Matilda, the insane man's friend, costumed as the Marquesa of Tuscany, as she had been during the pageant. Matilda's daughter Frida now looks exactly as her mother did twenty years earlier, and she is substituted for the painting.

But while this is being planned, "Enrico" turns out to have been quite sane for ten years, having chosen to continue the role-playing and live in history, where all is predetermined, concluded, and final. There, he feels that everything is known and safe, and he prefers a story that cannot change to life's frightening unpredictability.

"Enrico" finally reveals his sanity to the attendants, but before his friends know about it Frida is substituted for the portrait, and "seeing" the Marquesa (or Matilda) young again shocks the nobleman right back to "Enrico" and madness. Or does it?

He immediately strangles Matilda's current lover, which seems to prove his insanity, but he had hated him during his sanity (if he was sane then). He now insists that he is Enrico, but he had insisted that during the long pretense, so this doesn't prove insanity either. What we are left with is the puzzle of whether he was ever mad and whether he was ever sane.

But *Enrico IV* is about more than the nature of insanity. Like Pirandello's earlier *Six Characters in Search of an Author,*

166

it is interested in the nature of time and changing existence. It is also involved with the possibility—or impossibility—of real understanding between people. The soul of one human being may be closed to all outsiders ("a door that will never open"), and in any case, "to trust anybody completely—that is real madness."

Finally, as in all of Pirandello, there is an absorption with role-playing, the general attitude being that the character you play is the character you are. The nobleman may have believed he was Enrico during the ten years of madness (if he was mad), but even before then he had been inclined to act. As Enrico he identified people not by how they behaved but by what costumes they wore—again an existence through role-playing. Psychiatry, demanding reality, cannot accept this attitude, so the psychiatrist tries to destroy it with the Frida-Matilda substitution ("Delusion will collapse like a punctured balloon"). And in the process sends the nobleman back to his role-playing. Can humans live with reality?

These are among the fascinations of *Enrico IV*. In the Hartford production, Jacques Cartier has staged the play with a great sensitivity to both its theater magic and its intellectual questions. Unfortunately, his company is not entirely up to the play's tricky demands, although Charles Cioffi managed many of the endless subtleties in the character of the nobleman. Eve Collyer was splendid as Matilda—smug, vain, and very female while being extremely perceptive. And Henry Thomas was wonderfully oily as her lover. The others were adequate at best and often not that.

Mr. Cartier moved them trickily across his stage in spreading chamber dances and kept the play as the tightly controlled situation that it is supposed to be. He might have been more careful in the opening scenes, where the details of plot must be carefully explained to avoid audience confusion, but his job was generally excellent. Peter Hunt's lighting designs were brilliant, nightmared when necessary and arm in arm with the staging. But John Conklin's set was much too Fu Manchu (it was probably meant to be garish, but the effect was too cheap, and the bare floor, so exposed, should have been cleaned up or covered).

The Hartford Stage Company is one of America's exceptional resident theaters, regularly producing adventurous plays and doing them with excitement and professional technique. It is showing that audiences need not be "educated" over long periods of pap production. Its *Enrico IV* is still another example of the company's importance not just as a cultural asset but as proof that art theater can also be exciting theater.

Pressure Cooker (*April 28, 1967*)

A couple of weeks ago I received a letter from Jacques Cartier, the artistic director of the Hartford Stage Company, and I quote part of it:

> Our attendance this season has dropped from the 92 per cent [of capacity] of last year to 82 per cent and our deficit up from the anticipated one of $55,000 to $80,000 plus, and there has been a great deal of complaining about the obscurity of the titles for this season. It's been a hell of a job trying to program a better known season for next year that still turns me and the company on. Here's the list of 10, from which I will choose seven. I suspect you will be disappointed.

I was disappointed indeed. Mr. Cartier's list of ten plays included *The Misanthrope, The Homecoming, Room Service, A View from the Bridge, Under Milk Wood,* Sophocles' *Antigone, The Hostage, Tobacco Road, The Threepenny Opera,*

168

and *The Avant Garde* (three one-act plays chosen "from such as Ionesco, Pinter, Genet, Beckett, etc.").

Why was I disappointed? Because these plays represent the playing of things safe and a concession to lower-level audience tastes. You might say that there is nothing wrong with Molière and Dylan Thomas and Brendan Behan. You might say that *The Threepenny Opera* is, after all, Brecht's, that *Room Service* and *Tobacco Road* have certain American folk art aspects, and that *The Homecoming* is an undeniably brilliant and artistic play. You might say it. But you know and I know and certainly Mr. Cartier knows that they are either war-horses or chosen because, as he himself says, they are "better known." They have been done too often to excite either a director or a company and will turn off the more adventurous Hartford theatergoers who have often found better theater at home than in New York.

The most bitter pill of all is that whenever resident theater directors have tried to justify their programming of safe classics as being necessary for plain existence, I have always countered with the example of the Hartford Stage Company. There Cartier had maintained more than 90 percent capacity audiences at a 300-seat theater in a city with only 500,000 people while programming such plays as Beckett's *Waiting for Godot* and *Endgame,* Genet's *The Balcony,* Pirandello's *Enrico IV,* and Goldoni's *The Servant of Two Masters.* Moreover, the productions had been polished and exciting, not always entirely satisfactory but certainly respectable. Any time I had visited the Hartford Stage Company the audience was absorbed, appreciative, and highly stimulated during intermissions. Watching those Hartford audiences cured me of any prejudices regarding the so-called provincialism of cities outside New York.

Now the fact is, as Mr. Cartier points out, that attendance did drop ten percentiles, and that is no trivial matter, especially since it represents a $25,000 differential in deficit. But on the other hand, 82 percent is hardly an unrespectable figure, particularly when you consider that many theater people consider 75 percent a reasonable goal and that even the big Minnesota Theatre Company in Minneapolis ran at that figure last season (though 75 percent of a big house like the Guthrie is a good deal more than 75 percent of a 300-seat theater).

But there are other concerns. Did Mr. Cartier begin the Hartford Stage Company in order to create a continuing institution or did he want a theater where he could do the plays that excite him? What difference does it make if HSC continues to exist if it must produce ordinary, dependable, better-known plays to do so? Perhaps it will still be providing classic theater for Hartford, but it will make of Cartier only an official. Too, what about those audiences who were impressed with the previous, exciting programming? How will they feel about the toned-down artistic attitude? And what about the company, which had grown accustomed to constant stimulation and challenge? Once their theater had been different and had special attractions. Now it is going to have its season read like those of a dozen other resident theaters.

Mr. Cartier says that facts are facts and while some Hartford sophisticates have already complained about the watering-down, the letters responding to next season's programming have been heavily in favor of the change toward name plays. He says that by getting more theatergoers into his house he will be able to make them familiar with the stage and then will be able to return to more original programming. But even he is half-hearted about it. For the fact is that once audiences become accustomed to a certain kind of play they will ask for ever more popular works and not more challenging ones. The fact is that he is only losing whatever education he had already provided for his, all right, 82 percent. And the fact is that those resident theaters which have tried to present broad-appeal plays have found themselves continually pushed toward ever broader-appealing ones, finally ending up with Broadway musicals and comedies.

Mr. Cartier says he will leave Hartford before he does *Bells*

Are Ringing, but adds that he has a real obligation to the city, to his trustees, and to the audiences who have poured money and faith into his company. He says that he cannot abandon his and their theater until conditions are really impossible to bear.

I suppose that this is a sympathetic argument, and obviously it is easier for me to demand maximum standards when I need not answer to financial reality. But I think that the past experience of the Hartford Stage Company proves that a substantial audience was drawn and was growing accustomed to art theater. I think that only by continuing this policy can the HSC remain distinct and develop an audience for exciting stage work. I think that a concession to popular taste is the first step forward abandoning independence and high standards.

Mr. Cartier should not have been forced into this position. His company represents something important not only to Hartford but to the resident theater movement. Having gone so far without any assistance from major foundations, it now deserves and—demands—subsidy from the National Council on the Arts, Rockefeller, or Ford. If Mr. Cartier is forced to lower his standards, Hartford still will have a good theater, but American resident companies will have lost a real example of hope.

Postscript: Cartier resigned the following summer.

King Arthur (*October 31, 1968*)

The cultural insecurity and desperation that have traditionally dampened the armpits of society matrons outside New York reached its all-time, never-to-be-matched perspiration point with the opening of the Atlanta Municipal Theatre on Tuesday night. In the choice of the ridiculous and (rightfully) obscure John Dryden-Henry Purcell masque *King Arthur,* in the presentation of it as an extravaganza, and in the execution

171

of it as chintzy Walt Disney, the Atlanta Memorial Arts Center demonstrated the American culture center at its most bizarre and philistine and just plain inane.

John Dryden wrote *King Arthur* in 1691, one of his final attempts to create an English opera style. It is not opera as we understand it, but a *masque*—a combination of drama, music, and pageantry. These are never meant to blend, and in fact the music has only an incidental relationship to what is going on in the story. Still, the theory is amazingly like what Wagner and our few modern Broadway people speak of as music-dance-theater. Unfortunately, however, Dryden's libretto has even less value as a musical basis than it does as literature. It is incredibly naïve, awkward in the writing, and absolutely preposterous in the hearing.

The story is not about the King Arthur of Guinevere, Lancelot, and the Round Table, but that's all right—nobody even knows whether there ever was a King Arthur. Dryden's story is more medieval, involving Arthur with an enemy Saxon named Oswald and a beautiful blind girl named Emmeline (needless to say, Emmeline's sight is restored for a second-act highlight).

This story is told intermittently, regularly interrupted for Purcell's music, which is much the best part—indeed the only worthwhile part—of the show. Dryden had originally written *King Arthur* with a French composer named Grabu because he felt there was no worthwhile English composer (as have felt many people throughout English history), when along came the young Purcell. The difference in age between Dryden and Purcell is apparent through every silly moment of *King Arthur*, the music being fresh and alive while the document is sterile and stuffy.

To all of this—and it already involves massed forces of singers and actors—were added dancers because the Atlanta Municipal Theatre wanted a premiere production which would demonstrate the three companies (theater, drama and ballet) that would be working in the house. I think this foolishly motivated pride, though appealing in its innocence, shows just how unaccustomed these institutionalists are to a living familiarity with art.

So, ignoring the fact that ballet was not to be invented until one hundred years after *King Arthur* was written, the Atlantans introduced choreographic elements that ranged from country dances to classical ballet, most of it ordinary, none of it unpleasant, but all of it irrelevant. And the people kept piling up onstage, while the scenery and scenic effects accumulated behind them, whether as badly painted cloth backdrops, cardboard cutout flats, or fake waterfalls yet.

Michael Howard was assigned the task of directing this crepe-paper monster production from the adaptation by Blanche Thebom, who is the director of the center's opera contingent. Miss Thebom's contribution was in cutting the original in half, which must be considered some kind of mercy killing. Howard's work was of a more diverse and visible nature. He began by setting the stage as a salon, where the royalty was being entertained, first by a string quartet (another anachronism since the quartet was yet to be invented), and then by the masque itself. One of the royalists was to be the evening's countertenor, and the fruity handling of this person exemplified, I think, the low level to which the entire production was appealing. Mediocre minds notwithstanding, the idea of a countertenor is neither fruity nor funny.

In any case, the introduction is concluded with a prologue written by John Lewin in the style of Shakespeare (What's one more anachronism?) and presumably self-satirical about culture centers. Lewin's verse—"Well, we have culture if they have the loot. So come on, sirs, let's toot"—is about as sensible and witty as the whole evening.

Then the production, with its comic-book-story style, its ludicrous dialogue, and the onslaught of school-play spectaculars. The company, as best it can be sorted out, is strongest in the musical department, with very good and very well-trained singers. The ballet corps sometimes looked like an assembly line gone amok, but the principals were competent. Which is more than I can say for the actors (with the single, and impressive, exception of Claudette Nevins as Emmeline).

Howard seemed uncertain about how to approach the whole thing (as well I can understand) and spent a good third of the time putting the whole business on, which was about as senseless as everything else in this senseless production. Perhaps some confusion can be allowed England as it was muddling its way through both the Restoration and the Baroque, but the Atlanta Municipal Theatre has no such credit line. It had better try to relax, forget about trying to impress anyone (especially itself), and get on with more reasonable projects while keeping the big building and local social pressures at arm's length.

[The Atlanta Municipal Theatre collapsed as an enterprise immediately after the run of *King Arthur*. It subsequently reopened, but on a hand-to-mouth basis.]

The Guthrie Twins: Minneapolis and Stratford
(June 16, 1967)

The two major American festival theaters—the Minnesota Theatre Company and the Stratford (Ontario) Shakespearean Festival (it must be considered as much American as it is Canadian)—seem at last to be recognizing their own problems and have become intent on correcting them. Whether they will actually be able to revitalize themselves or whether their very size and nature make institutionalism inevitable remains to be seen, but at least they have finally shown some awareness of the sterility that an official theater can cause.

It is Stratford that really has the more absorbing problem be-

174

cause the company, within fifteen years, has developed a technique and polish which rival that of any English company
(and it is the first-class English repertory companies upon
which Stratford was modeled). Beginning with a big-money,
big-name policy, this theater was directed by Tyrone Guthrie
into classical discipline, ensemble work, fidelity to style, and the
traditional acting fundamentals: diction, movement, stage
definition, projection, and body control. The production assets,
such as costumes and wigs and lighting, were ultraprofessional.
And so the look of things was beyond reproach.

The problem, of course, was a concentration on surface and
an increasing lack of vitality and drive. It was not very long before Stratford's productions were veneer theater, more suited
for a museum than for living drama. This was fine for the tour-
ists, and Stratford proved an immense financial success.

But who in the theater—indeed, who interested in the theater—could care? It often seemed as if not even the participants
did. There was pride in the professionalism, but no excitement,
and without excitement a theater will die. In fact, Stratford,
while beautifully embalmed, has been dead for some time.

But something very interesting has happened this season. Michael Langham, who succeeded Guthrie not long after the theater had been established, had already committed himself to a
new theater festival in La Jolla, California [which never ma-
terialized] and this summer is to be his last as artistic director.
In a parting shot, he warned Stratford of institutionalization
and gave its all-Shakespeare policy another ten years at most.
On the surface, this didn't seem Langham's to say and sounded
tactless at best. After all, wasn't it Langham who had been as responsible as anyone for Stratford's sterilization? And wasn't it
tasteless for him to turn a back on his own company after having worked with it for so long? And wasn't it cowardly for him
to make the accusations when he already had another job and
so had nothing to lose?

I think so, and yet one must look deeper than his basic statement. What if Langham found the powers at Stratford beyond the fighting while he was actually working there? Stratford is a quasi-governmental theater and it is very much mixed up with political officials, business interests, and Canadian money-society. What if he decided that since Stratford had become a deadly theater place, he was in a perfect position to prompt public pressure for its vitalization? He knew that John Hirsch, his successor (in association with the Stratford veteran Jean Gascon), was a man of considerable theater vividness. Hirsch had established the respected Manitoba Theatre Centre in Winnipeg and had produced exciting plays there. If Hirsch were to be able to substitute adventurous plays for Stratford's war-horse repertoire, the stuffy powers would have to be shaken up a bit. Perhaps Langham thought that his strong public statements might help.

This year's opening production did not suggest a new energy as it began, except that its leading player—Alan Bates—was brought in from the outside. Although there is nothing more conducive to ensemble playing and company finesse than years of work together, a group of actors can grow stagnant and its habits ingrown. A new face can provide fresh inspiration, and between Bates and Zoe Caldwell and Christopher Plummer (who is coming later in the season) such inspiration was in the offing. But the opening night *Richard III* rolled along much as had any Stratford production: beautifully dressed, beautifully read, and beautifully dull. Then, as the play moved into its final battle scene, something startling happened. Mr. Hirsch, its director, abandoned the long-practiced Stratford concept of battle scenes (swords and banners and fanfares and stage crossings) for a highly stylized, even abstract, staging. Swords clashed only once, with a musical crack. Military movement was staccato, one step at a time. Snap! The lighting changed sharply from moment to moment, creating striking photographs of military theater (and remember that never before had Stratford made any creative use of its magnificent lighting system). Finally, the play's ending was changed and instead of Richard being killed in battle, he committed suicide by handing his knife to the opponent he had on the brink of death. It was a brilliant idea of Hirsch's, driving into a real understanding of the grotesque, monstrous, unloved Richard. But it was also untraditional, and that is something unheard of at Stratford.

The staging of the next evening's *The Inspector General* by Langham himself was no less adventurous (for Stratford), adding to the small revolution here by not only again making imaginative use of lighting but actually using scenery. The Stratford stage has a permanent portico set and there has never been use of scenery—an incredibly stupid, self-imposed, antitheater restriction. Langham staged the play as a broad slapstick, making regular use of silent movie techniques and using flickering light to amplify that impression.

Whether or not these productions succeeded, and neither did completely, their scheme was crucial to the future of Stratford. The try for change had begun.

At least Stratford had a justification of sorts for having fallen into a rut. Its theater may have become official and arid, but a finesse of craft had been developed. The Minnesota Theatre Company in Minneapolis had no such excuse. Arrantly modeled after Stratford, it began existence with a splashy theater, funded to the teeth, and with no artistic purpose. It proceeded to produce standard classics with neither drive nor craft. And without purpose, without direction, neither was developed. Except for an occasional excitement—1965's *The Caucasian Chalk Circle* and this year's *Thieves' Carnival*—Minneapolis productions were badly executed exhibits rather than dramatic experiences.

Now Minnesota's executive director, Peter Zeisler, is intent on injecting life into the company. But can he? Suppose that he can induce Douglas Campbell, his war-horse-oriented artistic director, to do plays of greater originality and modern art? Should an executive director so influence an artistic director?

No. Once chosen, an artistic director has to be given a free hand. Mr. Campbell was not an unknown quantity. If Minnesota was built on the reputation of Tyrone Guthrie and considered that reputation so important that it accepted Guthrie's protégé as his successor, then Campbell is what it deserved. Besides, since Minnesota has never been able to keep actors or associate directors, it has not developed a trained, familiar acting corps or a personality of its own.

So the Minnesota Theatre Company has a much more primitive problem than that of Stratford. Yet they are both fighting the specter of official, institutional, big-time festival theater. Whether that fight can ever be won remains to be seen. What is inspiring right now is that at least it has begun.

Serjeant Musgrave's Dance (June 18, 1968)

The idea behind *Serjeant Musgrave's Dance* is so appealing, and its pacifistic theme is so fashionable, that directors keep trying to do it despite flaws that make the John Arden play all but impossible to stage effectively.

The irony is that the qualities of *Musgrave* are on a rather high level—they are qualities of language and movement and style—and so the play attracts sensitive directors and serious theaters. You can't really blame them for trying it because there are few modern plays so original and so ambitious.

There are also few modern plays so exasperating. The *Musgrave* problem is in the play itself, and no director can restructure, reintellectualize, and rewrite a script, no matter how creative and positive he may be.

As produced by the Minnesota Theatre Company here [in Minneapolis], Arden's play remains a tremendously promising theater idea that has defeated its author. It is at once repetitious and confused, beautifully written and then overwritten. Mel Shapiro has staged it with what one can fairly call devotion, and he obviously wanted it very much to work.

But *Serjeant Musgrave's Dance* will not work—cannot work. It will always be too long, too wordy, too uncertain about what it wants to say and do and how it wants to say and do it. The play is trapped in its basic theme, forbidden to expand into the bounding theater experience from which it seems but one leap away.

The central idea is brutally ironic and altogether splendid. A career soldier who has been brainwashed with the idea of blind duty suddenly realizes the horror of war after witnessing the pointless death of one of his men. Breaking down under the conflict between regimented military thinking and his own awareness, he deserts in order to return the man's body to his village and teach the populace what their flag-waving patriotism really represents.

He aims to teach them by murdering them. That is the only way they can learn that war is not flags and banners and handsome uniforms and recruiting demonstrations, but guns and bullets and death, arbitrary and merciless. As Arden says in his introduction to the play, "I think that many of us must at some time have felt an overpowering urge to match some particularly outrageous piece of violence with an even greater and more outrageous violence."

As an approach to pacifism, this is a good deal more palatable, honest, and realistic than that of your run-of-the-demonstration flower child. It is very easy to preach absolute pacifism, but preaching peace away from the battlefield is no more sensible than preaching war away from the battlefield. Arden realizes this, and so his Musgrave, while outraged by war, releases his outrage with a violence no less bloody. The ardor of the pacifist becomes as brutal as that of the warrior.

This in no way weakens the purity of Arden's peacefulness; in fact and to the contrary, it strengthens it by making it plausible. What it does weaken, however, is the play, which must be terrifically well written if it is to carry arguments of such complexity.

It is a challenge that Arden does not meet. His approach to pacifism is never clarified until the play is almost over, and you get the feeling that the playwright himself was uncertain of his exact point until then. A parallel with union organizers in the village is attempted early in the play and is virtually forgotten.

A sequence involving the dead soldier's girlfriend, now a pathetically indiscriminate barmaid seeking another soldier to symbolize him, is very effective in itself but unmeshed with everything else. The relating of Musgrave to God is extremely vague, and Musgrave's dance itself, while a wonderful theater metaphor, is never realized. Since it is meant to be a climactic scene, this is a rather crucial fault.

Finally, the entry of the Dragoons, come to arrest Musgrave, smacks of high-school-play pageantry no matter what a director does. Frankly, I think Shapiro could have escaped this trap by avoiding super-soldier costuming.

But that was one of a very few ways in which he could have helped the play. In general, his capture of Arden's period unreality was precise and his reproduction of it as a parable was rich and colorful, as it should have been. The character of Musgrave is a brilliant one, shiny and stiff as if with mustache wax, and Shapiro helped Len Cariou stomp right into it.

A virtuoso actor could have even done more—the role is wide open for art—but Cariou's intensity and physicality did right enough by it. Roberta Maxwell was extremely touching and delicate as the barmaid, and the company supported consistently, if not as group participants. But for all the work, the production is doomed to the confusion and lethargy of the play.

New York's Companies

APA—The Craft but Not the Taste (*April 16, 1965*)

I T looks as if the Association of Producing Artists has passed its major hurdle—the commercial one—in New York and will be settling down to a few more seasons at least. The fact remains that the company did not deserve the critical reception that made all of this possible.

It is depressingly obvious that had APA received the criticism it rated, New York audiences would not have come and it simply would never have the chance to develop. So, in a way, the unwarranted notices served a good cause. But this still-immature repertory company will collapse if it relies on continued blind luck. It has much work ahead, much training to be filled in, and much more care to be exercised in its choice of plays.

Choice of plays is actually the prime problem. The weaknesses in acting and directing are ones that will, in time, be corrected. APA has some lead players who are going to have to be weeded out—there is too much flamboyance and floridity there. And its direction has been altogether too erratic, with productions leaning toward physical movement for climaxes when intensity should be growing from within. But such problems can be solved, with practice and consideration. The matter of play selection is much more complex. It is a question of taste and judgment and is tricky in the correction.

In its two seasons at the Phoenix Theatre, APA has done a worthless, crude play by George M. Cohan, a trivial pair of Molière comedies, and Gorki's turgid, stolid *Lower Depths*. These were pure waste. It also produced an adaptation of *War and Peace* that, while generally effective, had only passing value. The company's *Man and Superman* was not at all well done, mostly because few of the actors were yet capable of Shaw, and certainly not the director. The most recent production, that of Giraudoux's *Judith,* worked to a very great degree, but the only entirely successful presentation over the two-season stretch was that of Pirandello's *Right You Are (If You Think You Are)* last season.

Of these productions, only the Shaw, the Pirandello, and perhaps the Giraudoux were really worth trying. Even if the others had been altogether successful in their production, they could not have been justified for repertory theater. APA's problem is that either it is selecting its plays haphazardly or it is doing only works that it thinks it can do well. Neither method is wise.

If you will notice, all six of the plays have conservatism in common—they are what I have taken to calling "right-wing theater." There is no adventure in any of them except the Pirandello, and even Pirandello has come around to acceptance in traditional theatrical circles. APA is not dominated by behind-the-scenes financiers or a stultifying "festival" image. Why does it lack the drive and curiosity a young company should have? Why is it so old?

The company also seems inclined toward spectacle plays that utilize large casts, much like a children's summer camp theater. It is as if all the actors have to be given a chance at a stage appearance. This is no way to run a theater. Nor is a scheme of selection that appears enmired in what was once conceived of as "classics" (a classic being anything that is acceptable for an eighth-grade reading list compiled by, say, William Jennings Bryan). This, again, is right-wing theater.

I have no intention of suggesting what APA should be doing. That is completely their own business. But in complaining about their past choices I am pleading for a little vitality, a little adventure. A repertory theater, especially one that is making it on its own (as opposed to one financed by the ruling "cultural" powers), is obliged to dare, to try the new or the overlooked. It really doesn't matter whether the plays are good, because, after all, "good" is an entirely subjective term. What does matter is that there should be a healthy influence from the left wing—the wing of change—which is badly in need of productions of technical maturity.

Perhaps, as APA approaches such technical maturity (and it is beginning to), its taste will grow bolder. It possesses some perfectly decent actors and a first-class leading lady in Rosemary Harris (if she rids herself of some grande-dame mannerisms that cropped up alarmingly in the recent *Judith*). If it can find its youth after having been born middle-aged, APA could be a godsend. Granted the landslide of undeserved support, it will have no excuse for not developing.

You Can't Take It with You (*November 24, 1965*)

The artistic director of a repertory company has every privilege of indulging his private whimsies, I suppose, but he hardly has the right when the company is presenting itself as seriously theatrical. Ellis Rabb apparently finds the pure-thirties quality of *You Can't Take It with You* attractive, but its attractions were not of a serious sort. There is no artistic reason for reviving this appallingly dated 1936 Moss Hart-George S. Kaufman nonentity, but merely a pseudo-artistic reason. And that reason is clearly that the production is a 14-karat camp (please pardon the use of that overworked term but it is really the only one apt).

There is no denying the perfect fit of this play into the stereotype of a thirty-year-old Broadway comedy. Every rich boy-poor girl situation ("You're of a different world—your family and mine—it wouldn't work, Tony, it just wouldn't work"); every character cliché (the drunk actress with bleached blond hair, black satin low-necked dress, strap shoes, and sailor songs); every curtain situation (the stageful of everybody being hauled off to jail, including the boy's stuffy parents); and every awful joke (HE: I wouldn't trade this evening for all the rice in China. SHE: Is there much rice in China?). It is all there, meant to parade in sentimental vulgarity, not for its original purposes but as reverse effete.

Mr. Rabb brought his Association of Producing Artists back into New York last night for a limited engagement at the Lyceum Theatre, hoping to prove that it deserves a full-time Broadway house for its repertory. In the past, APA has displayed very inconsistent taste, and this production is the second to be of the in-group sort (Cohan's *The Tavern* was the first). Broadway cannot afford to reject any repertory company these days, but APA would be far from a bargain.

It should be said that Mr. Rabb's staging for the Kaufman and Hart is about as good a job as he has ever done, apparently prompted by material and style that he really enjoyed. There is not a single step that he misses in re-creating the stage style of the past. A stage alive with a director's interest is a stage alive, and the company moves across the Lyceum's in a kind of perpetual motion of the past. What's more, most of its performances are just what Rabb was after—not mimicry or burlesque but *duplication* of the old style. And Rosemary Harris leads them all in a stunning display of acting virtuosity used for the most reprehensible of theatrical perversions. Miss Harris, one of the finest performers in this country, actually became an *actress* starring in a 1936 comedy. Clayton Corzatte was not quite in that class as her boyfriend, but his Jack Armstrong quality was admirably assumed. The remainder of the company stayed right with it.

As a play to see in 1965, *You Can't Take It with You* has absolutely nothing to offer except the shock of past tastes (Could George S. Kaufman have ever seriously been considered a wit? Will our own wit appear this moronic in 1995?).

But perhaps you are eager to see a revival of a comedy performed not for intrinsic qualities but for quaint outer style. Perhaps you might break up seeing how Negroes were once played (as domestics, of course, in saddle shoes and with lines like "Y'ever notice how white folks is always gettin' theirselves into trouble?"). It is a big, big laugh for Mr. Rabb. Whatever you say, sweetheart.

Right You Are (If You Think You Are)
(November 24, 1966)

Luigi Pirandello's *Right You Are (If You Think You Are)* always impressed me as the best production in the Association of Producing Artists' repertoire. Not just because it is a very good play but because the company seemed best mated to it and capitalized on its ensemble writing to present more of a company performance with this than with anything it had yet done. As given last night at the Lyceum Theatre, it remains excellent —in fact, the most stimulating and genuine-theater production presently available in New York.

The work is a perfect example of playwriting, in the most literal sense of the term. *Right You Are* is indisputably *written* as opposed to a stage conception. It carries a lucidity of argument, a fluid vocabulary, a structure necessarily put down on paper before it could be transposed to the stage. Nor does this detract from its stage vibrancy. This play is very much of the theater.

It is based on a premise typical of Pirandello: that humans need and demand absolute truths; also on a question typical of him: What is the nature of truth? And an equally typical answer: the only truth is what you believe, no matter what the absolute, abstract truth is. In fact, according to Pirandello, such truths (particularly when they apply to human matters) seldom exist, absolutely.

In order to deal with this question, he sets up a mystery play. A Signora Frola moves next door to the nosy household of Councillor Agazzi. She is presumably in town to be near her daughter, who is married to Ponza. Ponza will not allow the mother to visit the daughter, and this naturally arouses the curiosity of the Agazzi entourage. Probing, they hear two stories. The mother says that after the son-in-law mistakenly believed his wife to have been accidentally killed, his emotional stability was so upset that he had to marry her all over again, believing she was another woman. But the son's story is that his wife, in fact, *was* killed, and that her mother's sanity was shattered by the shock. Now, he says, his mother-in-law insists that the second wife is her daughter.

Councillor Agazzi, his wife, various neighbors, and local officials demand an explanation, insensitive to the privacy of the people they are intruding upon and heedless of the advice of Agazzi's brother-in-law, Lamberto Laudisi. Laudisi keeps insisting that truth is relative and that it will not—cannot—be delineated by logical procedure.

This presents several problems. As a philosophical argument it is fascinating, but as a hypothetical situation it is irksome. Pirandello is perfectly correct—if the mother believes the wife to be her daughter, then in a real sense the girl *is* her daughter. And if the husband believes her to be a different, *second* wife, then that is true too. But in the situation as presented, we know that there is a *fact* involved, and when the daughter finally appears to confirm both stories in flagrant inconsistency, we are bound to feel frustrated by a too obvious dramatic mechanism. The daughter confirms both stories only to confirm the playwright's thesis. I think that Pirandello might have imagined a more airtight example, and this is a definite flaw in his play, but the situation is so entirely interesting and provocative that there is hardly any reason to dismiss the whole business because of it.

Another problem is Laudisi himself, who exists as the playwright's mouthpiece. The character is much too smug, much too superior to his naïve and cruel company, to be very sympathetic. Called upon at each act-ending to laugh archly at their foolish search for a truth that neither exists nor matters, he grows unbearably obnoxious.

It is hardly the fault of the actor who plays him. Donald Moffat minimized this irritating trait as much as possible without conflicting with the script. Very often he is called upon to sit with terrible wisdom, observing the follies of his silly fellow humans. It is a terrible burden for any actor. Too, he must play an extremely precocious scene with his mirrored image. Between these extremes, he spends the evening repeating Pirandello's point about truth's relativity. Despite such weights, Mr. Moffat managed the role with a great deal of charm, lending it a style that led the way for the production in general.

That style was impeccably followed by a cast performing in an ensemble manner that could well be envied by any resident company in the country. Stephen Porter, who originally staged this production for APA, drew this cohesion from his cast in the first presentation of it some years ago, and if anything, he has improved upon it since. As the husband, Sydney Walker deliberately confused the audience about his side of the question, playing the role as believable in either direction (madness or sanity).

But most impressive were the assorted old ladies, cackling, popping in and out, and generally pressing recklessly for gossip. Mr. Porter kept them precisely within the Pirandello style of period drawings, and they worked beautifully, every one of them.

The lone misperformance of the evening was that of Helen Hayes as the mysterious Signora Frola. Working in a thin, colorless voice and apparently acting off the top of her head, Miss Hayes seemed entirely unaware of the rigors of style or the demands of group acting. Off somewhere on her own, she missed the not-terribly-difficult details of her interesting character.

The production was beautifully mounted by James Tilton, rising high into the Lyceum's flies before a blacked-out stage. APA ill-advisedly skimps on wigs, and these invariably give its actors an amateur-night look, but Nancy Potts' costumes were neat and bright without being overdone.

There is, then, a general excellence to this production, and the faults notwithstanding, it is exactly what one might most desire from a resident, repertory company.

The Repertory Theater of Lincoln Center— *Danton's Death* (*October 22, 1965*)

In opening the Vivian Beaumont Theater, Herbert Blau insulted a great play, the idea of professional theater, and the hopes of all of us for a respectable repertory theater in Lincoln Center. It came as a devastating shock to find his new production of Georg Buechner's *Danton's Death* a leaden, barren, dramaless shell of the important and exciting play it really is.

There is no question that the fault is Mr. Blau's. In adapting the play, he senselessly cut the most vaulting speeches, rewrote them in the most prosaic style, dropped essential scenes, and blurred nearly all of the dark color. In directing it he seemed nearly amateur, apparently rattled by the awesome versatility of the new theater and unable to use its shapes. His control of the large cast seemed limited to a concentration on central characters, leaving everybody else to wander the open spaces. And his handling of individual performances reduced proven actors to parodies of their own abilities. As for the actors that Blau brought in from his San Francisco Actor's Workshop, the bulk of them seemed unprepared for major work. Finally, Blau chose a near-incompetent for the leading role.

That was an even more crucial error than it ordinarily would be. *Danton's Death* is, in the deepest sense, about Danton himself and his life-and-death situation. The play is perfectly titled —it is about the death of Danton: what that death meant in terms of his attitude toward life, what that death meant in terms of the death of all of us, what that death meant in relation to revolutions and history.

Buechner, although virtually unproduced here, is generally (and deservedly) given credit for the development of drama among the German expressionists. There is no question that Brecht was inspired by Buechner's trail-blazing, and Max Frisch after him. Furthermore, if Samuel Beckett's philosophical orientation is timeless, its expression is clearly out of Buechner. In fact, Buechner provides the most logical link between Shakespeare and modern theater.

Danton's Death, which was Buechner's first play, is laid in the aftermath of the French Revolution and concerns the bloody in-fighting among the Republicans that made them victims of their own cause. To a degree, it is about the horrible weakness of man in the face of churning history.

It is also about much, much more. Georges Danton, as the play begins, has really lost all interest in politics. Aware that it is not merely this revolution that is out of hand, but that all revolutions will defeat revolutionaries, he has given up. The only thing with real meaning for Danton is Life—the flesh, the joy, the love of things living.

His antagonist is the self-righteous Robespierre, who equates pleasure with vice and uses that equation as a tool for a tyranny no better than that of the defeated aristocracy. For Robespierre, "Morality must rule by fear." His violent asceticism is in mortal battle with Danton's humanism.

In the multiple significances of this, all of which lead to Danton's suicidal giving up of life, Buechner managed a ranging drama of intense depth and fiery theatrical life. In Blau's inability to grasp either the meanings or the drama—to sense any rhythm—the play was shamed.

Curiously, it was not Blau's annoying credo of politics-in-the-theater that led to the destruction last night. In fact, for all of his talk about bringing contemporary politics into plays (whether or not those plays were intended as political) there were no such objectionable interferences in *Danton's Death*. The parallels with some modern wars are apparent and Blau left it at that. What was the matter was plain and simple amateurism.

Alan Bergmann had no business being cast as Georges Danton. Mr. Bergmann has a face that not even a fly could twitch—there is not an expression, a glance, an emotion, that could cross it (not even, I suspect, a shadow). As crucially, he does not seem to have the faintest idea of bodily movement, and all of this does not do wonders with the heroic speeches he is called upon to make.

On the other hand, Robert Symonds was a perfectly splendid Robespierre (and in all fairness it must be pointed out that he is one of the people Blau imported from the West Coast). Mr. Symonds created just the sort of superpious fanatic that Buechner wanted—a man who could well be driven to blood by the vicious St. Just.

Mr. Symonds, unfortunately, had little genuine acting company. Claudette Nevins did a very fine job as Danton's tragic wife, and Robert Stattel was a touching Camille, but that was just about it. The disappointments were provided by two excellent people—Roscoe Lee Browne and James Earl Jones—who, I hope, were simply the victims of Blau's mixed-up direction. The remainder of the cast seemed left on their own and without much capacity to do anything about it.

There is no justification for Blau's tampering with the Buechner script just because there is no copyright on it. It is rare, indeed, that any director will rewrite any play to an appreciable degree, and when the play is the work of an artist it is shameful. A new translation is one thing, an adaptation something else.

Hopes for this opening were very high. The new theater was bringing with it a completely overhauled company and a pair of new codirectors. To be sure, the selection of works for this season is very respectable. Unfortunately, taste is not necessarily indicative of ability. But with the handsome red-and-brown theater and its extraordinary physical capacities, it must be hoped that technological progress will not outstrip artistic capabilities. There is too much at stake for the New York theater.

The Taste but Not the Craft (*April 21, 1967*)

It is ironic that after this fourth season of the Repertory Theater of Lincoln Center, when some sort of light has finally begun to peep through what had once seemed an endless darkness, administrative interference with the basic idea of the company has reached its most offensive state.

There has flowed a lot of water under the bridge—enough, it

sometimes seemed, to drown the whole bridge, lock, stock, and hope. The Broadway taste, professional assurance, and classical inability of Elia Kazan and Robert Whitehead were rejected after two years at the temporary ANTA-Washington Square Theatre, following a series of inappropriate selections (*But for Whom Charlie, Incident at Vichy*) and sensational fiascos (*The Changeling*). Herbert Blau, who with Jules Irving replaced them, proved, expectably enough, to have precisely the opposite taste and scheduled two seasons of resident theater dream plays, ranging from Brecht's *The Caucasian Chalk Circle* and Buechner's *Danton's Death* to Lorca's *Yerma*. Unfortunately, Blau and Irving were the opposites of Kazan and Whitehead in more than this respect and proved entirely amateur and distracted with irrelevant, political connotations. Then Blau resigned over a combination of critical rejection and administrative pressure. It was perfectly apparent that the Repertory Theater of Lincoln Center needed the Blau-Irving producing taste but someone else to direct—someone who had classical theater technique at his command. Midway through this season, they found him in John Hirsch.

Mr. Hirsch had been director of the Manitoba Theatre Centre, a Winnipeg resident company that had (and has) as formidable a Canadian reputation as that of its more publicized neighbor, the Stratford Shakespearean Festival. Though I have never been to this theater, I have heard marvelous things about it, and its play selections have always been serious and sometimes adventurous (it reportedly did a fine *Mother Courage* with Zoe Caldwell). In the past few seasons, Mr. Hirsch has been guest-directing at Stratford and has now become artistic codirector; there his work is entirely professional, well-organized, and knowledgeable.

It is not, however, terribly exciting. Stratford, like most theater institutions, grew very official as its technique developed. It is indisputably the finest resident company on the North American continent, but watching the productions there, one always feels that everything is kind of under glass. Polished, yes, but sterile.

Hirsch's work reflected this sterility, and while no technical complaints could ever be lodged against either him or his actors there would always be a nagging for just a little amateurism, a little enthusiasm, a little daring. Stratford, however, was not about to dare anything and comforted itself with perfection.

Coming to Lincoln Center as a guest, Mr. Hirsch must surely have felt a certain unease about applying such perfection to a company of typically untrained American actors. Although Blau and Irving had rid their company of many of the faithful beginners they had brought with them from San Francisco, the actors Hirsch found were hardly comparable to the deeply trained, familiar-with-each-other, ensemble people who spent summer after summer at Stratford, rehearsing over long periods and then playing in the rotating repertory that is necessary for a real stage education (and which is not used by Lincoln Center).

Still, he found an improved company. Unaccountably though, the Repertory Theater had signed some actors for individual plays rather than the entire season, preferring to have somebody good for a single production rather than not having him at all. It finally brought some of America's finest actors into major New York productions of classical theater, particularly Michael O'Sullivan (for *The Alchemist*) and Frank Langella (for *Yerma*). Others were available for the whole season— Philip Bosco, George Voskovec, Aline MacMahon, George S. Irving, Stacy Keach, Shepperd Strudwick, Ted van Griethuysen, Ronald Weyand, joining the more talented of the original Blau-Irving company (Robert Symonds, Elizabeth Huddle).

After the 1966–67 season had begun in the same abysmal rut as the preceding one, with a completely botched *Alchemist*, things began to pick up. Robert Symonds, an assistant director, staged a new drama called *The East Wind*, and although the play was disorganized and dull, the production craft was at last good. It was a sign.

A sign that would prove more than just a sign. Hirsch came in to do both *Yerma* and *Galileo,* and although neither production was really satisfactory they were at last examples of professional technique, true acting, confident use of the physical theater and ensemble performance. There were still indications of the more annoying Blau-Irving habits (particularly the extensive and unjustifiable rewriting of *Galileo*) but now at least there was a firm hand on the staging and a company capable of following its lead. Actors could read, they could move, they could *act.*

At the same time, and most oddly of all, the productions assumed that same, Stratfordian, coldly uninspired look. Stratford's system is one of book-following, playing a script line by line, exactly as its author intended, with a running conservatism. It is an attitude encouraged by long work with fundamentals and an emphasis on finesse. Since Lincoln Center's history was hardly one of either fundamentals *or* finesse, this banking of fires was as surprising as the sudden acquisition of polish.

Now perhaps you can't have one without the other, but there are English resident companies that have proved otherwise (the Royal Shakespeare Company's *The Homecoming,* currently on Broadway, is one example, and various productions by the National Theatre of Great Britain are others). Perhaps if Mr. Irving, as producer, could recapture the excitement that drove his Actor's Workshop while retaining the present refinement of craft, this ideal combination might make the Repertory Theater of Lincoln Center the leader it should be for America's resident theaters.

But recent administrative decisions at Lincoln Center would seem to make this unlikely. The Vivian Beaumont Theater has been made into a booking house for the first time in its brief history. An outside production of a new Peter Ustinov play is to play there this summer and a revival of Lillian Hellman's

The Little Foxes is slated to open in late October for a nine-week run. Lincoln Center has been trying to palm off the Hellman as a production by the Repertory Theater simply because it will be part of the subscription season but the fact is that it will be produced, directed, and acted by outsiders and is a private investment enterprise that was actually planned for Broadway. Because of it, the Repertory Theater season will not truly begin until mid-January and there will be only three productions instead of four.

This is a very bad thing for New York's theater present—and future—and the great pity is that it comes at just the time when hope was showing its first glimmer at the gorgeous and troubled Vivian Beaumont Theater. There is nothing quite so depressing as a gloomy note striking at just the moment when circumstance called for an optimistic one.

Tiger at the Gates (*March 1, 1968*)

The Repertory Theater of Lincoln Center has recently been managing to win the praise that painfully eluded it for so long by presenting war-horse plays with institutional craft. The praise has never been deserved. Although the craft has been welcome after so many years of ineptitude, the institutionalism is dull and the war-horsism cynical. But even that, I think, was preferable to the industrial show slickness with which the company's *Tiger at the Gates* was presented last night at the Vivian Beaumont Theater.

The industrial show is a peculiar theatrical phenomenon. It demonstrates the impressive finesse of business art while insulting the very nature of the theater. It is plastic personified. The Repertory Theater's production of Jean Giraudoux's play last night, from its motel-decor settings to its over-made-up actors to their hollowly professional performances, was not much different from a World's Fair exhibition designed to plug a product. Sleekly confident and all veneer.

The play itself has never offered much. Pseudoclassical with typically French pretensions to wisdom, its point is that pacifism is futile because men want to fight wars and destiny insists on it. But the "destiny" that M. Giraudoux's "tiger" represents is only the fact that the Trojan War really did happen. Since his play is set before the war begins, and since his characters are trying to prevent it, he insists that there was nothing that they could have done about it. This is patent nonsense. The war really *didn't* have to happen. Few wars do.

In *Tiger at the Gates*, Hector is trying desperately to avoid battling with the Greeks. The prospect of war for the sake of a woman strikes him as idiotic and that Helen isn't even in love with Paris anymore makes it lunatic. But because the older men are dazzled by this beautiful lady ("That's how impotent men make love") and because they are moronically obsessed with trivial conceptions of honor and reputation, they refuse to help Hector. They insist on war, even when Helen agrees to return to Troy and despite Ulysses' willingness to go along with the plan. No matter how often Hector insists that "there will not be a Trojan War," history—destiny—dictates it, according to the playwright.

The play has an obvious relevance to the present war in Vietnam—a war so concerned with honorable solutions. But is the attitude of this production that nothing could be done about it? I doubt that this has been thought through. But it makes little difference because no matter how anxious theater people are to press points, they are there to create a stage show (make theater, not statements). The stage show at the Beaumont has only intermittent theater value.

The reasons are in both the writing and the performance. *Tiger at the Gates* gets off to a very slow start, slopping in the wisdom from the very start and getting into a repetition habit very quickly. Giraudoux says nothing without saying it three times over. Since his play is little more than third-rate Shaw with a French accent, once is enough for most of the statements. The characterization of Helen as a bitchy girl-woman is enchanting, and the whole business of making legendary people into foolish humans is always a nice stage device. But the entire play is based on a single gimmick—our knowledge that the Trojan War happened—and it could have been in one scene as easily as two acts.

The performances are nearly all exhibitions of craftsmanship but no more. Philip Bosco was humane and heroic as Hector and it was good to see him get a crack at a major role—he has long deserved it. Robert Symonds, a continuously impressive actor, was hatefully stupid (as opposed to hatefully evil) as a Trojan senate leader with his heart set on war. Jennifer West's Helen kept switching from put-on to genuine silliness, but there's no denying the charm or the truth of the type. And both Tony van Bridge and Ronald Weyand proved how wonderfully makeup and character acting can combine to assist the serious actor—theirs were the only true characterizations of the evening. More typical of it were Diana Sands' excessively mannered Cassandra and Anthony Quayle's callow, stand-around-and-watch direction. At least there is an interior to match Lincoln Center's exterior, suitable for framing.

The American Place Theatre—*The Old Glory*
(*November 2, 1964*)

Last night the American Place Theatre at St. Clement's Church introduced poet Robert Lowell as a playwright, and

Mr. Lowell's play, *The Old Glory,* introduced the American Place Theatre. In both cases, the first meeting was impressive, although some serious reservations must be made.

Mr. Lowell's title covers two one-act plays, each based on a short story—Nathaniel Hawthorne's "My Kinsman, Major Molineux" and Herman Melville's "Benito Cereno."

Let us get to the Melville at once, because with it Mr. Lowell establishes himself as a playwright of such enormous talent that it is difficult to restrain oneself from throwing hats in the air, crying hurrah, hurrah, and going through the nonsense that proclaims exhilaration. *Benito Cereno,* for all of its cutability, for all of its excessive talk and unnecessary length, is a work of vicious theatricality, of marvelous language, of bruising power and honest-to-God excitement. It was perfectly performed last night.

It is set primarily on a Spanish slave ship in 1800. The United States is in the first flush of its independence. The Spanish Empire is entering its death throes. Caught in the middle are the African slaves, being passed from a perishing colonial Europe to a thrashing young country.

Mr. Lowell has taken this historical situation, whose ramifications are all too violent today, and reduced it (via Melville) to three men: an American captain, a Spanish captain, and an African tribal king en route to bondage.

The American is established at once as a caricature of uneducated power—he claps his hands behind his handsomely uniformed back and stiffens himself. He pops his corncob pipe in his mouth, snapping on its stem. He is knowledgeable, he is sophisticated, and he is a mockery of imitative aristocracy ("Oh, the French are like the rest of the Latins—hardly white people"). Lester Rawlins is not one jot short of brilliant in the role.

The Spanish captain is the victim of a mutiny. His crew has been decimated, and of the more than 300 slaves only some 80 are left. The American is told that the ghostly ship was the victim of a jaundice epidemic (when he finally realizes that the story is not true, Rawlins passes his hat before his face to throw the very shadow of shock).

As the play moves unsteadily, stepping here in gorgeous theater and there in waste, it builds up to a power that is finally beyond bearing, never stopping to fit itself awkwardly to its allegorical clothes (although stopping long and often just to dawdle).

As the Spanish captain, desolate and destroyed, Frank Langella is superbly the shadow of a shadow, nearly as dead as the skeleton that remains of his ship's owner. Roscoe Lee Browne plays the African king with a mocking bitterness masked by childishness. Almost as much as Lowell, Browne magnificently underscored the play's references to American Negro cynicism. And Jack Ryland is touching as the American captain's aide, human and frightened.

As for the first play, Hawthorne's "My Kinsman, Major Molineux" was turned into a confused and confusing abstraction, done up in chalk face and nonsense. In its own way as vicious about America the Beautiful as the second play, it was more the work of graduate school artsy-craftsiness than professional theater.

Jonathan Miller's direction is wonderfully organized when the play is active, but when the script gets tedious, so does he. Nobody was credited for the lighting, and small wonder. Such disorganized work is astounding in the professional theater. Finally, the St. Clement's acoustics are so terrible that when actors face rear they are thoroughly inaudible.

The American Place Theatre is partly designed to promote the plays of serious writers who are turning to drama from other literary forms. In its first production it has given us Poet Lowell—quite clearly a playwright of brilliant promise. It has all thanks.

Journey of the Fifth Horse (April 22, 1966)

If the American Place Theatre does nothing else—and it has done more already—it will have introduced and nurtured a superb new playwright for the American theater. Last season, it presented Ronald Ribman's first play: the tremendously exciting and deeply sensitive *Harry, Noon and Night*. Last night at St. Clement's Church, it presented his second, *Journey of the Fifth Horse,* a terribly compassionate portrait of human loneliness. It is a real play, and Mr. Ribman is a real playwright.

Without taking any of that back, it must be said that this play is not perfect. On a couple of occasions, the back and forth of its technique slip away to become weighted down by wandering irrelevancy. I think that a couple of occasions, considering the excellence surrounding them, can be discounted, even as we wish they had not happened.

The play is drawn from the Ivan Turgenev novella *The Diary of a Superfluous Man,* a touching but by no means great story of a character type that was to become popular in subsequent Russian fiction. It introduced the Russian version of the victim-hero—a man whose awkwardness, loneliness, and insecurity become self-defeating, prompting the very solitude he fears. By anticipating rejection he prompts it.

But while the Turgenev mood of pathetic paranoia is pervasive, the structure and story of the play are almost completely original. *Journey of the Fifth Horse* is constructed in two interchanging parts. Zoditch is a reader in a publishing house, masking his clumsiness and desperate need for love with sarcasm and cruelty. When a diary is submitted to the firm, he cruelly mocks it only to be slapped down by his more understanding superior. He is told to read it and returns to the little apartment, where he is beset by the hallucinations of the world he fears—the world where he is tormented and humiliated—the world he avoids by his complicated defense mechanisms.

The diary has been written by a man exactly as lonely and wretched as he, but entirely without those defenses. Nikolai Chulkaturin went naked into a life which gave him nothing because he was too desperate in his need. Openly asking for love, openly aching for involvement, he found himself unable to assert himself and become somebody. He was useless, a fifth horse running pointlessly beside a carriage already horse-drawn. The only difference between Chulkaturin and Zoditch is that Chulkaturin sees his misery and *physically* dies of it while Zoditch cannot see it and *emotionally* dies of it.

Ribman's play weeps this inside a wonderfully fluid use of stage possibilities. The scheme is simple enough—as Zoditch is reading the diary on the upper level of Kert Lundell's fine set, Chulkaturin's tragedy is seen below. This is entwined with parallel setbacks for Zoditch. So while Chulkaturin is futilely courting a girl who is in love with a flashy officer, Zoditch is hallucinating a seduction by his landlady. And while Chulkaturin's openness is scarring him, Zoditch's compensations are scarring others.

Ribman keeps this pattern weaving between bursts of ironic humor from the observing Zoditch and sad confessions by the vulnerable Chulkaturin. The writing is sure and literary, in keeping with the style and mood, and is very often genuinely poetic. The humor is always apt and funny, and in the hallucination of the landlady's seduction, hilarious. The tragedy is continuous, and finally, when Chulkaturin reaches out to Zoditch as a love gesture to an alter ego, it is heartbreaking. Zoditch can't even love himself.

Two of the performances were brilliant—Dustin Hoffman's as Zoditch and Michael Tolan's as Chulkaturin. Many of the others were very good, especially Susan Anspach's as the dream girl in their lives, Catherine Gaffigan as the landlady, and William H. Bassett as the captain. Larry Arrick's direction was usually very good but did not help the problematic moments when blackouts murdered mood. As for Ribman, his second play is clearly out of the same sense of humanity as his first, and that is the way an artist grows. He is part of our theater's great tomorrow.

A . Place . for . Writers (*June 2, 1967*)

The American Place Theatre is concluding its third season and remains very well subscribed, newly loaded with foundation funds, still true to its original artistic premises, and, strangely, almost unknown to the mass theatergoing public. It is a phenomenon in the American theater.

A phenomenon for several reasons. In the first place, it is neither a resident theater nor a commercial one. Its company of actors changes from production to production and it chooses directors on a play-at-a-time basis. Yet it does not aim for the commercial-theater public and even allows its playwrights the choice of not being reviewed at all (this season, two of the four plays were, in fact, not reviewed). Its audiences are mostly subscribers who have found APT's past productions worthy of faith and so they subscribe blind. But there are still other reasons why APT is unusual. Wynn Handman, its serious and idealistic artistic director, does not choose plays because they are completely achieved works. He chooses them because he finds them interesting, artistically ambitious, and serious. And even when a play is acknowledged to be unconsummated, he will produce it as long as it commands his respect.

This does not mean that APT constantly presents unfinished work. Its record proves otherwise (Robert Lowell's *Benito*

Cereno, Ronald Ribman's *Harry, Noon and Night* and *Journey of the Fifth Horse*). But it does mean that the emphasis is on the theater rather than on what would "work."

Still further, the emphasis is on the play and the playwright rather than the actors and the production. That is, APT is a place for the *writer* and it is *his* interest that comes first. Mr. Handman says that directors are chosen on the basis of their compatibility with the playwright and their eagerness to do the play as *he* envisions it. He says that conflicts between director and playwright are invariably settled on the side of the playwright. Not only does Handman say this, but playwrights who have worked with APT verify it.

This writer orientation is completely against the trend of the most modern international theater, which is moving away from the literary script and toward the stage as a place for production. It is a trend toward creative direction, toward the idea that the stage is a place where theater things happen and not merely for the simple translation of work from the written page. And it is a trend with which I wholeheartedly agree. The most exciting works that I have seen lately came out of it, from Judith Malina and Julian Beck's Living Theatre to Joseph Chaikin's Open Theatre, William Ball's American Conservatory Theatre, Peter Brook's work with the Royal Shakespeare Company, and the more driving of the resident theater directors.

Yet, for all my enthusiasm for stage-oriented direction, I think it necessary to have a countervailing force pressing for literary respect. All theater cannot be production theater, and playwriting must not be buried. The stage will always be a place for writers as well as directors, and dramatic literature will have eternal validity.

Besides, there are very talented, very modern playwrights whose work just is not geared for production theater—their scripts, their language, their stage directions, *must* be followed, at least in the original productions (Harold Pinter is the most obvious example of such a playwright). And the American Place Theatre is defending this tradition.

It is doing very well at it. It is relatively free of the hit-or-miss syndrome of today's Broadway and off-Broadway because its subscriptions guarantee audiences. When plays are interesting but not quite stageable they can be given dramatic readings. Foundation funds support this, as well as make up for the inevitable deficits.

But I think that the American Place Theatre is making a serious mistake in avoiding criticism, and I mean criticism—literally—rather than raves and pans (which, of course, are not criticism at all). Without a professional, objective, educated comment, APT will never know whether it is achieving what it is setting out to do. The critic should be defending a theater—and a set of standards—that is no different from the one that APT is trying to match. Ideally, they ought to be sympathetic opponents, one playing the loyal opposition to the other. That *is* an ideal situation, I grant you, but even though it may not be realistic right now the ruling out of criticism denies even the possibility.

Another problem APT faces is its reliance on subscription audiences. In the first place, many in those audiences have built their faith on last season's reviews. Too, they are likely to be a homogeneous group, and a thriving theater needs diversified audiences.

Box-office dependency, the challenge of reaching an audience —an unguaranteed audience—can be very stimulating to theater creativity. Just getting those people in through sheer excitement, whether it is word-of-mouth or curiosity, is a basic challenge. It is short indeed on financial stability and makes for unnecessary budgetary headaches; it certainly applies pressure to give audiences what they want.

So, everything isn't perfect at APT. Still, it is a remarkable theater adventure for New York—indeed, for our country—producing new American plays by new American playwrights. And choosing them on an up-to-date intellectual basis. That it is doing so well is a pleasant glow in our too-otherwise-gloomy (and backward) theater atmosphere.

The New York Shakespeare Festival—Doing Good or Doing Well (*June 30, 1967*)

The New York Shakespeare Festival opened its mobile theater for the fourth season Wednesday night, continuing a remarkable story of hard-nosed faith. It was lovely to see Ming Cho Lee's portable theater spread out near the arch in Washington Square Park—spread out with the confidence of experience and quite ready to do its job. The grandstand seats waited for the long line of shirt-sleeved theatergoers to occupy the. The gangling lighting equipment waited for the sun to set midway through the performance so that they could give David Mitchell's set the colors he meant for it. And Joseph Papp waited for the continuation of a private fantasy that has managed to step out of a dream world and into a real one.

That his mobile theater even exists seems dreamlike, but then so did the idea of free, professional productions of Shakespeare. Yet the New York Shakespeare Festival's *Comedy of Errors* is presently splashing almost lavishly in the handsome Delacorte Theatre in Central Park. What's more, Papp is about to open a couple more theaters for modern American plays down around Lafayette Street. They won't be free but they'll be close to it. How can all of this be happening, and if it is happening how does it fit into the grave that everybody has dug for the New York theater?

It is happening because of Mr. Papp alone—because of as well as in spite of his dedication. He is a do-gooder and he is a practical, working theater man. He dreamed up the free Shakespeare as a public good, with all the culture-mongering that such thinking implies. Yet he pushed it through. He convinced the actors to do the work and he convinced the Parks Department to give the space. He collected the money and directed the plays. And the company tramped from place to place. Each season the New York Shakespeare Festival grew more polished, and by the time the Delacorte Theatre was built it was costumed, set, and controlled well enough to compete with any professional company in the country. Tonight, when it presents *The Comedy of Errors* once more, its audience will be seeing Shakespeare done as well as anywhere in this country. It will watch a delightfully inventive set by Mr. Lee. It will listen to John Morris' charming musical score. It will have the benefit of the company's inventive and disciplined artistic director, Gerald Freedman (Papp wisely handed the artistic reins over to Mr. Freedman when administrative and producing responsibilities grew too great). It is a going operation.

Now so is the mobile theater. Nobody was any too sure when it gave its first performance in Mt. Morris Park in 1964.

At that time there were annoying aspects to the whole idea as well as rude awakenings that were soon to occur. What was annoying was that the mobile theater was conceived to bring culture to the slums, working from the premise that art is beauty and drawing the inference that beauty will reach and gratify the deprived. It was condescending and it was illogical. New York's slums are terrible places and the people who live there are in terrible situations. There is little food, there are few jobs, there are disgusting living conditions—rats. There is a great resentment born of ghetto living and the pain of prejudice. Who wants white men coming in with art? What could be more insulting?

Papp was an innocent who was soon to learn better (a trait that has carried him through so far). On that very first opening night the scent of problems was in the summer air. The audience—much of it undoubtedly experiencing an initial theater experience—was restless. Some people listened to transistor radios during the performance. Others chattered. It would probably have been pleasing in a phony way to see fat ladies watching the play with infants on their laps, and I suppose a little breast-feeding would have sent the Festival into ecstasies of arty-smugness. In fact, the whole situation smelled of theater for nontheater purposes; theater for social welfare.

Yet that performance of *A Midsummer Night's Dream,* for all its self-conscious slapstick, had a vitality and an excitement that has disappeared from the Delacorte branch of the Festival. It had a tackiness, an amateurism, a basic openness of theater that comes from life, just plain life, on a stage.

Papp was to learn some lessons. As the mobile theater began its first tour through the city's boroughs its audiences proved to be a little less than ready for culture's beauty. Slums are tough places and they breed tough kids. Actors grew frightened and for good reason, dodging bottles and rocks. Some threatened to quit. Others worried as much about the audience as they did about their lines. The chatter sometimes grew impossible. And still the mobile theater toured.

This year's opening performance was Ben Jonson's *Volpone,* a play that often seems to have an academic respect unearned on the stage. The respect was earned Wednesday night in a breakup performance that sometimes came very close to overplaying but never went over the line. George L. Sherman staged it with speed and straightforwardness, keeping the italics under both the story and visual humor. He provided allowances for stepping up the slapstick if the audience needed it, but I would not call this a condescending production.

Alexander Panas played the greedy Volpone wide open, almost as Groucho Marx, unabashedly wearing his body microphone as practically an advertisement of the company's freedom from nuances. Leading his trio of would-be heirs on a merry chase, he managed to be simultaneously sly and dumb (sometimes nearly a nitwit).

Roscoe Lee Browne has allowed vocal mannerisms to get the best of him and now cannot help but say everything with a double-edged attitude and an African-esoteric accent, and his Mosca seemed too much like the mock-obsequious slave he played in *Benito Cereno*. But still the performance had a great fun to it. As did most of the others, even when they were ragged, which was occasional. But there could be no complaints about the trio of money seekers begging a place in Volpone's will. Alfred Leberfeld's Corvino was a dumb merchant, perfectly capable of trading his wife's bed for an inheritance. Paul Hecht made Voltore a stuffy lawyer, easily tricked. And Fred Warriner had a field day with the old fool Corbaccio. Mr. Mitchell's set was gilted Venetian and structurally clever, and even David Amram got out of his quasi-Elizabethan rut to compose a rowdy, cornet-and-snare-drum musical score. What became of all of it was true theater—out in the open, out on a stage, in *performance*. Just messing around. Just putting on a show.

Now come the problems. Washington Square Park is one thing. The audience is local and tame. Now the touring starts. But it is the fourth year and lessons have been learned. The save-the-world-with-art attitude has been tempered by experience. And something very, very good is being done.

King John (*July 14, 1967*)

There are people—and I am one of them—who constantly complain about repetition in the production of Shakespeare. Our line is that the same plays are always being produced and that we never get a chance to see any of the lesser-known ones. We are terribly serious about this and of course anybody who is terribly serious manages to end up being terribly ridiculous. The silly thing about the Shakespeare complaint is that the plays that are produced are the good ones and the plays that *aren't* produced are the bad ones. When somebody finally mounts one of the plays that we have all been crying to see, we end up being bored. And after all the complaining.

The New York Shakespeare Festival is going all out for the overlooked plays this season. Two of this season's three productions are ultra-overlooked, never-produced, completely ignored Shakespeare: *King John* and *Titus Andronicus*. At last we are satisfied. Yes, and at last we are appalled. Why haven't we seen *King John?* we have asked. Because it is terrible, we learn.

As produced at the Delacorte Shakespeare in Central Park, *King John* is a chronicle play in the worst and really dreariest sense. Shakespeare may have been absorbed with the English crown—its history, its nobility, its necessity, and its supreme importance—but this story of a minor monarch, and the details of his succession and supercession is no more than a series of quasi-historical facts with few redeeming dramatic qualities (that was a reviewer's cliché passing in the breeze).

The odd thing about *King John* is that while it was written by a young but mature Shakespeare (between *The Merchant of Venice* and *Midsummer Night's Dream*) it has neither the poetic beauty nor the dramatic structure that marked all his other work of the period. The play is shabbily written, quite mediocre in its language, and entirely dull in construction. It has not a single full-blooded character and only one of any interest at all. This is Philip, the Bastard, whose illegitimacy has destroyed his claim to the throne, even though he is perfectly equipped, intellectually and personally, for ruling. Philip is interesting because he is entertaining—ironic and idealistic, scornful and bold. He is a precursor of Hamlet but of course has only that one charming side and it is hardly enough for a character. Robert Burr indeed plays him as Hamlet and for a while is quite enchanting at it, but unfortunately Mr. Burr has not the slightest interest in movement and spends most of his speeches with arms and legs locked.

The blame for this is difficult to ascribe, since director Joseph Papp has not allowed any movement to smudge the sheer inaction of his production. At times as many as fifteen people are onstage, not a one stirring. Just posing while a hopelessly inconsequential conversation drones along between two inconsequential characters.

Now there's no denying that no matter how lifeless the play, a director can stir up some life. I see no sense in creating an entire production out of irrelevance, but given the decision to mount *King John,* I think Mr. Papp might have done more than light his usual torches. James J. Sloyan had the right idea with the battle scenes, which he staged with real imagination, at one point choreographing them in stylized slow motion rather than falling into the usual banner-waving rut. I suspect that Mr. Sloyan may have been at Stratford, Ontario, recently, where John Hirsch did very much the same thing with the *Richard III* battle scenes, but in any case his work came as a refreshing dose of real theater during an evening fraught with inaction.

The remaining performances were perfunctory except for Mark Jenkins as the tragic Arthur, who escapes King John's murder plot only to die in an accident. And Marion Winters as his mother. Miss Winters was frequently shrill, but then so are Constance's speeches. In her final capitulation to tragedy, Miss Winters was terribly moving. Much more so than the play could ever be.

One is now supposed to congratulate the New York Shakespeare Festival for producing a play so seldom seen. One is also supposed to regret that no more was done with it, even allowing for the play's weaknesses. I think that it would be better to treat this as a lesson learned—before complaining about a play's being overlooked, it should be ruthlessly examined for worthiness. The fact is that *King John* just isn't worth the production.

The Memorandum (*May 6, 1968*)

The New York Shakespeare Festival's first season at the Public Theatre has been—up until now—a terribly professional, terribly earnest, terribly stiff succession of middle-aged attempts at the avant-garde. *Hair* (in its original form) was a rock 'n' roll musical as only a nonmember of the rock 'n' roll generation would see it. Both *Hamlet* and *Ergo* were products of tired middle-European, neo-Expressionist theory. Vaclav Havel's *The Memorandum* continues along this line—it really is no more than warmed-over Kafka-Brecht—but it also happens to be a generally delightful stage production, funny and intelligent and beautifully directed. Although it is consistent with the tedious theater thinking of this group's first season, there is no denying its charm, and so it deserves better than left-handed praise. Indeed, it is one of the highlights of this season.

The play is an appreciation of human frailty, an enjoyment that this frailty will defeat any attempt to systematize human life. Its specific target is Communism, and it is a wonder that the Czechoslovakian government allowed its production. Either Czech officialdom is more permissive than we have been led to believe or else it is more stupid, and that wouldn't surprise me of any government. But Havel's play goes beyond any target as specific as Communism. It is dubious about any scientific organization of man's life and revels in man's incapacity for logic. Such humanism is obliquely anti-intellectual, but there is no sense getting into a hassle over it when the play is so amiable and the fun so good.

True to type, *The Memorandum* is set in a civil service office and its characters are middle-rank clerks. The office chief is being undermined by a slippery subordinate who has introduced a synthetic language into the bureau. This language, called "Ptydepe," is supposed to be more precise than the native language, and all employees are directed to learn it. The chief, an intellectual and a humanist, criticizes its dehumanizing effect and resents the high-handedness of his subordinate. But the bureaucracy works against him and the subordinate takes his job.

However, nobody can learn the language because it is hopelessly complicated and they are silly and too sloppy. This silliness, this sloppiness, is—for Havel—the defense of man's niceness: our natural cultures are the bases of our humanity. The new language may be theoretically exact, logical, precise, scientific, and proved-perfect, but nobody believes in it. It is entirely too scientific to have any relationship with life and reality. Finally, the office becomes a revolving door of noncommunication.

Havel has placed this amusing parallel of Communism's scientific method upon a structure of near-farce, his petty bureaucrats tearing about in vaudevillian circles. And this running-around-in-circles structure has been just about perfectly maintained by Joseph Papp, who has done probably the best directing job of his career with this production.

Drawing an ingenious turntable set from the extremely talented Douglas W. Schmidt—a set that absolutely matches the technique, the style, and the structure of both play and production—Papp kept his company liquid, open-faced, and cartoony, matching the sense of the production with the sense of the play. This is ideal directing.

The performances are splendid. Paul Stevens is straightforward and devoutly cowardly as the office chief, a humanist as mixed up as the scientists. John Heffernan is oily and sneaky as only a power-hungry junior executive can be, and George Bartenieff is priceless as his silent partner (although he should not have been allowed to speak a single word, as he does at the end of the play). Bartenieff's is a dazzling comic performance, artistic and disciplined in every way. Robert Ronan, while doing set pieces as he parodies academic foolishness, is hilarious as a teacher of the new language, and Olympia Dukakis is very funny as one of the clerks, although her use of brassy show-biz mannerisms (whether the fault of translator Vera Blackwell or of Papp) is very much out of place. The out-of-placeness is what makes her so funny, but that may not be enough of an excuse. Still, carping is extraneous—this production is a theater whole, perfectly integrating script and staging and performing, and as a whole it is grand and brainy fun.

The Negro Ensemble Company (*January 5, 1968*)

On Tuesday night, the Negro Ensemble Company gave its premiere production, becoming the first major Negro company in New York and confronting us with the stage segregation problem in still another context: the all-Negro theater created by Negroes themselves. Is it "right"? Is it "wrong"? Does it make a difference or are the productions our only concern?

It takes no great intelligence to realize that an all-black theater exists only because there was an all-white theater before it. If our theater had not been so awfully and stupidly restrictive to Negro actors and Negro playwrights and Negro themes there would not have been the necessity for a Negro Ensemble Company. But the necessity goes beyond that. This new company has not been formed merely to give work to Negroes in the theater. It has been inspired by the Negro revolution—a revolution prompted by incredible American injustice and ignorance and a revolution much belated. Having put up with primitive treatment through the history of this country, the Negro has at last decided that he is fed up with it. The Negro Ensemble Company, whether it announces as much or not, is dedicated to a theater that will lead and reflect the change in racial America.

So this new company is not a make-work program. Nor is it an ethnic theater, designed like the old Yiddish theater to provide familiar, folk entertainment for a group. But it is indeed all-Negro, designed primarily *for* Negroes.

Now to the main question. Is an all-Negro theater—an all-anything theater—ethically acceptable? To be sure, this new all-Negro theater is hardly the same as, say, an all-Negro *Carmen Jones* or *Hello, Dolly!* Those are white productions, designed for white audiences and financed by white producers, and they use the Negro companies primarily for freak purposes. The show, practically, is the color of the performers. Moreover, those are producers who do not cast Negroes in usual productions except, these days, for the obligatory colored chorus boy or girl.

Still, the Negro Ensemble Company *is* all-Negro and there's no getting around that. It is segregation, even if it is self-segregation, and while the Negro's retrenchment into pride is understandable, whatever its childlike and even neurotic aspects, it is segregation still. But considering America's traditional mistreatment of and condescension to the Negro, and the Negro's parallel acceptance of it, a reaction into racial assertion was predictable. And racial pride was long overdue after centuries of outrageous humility. It is this reaction that the more radical Negro leaders are encouraging as well as capitalizing upon.

But can segregation, whatever its purposes and however understandable its self-infliction, ever be acceptable? If the whole reason for Negro resentment is their treatment as "different," why should they think it progress to construct their own ghettos? If Negroes resented their exclusion from all-white theater, why should they want an all-black theater?

216

Well, there are the black nationalists. In a recent issue of *Evergreen* magazine, LeRoi Jones put down every well-known Negro actor for trying to make it in the white theater. Mr. Jones, an ardent racist, thinks that any Negro working in today's theater is only accepting the white hierarchy and even trying to become white—to be accepted on any terms. And he includes two of the Negro Ensemble Company's directors (Douglas Turner Ward and Robert Hooks) among these.

Forgetting about most of Jones' arguments, which are too emotional, hateful, and exaggerated for discussion, there is a point in there. Certainly the funding of this new company by an enormous Ford Foundation grant represents a striking irony. The Ford Foundation, more than any other such body in the country, represents the white, do-gooding, cultural establishment. The Negro Ensemble Company may think it is neatly putting down white America by appropriately stealing away with Ford money (indeed, this was the attitude of Mr. Ward's play *Happy Ending*), but the fact remains that it is accepting—not even stealing it. Jones, a racial extremist, demands absolute aversion of the white world. The Negro Ensemble Company—for whatever reasons—refuses to go his distance and is trying to play things both moderately and militantly.

Yet if the Negro Ensemble Company uses only Negro actors, and concentrates on Negro-theme plays by Negro playwrights, it still exists only because of white generosity and guilt. Almost a half million white Ford dollars to finance a Negro theater. Now how about that?

Well, it is all wrong for a theater to be staffed according to race. Ward and Hooks say that when the need arises, white actors will be used, but at the moment it is obvious that white actors were not eligible for the company—that the first requisite for employment was blackness and not ability. No art can be made that way, nor should art be made that way. Nor is segregation acceptable on any basis. The all-Negro production is as obnoxious as the all-white one. It is also detrimental to theater

because when a cast is all-Negro that is the first thing you notice and it has an immediate, emotional effect on you. That is
fine for a particular production designed for just that effect, but
when *all* the productions are going to work that way there is an
extratheater pressure working beyond the particular play.

Okay, enough of that, because as it happens the first production of the Negro Ensemble Company turned out to be an extraordinary one, and it had every reason to be performed by an
all-Negro company (even though, ironically, the playwright
was white). Peter Weiss' *Song of the Lusitanian Bogey* is a theater work of great artistry and brutal power.

It is full theater, building a disgust with African racism upon
a structure of music, dance, mime, vaudeville, comedy, and
irony. Some of the devices are Brechtian and others are as unlikely as Japanese puppet theater, but Mr. Weiss is not derivative so much as he is a modern representative of all-element
theater. As with his earlier *Marat/Sade,* he provides a director
with every support for a spectacular stage presentation. Since it
all converges upon his undeviating and justified rage, the evening builds art upon intellect. It is superb theater for whatever
its lacks (and there are some).

So I am trapped between personal conviction and an artistic
truth. There are wrongs with an all-Negro theater and they remain wrongs. But *Song of the Lusitanian Bogey* is art, and art
cannot be denied.

Ceremonies in Dark Old Men *(February 6, 1969)*

It looks as if the Negro Ensemble Company has found itself
what every resident theater dreams of—a playwright suited in
purpose and style to its own—and if Lonne Elder III develops
as he should, the relationship should be fruitful for himself, the

company, and its audience. Mr. Elder's first play, *Ceremonies in Dark Old Men*, is not the best work to have been presented by the Negro Ensemble Company at the St. Marks Playhouse, but it is certainly the most fitting one. And the most affecting, given the company's purpose.

The purpose of the Negro Ensemble Company is to address the black community with a theatrical combination of art, entertainment, and pertinence. Mr. Elder's play does exactly that, going directly to today's Harlem and its conflict between traditions born of ghettos and suppression and the new racial pride and rebellion. What's astonishing is that it is the first full-length play the company has produced that is set in Harlem.

Elder's story parallels the situation, the problems, and the background that prompted the present of today's Harlem blacks. There are reflections of the Moynihan Report's insights and a pervasive warmth and understanding of the Negro situation that only a black man could have. The combination of love and perception is what makes the play.

Ceremonies in Dark Old Men is about a motherless Negro family being supported by a sister. The father uses a barbershop as a cover for loafing, and the two brothers don't bother with a cover. The older is in bitter withdrawal; the younger is an experienced shoplifter.

When they mix a batch of good corn liquor, a Harlem crook moves in and starts a bootlegging business, dealing in numbers on the side and also selling dart targets of Southern racists. He identifies himself as the prime minister of "The Harlem Decolonization Association," whose purpose is "to get rid of white businessmen in Harlem." With this one device, Elder blends the new black militance with the old Harlem traditions, explaining the hopelessness that led to illegality as a custom.

The bootleg business is successful, though the older brother finds himself working overtime while his father cats around and his brother is dragged into full-time burglary. The sister abandons her white-collar job for clothes and a boyfriend, both flashy. And finally, the whole illusion of escape from ghetto-imposed lethargy, frustration, and poverty dissolves, inevitably, into tragedy.

The story is told in straightforward, folksy terms, but only because of the playwright's uncertainty about more provocative styles. Elder has an obvious inclination toward the poetic and on several occasions indulges himself in soliloquies about sex and love, Harlem sharpies, and the past as vaudeville. While these contain some stretches of beauty, they really are of the page, not the stage. Yet he is by no means a nontheatrical writer, and the dialogue is regularly marked with that most difficult of tricks—the line that works as both specific and broad: "What kind of house are we living in? You think we gonna let some woman tell us what to do?" (with its references to blighted Negro masculinity in a matriarchal system); "Mama killed herself because there was no order in this house." "I never have been lazy. I just didn't want to break my back working for the Man." "You do anything to keep alive. But you get killed anyhow." And finally (I'm paraphrasing), "If I can move out of here—love a girl and not kill anyone—then that's a victory."

Though the play sprawls, is way overlong, and has scattered inconsistencies of fact, these are minor faults considering its masculinity, its confidence, and its good humor. Edmund Cambridge used the St. Marks' open spaces too restrictedly, as if it were a proscenium house, but made the family a family, and this "familiarity" reflected the company's experience in working together. Douglas Turner was wonderfully loose and altogether excellent as the father, and William Jay was pained and hungry as the older man (though he only opens one eye and that rarely).

Despite a badly inconsistent role, Rosalind Cash was very good as the sister, helped by the author's uncommon ability to write dialogue of gender as well as of character. Each person sounds like a person, and the men sound like men, the women like women. That is the talent of a natural playwright, as indeed Mr. Elder is. *Ceremonies in Dark Old Men* needs no first-play excuses, though it is imperfect. The play is rich with the best theater values, and its author is just the man for the mood, the needs, and the aims of the Negro Ensemble Company and its audiences.

...And Race Theater Generally

Up Against the Wall (*May 22, 1968*)

STRANGE is hardly the word for a night in the theater where somebody tells you he hates you and intends to kill you. No "you" meaning everybody in general but "you" meaning white people. Walking into such a theater, to watch a rally for a militant Negro organization called the Black Panthers is not much different from a Jew walking into a Nazi rally.

But the situation itself was only one among many weird aspects to the Panther rally Monday night. The location itself—Fillmore East—was odd enough. Fillmore is a converted movie theater on Second Avenue, ordinarily used for weekend rock concerts. The music, aside from being the most creative and exciting cultural phenomenon in today's America, represents a broad point of view that has love as its base. You might say it's a little odd to find violence and hatred being boomed through a place that only two weeks earlier had housed the Jefferson Airplane with its love-your-neighbor message. But dig a little deeper. Jefferson Airplane, as all modern popular music, never would have happened without the original rock 'n' roll, and that of course is pure Negro rhythm-and-blues music. Moreover, though the reasons are perfectly innocent, the new music has become white in both sound and personnel. You will almost never see a black musician on the Fillmore stage because there are virtually none of them playing post-rock-'n'-roll pop music.

The Black Panthers would say that the white race stole the black race's music just as it has stolen rhythm and athletics and even the peanut. It's funny that these racial characteristics, so recently mocked as clichés of prejudice, are now being parlayed for Negro self-pride, but that's how complicated and inverse the militants have become.

But on to more strangeness about the Panther rally. For example, though the message was murder, the audience seemed at least half white. Since the militants have left no road for the liberal to take, the only thing he thinks he can do is accept death as a purge of his own guilt. It is, of course, choosing to be loved by the blacks rather than choosing to do what makes sense. It is a ridiculous and pathetic choice.

Perhaps the strangest thing of all is taking such a rally as theater when its purposes are so ugly (Would you discuss the sound of an exploding atomic bomb as an artistic exercise in pure sound?). Yet it was theater—not merely because people on any stage, for any purpose, make for theater but because, plainly and simply enough, several short plays were presented.

Two were especially significant because of their authors. Ed Bullins was recently represented by three one-acters at the American Place Theatre, and they showed him to be a talented and driving playwright, intelligent, artistic, and committed enough to apply the black revolution to the stage. His play that was done at the rally was a simple propaganda piece, as it had to be. *How Do You Do* does not try to use dramatic subtlety—it means to fire a mass of people. Yet its concerns are identical to those in Bullins' more sophisticated pieces: the conflict a modern Negro finds in trying to be, simultaneously, a soul brother and an educated man. His little tale about a couple of blacks affecting white mannerisms amused and excited the crowd. The pity is, and I'm sure Bullins knows it, he was exciting to them on their lowest and most irrelevant level. That is how mass propaganda theater works, and it insults both the theater and the crowd.

Bullins wrote down to his audience and succeeded. LeRoi Jones wrote on his own level and, predictably, failed. *His Home on the Range* is a combination of poetry (a half-hour prologue of it) and art theater. As it happens, and aside from its subject matter, the stuff is nearly all crap, but even had it been wonderful this is no way to reach a crowd of more than 2,000 people.

Jones' play, after its endless introduction praising the wonder of blackness, is a physical imitation of Ionesco with a content devoted to the mockery and then the murder of a white family. Unfortunately, it does not capitalize on Jones' most upsetting attitude—that when all the violence is done, it will be the blacks, not the whites, who are exterminated.

But the evening's most spectacular performance came not from the plays but from Bobby Seale, the Black Panthers' chairman. Seale is an up-to-date Holy Roller, a groovy Oral Roberts complete with vocal stops and side jokes. He flashes from philosophy to in-the-gutter obscenity. His physical presence and voice control should be the envy of most American actors. His tone, from glibness to hatred to sweet peace, is mesmerizing and his storytelling ability delightful. I'm sure it's strictly instinct, but his technique is classical—the repeated phrase, for example —and his use of fawning bodyguards is traditionally dramatic. What he said was something else: garbled and inconsistent and giddy with fright. As far as his message goes, who knows what it will lead to? If he says, "A spontaneous riot is an incorrect tactic, there's too many black people killed," is it a hope for less blood? Can the Black Panthers really instigate, control, or affect riots? When he says, "I will kill you . . . if you shoot at me," does it mean that the Black Panthers Party for Self-Defense is just that?

And what about the white people at the rally? Are they really just middle-class lambs walking to the slaughter to prove their liberalism under the knife? They bought those tickets to finance the purchase of guns—guns meant for them. Max Frisch, the Swiss playwright, wrote a play called *The Firebugs* that was about the German people's comforting themselves with lies while Hitler built his Nazi Party in open view. Are the black militants no less evil? Are the white liberals no less stupid?

Or is Bobby Seale right when he says that the white race went to Africa and abducted the black people, deprived them of their freedom, their way of life, their governments, their dignity, and their humanity? Now, he asks, what white man can stand up and deny the black man anything?

It is all very complicated, very frightening, and very strange. The most terrible thing of all is that nobody—no white man, no black man—can figure the whole thing out, and in the midst of the confusion are guns. A silly rally, silly speeches, silly theater. And a half dozen not so silly Black Panthers dragging a white man out of the audience for standing up and denouncing the whole business.

The summer begins one month from now.

Theater in the Streets (*August 21, 1968*)

This is a time for involvement, but "involvement" can mean different things to different people. For some it is an extended trip to South America to work with revolutionaries; for some it is a summer spent registering voters in the Deep South; for some it is a march on Washington, D.C., or Selma, Alabama; for some it is participation in the political process. Everybody agrees it is a time for doing something instead of writing or saying it. The problem is that they sometimes make more of a mess than they found.

Providing theater in the streets of New York's racial ghettos has become the involvement outlet for many people who want to do something, and it has produced situations ranging from the mildly dangerous to the vaguely ridiculous. In most cases it has provided mild entertainment for the audiences and a strong sense of self-satisfaction for the producers. But it has also lumped together a great many theater people who have very different conceptions of theater in the streets, and it has in many cases offended the very cause with which these people sympathize.

Theater in the streets is a catch-all phrase that covers such social projects as the mobile theater of the New York Shakespeare Festival, which presents Elizabethan plays to bring culture to the masses; the Puerto Rican Traveling Theatre, which presents melodramas vaguely pointed toward matters of injustice; the New York City Theatre Workshop, which gives an almost Broadway-size musical.

But there are other theater companies that have much more radical purposes: the Living Theatre (long exiled because of a legal hassle, but soon to return for a visit) means to bring reality to the theater by bringing the theater to reality—for political but mostly for artistic purposes. There are companies on the West Coast like the San Francisco Mime Troupe and El Teatro Campasino that exist entirely to further particular causes (like the problems of migratory farm workers). And there are guerrilla theaters designed to undermine the American system and instigate honest-to-God revolutions, like the Gut Theatre and the Black Arts Theatre.

As you can see, it is a wide range of theaters, but much more so in purpose than in technique. For the most part, these theaters function in an atmosphere, with a personnel, and under budgeting circumstances that prevent even an approximation of professionalism. Nobody has been able to devise a sound system capable of clearly amplifying stage dialogue. It is extremely difficult to keep the attention of an audience that is sitting (usually standing) on hot concrete, especially when the composition is multilingual and covers a wide range of ages. Finally, none of these theaters (at least the ones I've seen) discovered a technique for effective street theater. They are all merely transferring indoor theater methods to outdoor productions.

The most offensive are the ones supported by the city of New York, not only because they stink of do-goodery but because they are so hypocritical. It is the city of New York that is responsible for the rat-and-roach-infested confinement areas in which these theaters perform. After all, what is "the city of New York" but an official name for the individuals who power that city? The thought of these seersucker-suited, Dacron-underweared people discharging their liberal consciences with a children's show (or Shakespeare) is obnoxious and demeaning. What could be more aggravating to a Negro or Puerto Rican than a show trying to make him happy in his slum? Especially when that show is sponsored by social-work-inclined whites? At best, it is a welfare check in stage makeup.

Even the Puerto Rican Traveling Theatre is irritating, though it is run and mostly staffed by Puerto Ricans. Last summer it presented *The Ox-Cart,* which seemed apt enough, written by a Puerto Rican in the melodramatic style so beloved to Spanish-speaking people. But the point of this play is that Puerto Ricans should go home—should never have left their farms for New York in the first place—and the idea of its being sponsored by the city government is positively disgraceful. This summer the play is *Winterset,* Maxwell Anderson's archaic verse drama. The producer claims it is relevant because of the play's involvement with the Sacco-Vanzetti case, though nobody would ever gather that from the unintelligible, chopped-up version being presented.

The most professional show is *The Flying Sunflower,* a big musical that even has a full-size orchestra. Because the music is catchy (and often good) it certainly entertains its audience, and that is nothing to be overlooked. But part of its success is due to its being written as a children's show, which isn't exactly flattering to its adult audience. Like the other shows, it indulges in such fashionable liberalism as putting down the police, but when the message finally arrives it is the disgusting advice to "fix up your own streets, pull yourselves up by the bootstraps." When you look up and down the filthy streets with their crammed-full tenement apartments, and you realize the circumstances that have forced these people to their knees in virtual slime, you wonder how anyone—particularly the city itself—would have the effrontery to give such advice. You can't pull up any bootstraps when society has locked them to the ground.

The guerrilla theaters are suggesting that those locks be shot off, and it is no wonder they are reaching the ears of the people. Perhaps just as expectedly, their productions are more effective even though they work on minimal budgets. The drive is there, the anger is there, the plays are written specifically for the streets—and for propaganda—perhaps crude but direct. The projects aren't powered by troubled white consciences but by furious black determination. Just how effective these theaters are remains to be seen, but it makes no sense to sit and wait and wonder whether these audiences will take the advice and make Molotov cocktails. If the "good guy" street theaters ever hope to counteract the "bad guy" street theaters—or hope to accomplish anything at all—they must, like any other theater, learn about their medium, their tools, their audience, and most of all, their purpose. Until then, the situation will remain, to repeat, mildly dangerous and vaguely ridiculous.

Big Time Buck White (*December 9, 1968*)

I'll do an ego thing for a change, by admitting several prejudices just so I can prove myself okay by (a) admitting them
and (b) demonstrating how I have overcome them. I am prejudiced against do-good theater, I am prejudiced against amateur
theater, and I am prejudiced against pro-Negro anythings when
they are done by white people. What overcame these prejudices
was the play *Big Time Buck White,* which grew out of the
Watts Writers Workshop in Los Angeles, a help-the-blacks amateur theater organized by (the white) Budd Schulberg and
written by (the white) Joseph Dolan Tuotti. It opened last
night at the Village South Theatre, and it is an exciting production, tackling a problem whose complexity cannot be
overstated and doing it with theatricality, sense, humor, spirit,
and a real dose of the real fright that smacks any white man
who understands what's going on in black America.

The play is set in the meeting hall of the Beautiful Allelujah
Days ("BAD") organization, which could be any one of the
black groups organized under the poverty program. It is simply
enough presented as an actual meeting of the group with us as
part of it. The play introduces the group's core members in
mounting levels of hierarchy from the simpleminded hangers-
around all the way to the leader and, finally to his star (sort of
King Kong)—a black militant generally modeled on H. Rap
Brown.

This beginning is more or less black folk theater, and it turns
me off, but things grow sophisticated pretty fast. The easy (and
ironically so much like *Amos 'n' Andy*) laughs go by, the play
moves into the tricky area of brainy-versus-demagogic black

militancy. This is when Jive, the leader of the group, introduces his race preacher, Buck White.

Now Buck White is a fabulously conceived character, thanks to a brilliant performance by Dick Williams. I don't know where to divide the credit for this person, between Mr. Williams and the author, since the play is admittedly conceived in both writing and improvisation. But the character manages to almost consistently walk the squiggly line between parody and legitimacy.

On one hand, Williams plays Buck White as hopelessly confused preacher, mangling thoughts in ungrammatic, illogical, and very purple prose. But on the other, he can make the most direct kind of sense, just like Brown and Stokely Carmichael and Eldridge Cleaver. The question is: Who listens, how much do they accept, is the nonsense swallowed as much as the sense is, how much of an effect does it have on actual behavior (the causing of action as well as the stopping of it)? These are big questions, of course, and Buck White doesn't (can't) answer them, but in mocking the foolish and defending the sensible, he sorts out the bluffing from the dead serious.

Following this big speech, the evening turns to audience participation, as straight question and answer. The theater part comes when the members of the group onstage begin to intimidate the questioners, either by demanding money for the right to ask a question or in threat-response. One member of last night's audience was particularly intimidated, and I was really frightened to death over what was going to happen because he seemed up-tight and his treatment was pretty shabby. But toward the end, when he was practically chased out of the house, one had to assume that he was a ringer. If so, he is one hell of an actor and I wish I could give him credit, but he isn't listed in the program.

The others, however, are indeed in the program, and if they were amateurs when the production was first presented, they are amateurs no longer. In most cases, the longer a company works, the more bored the actors grow. With this one, the result seems to have been an absolute onstage security. In the direction by Williams and in every individual performance, there is a kind of vigor and confidence and interplay that marks only the best of ensembles. For individual names, Arnold Williams was scary, groovy, and ultimately cowardly as a ghetto-tied spade. David Moody was just-right silly as a would-be leader. Van Kirksey was fishtail Cadillac as a business success, Kirk Kirksey was funny as comic relief, and Ron Rich cool as the head of the house. But Williams, above all, was staggering in his massive natural hairdo, black-cape-and-bells regalia, and flashy slinking between Holy Rolling and hard sense. In his playing lies the key for those of us who understand the need for black power but shrink from violence. Williams will help you understand Cleaver and Carmichael and Brown. It is a helpful and desperately needed hand he is holding out, and it emerges from an extremely effective theater piece. *Big Time Buck White* is as successful as it is important. (I should like to add that Edward Burbridge's set was as exactly right for this play as was his work for last week's *Jimmy Shine*. He deserves a great deal of praise for both. He is one of the best designers in New York.)

Brecht

The Berliner Ensemble (*September 16, 1966*)

IT is strange visiting the Berliner Ensemble here in East
Berlin. Strange because the company is legendary and you
feel kind of unreal when first seeing it. Strange because it is
Bertolt Brecht's own creation, and such a theater has been made
by no other playwright of our time. Strange, of course, because
the Ensemble is here in East Berlin, a secure bundle of sub-
sidized art in the midst of a sadly poor, bureaucracy-ridden, and
thoroughly spiritless place.

But once in the theater, all externals are forgotten and the
matter is the stage. The house itself is impossibly neobaroque,
a gorging of gilt Cupids. When the East German government
decided to give Brecht a theater, he chose this one out of sentimental perversity. Sentimental because the Theater am Schiffbauerdamm was where his *Threepenny Opera* had its successful world premiere in 1928. And perverse because he
thought its old-fashioned ugliness a curious contradiction to the
new-style theater that he was creating. But physically, it was
quite satisfactory. The 900 or so seats provided the right size au-

dience, and the stage was large enough to handle all the equipment he needed (it is about as deep as the auditorium).

The Berliner Ensemble was formed by Brecht not so much to
present his plays as to present his theater theories in the form of
productions. While many of the plays were to be his, there were
to be others, too. Brecht believed that he had developed an entirely new approach to the stage—an approach he was sure
would supersede the Stanislavskian realism that had revolutionized the world's stages during his youth.

He was after ultrarealism, which would seem strange since
Stanislavski stood for realism, if nothing else, and Brecht's plays
were beyond realism and into surrealism and caricature. But by
"realism" he did not mean a play that looked realistic. He
meant a realism that never let an audience forget it was in a
theater and watching actors.

There was another purpose to his theory. Brecht considered
the theater a place for enlightenment and prodding to constructive social action. He was disgusted with the theater that meant
only to entertain, and he called it "culinary" theater because it
was as self-indulgent as most diners. And even wrote an early
(and magnificent) work with Kurt Weill mocking it—*Mahagonny*.

While these purposes seem simple and logical enough, Brecht
considered himself a philosophical theorist and wrote endless
essays and dialogues winding through an assortment of pretensions and complications that only confused this simplicity.
One of those dialogues, called *The Selling of Brass* (*Der Messing Kauf*), is in fact being presently staged by the Ensemble. It
is as determinedly and adolescently profound as the long-
winded discussions in any Viennese coffeehouse.

Being a theater person, basically and professionally, Brecht
was much more specific in the actual stage implementation of
these theories than he was in their elucidation. He wanted to
remove his audience from the possibility of blinding rapture
and so asked for actors who did not "become" their characters

(as Stanislavski wanted) but who "stood beside" those characters. He wanted the audience to never forget that it was an audience, in a theater, watching a play.

So he used titles, flashed slides, to forewarn the spectator of the action about to occur, eliminating surprise elements. He staged songs to emphasize that they were songs. The band was placed onstage and the singer was instructed to be emphatically artificial in his delivery. Sometimes, irrelevant props (such as a suspended spinning, lighted wheel) were used, to underline the "number" nature of the song.

He also made great use of extravagant makeup, masks, exaggerated gestures, and overamplified sounds to promote theater artificiality. The Berliner Ensemble was formed to practice all of these devices.

It is perfectly obvious, though, they were not theoretical but the substance of the Brecht style of playwriting and production. The theory of alienation was only so much nonsense, disproved by the sheer theatricality of all of his better works. The manners of staging were merely the physical aspects of his personal style of writing. It would be foolish to say that the Marx Brothers' style was rooted in comic theory. It was their act. This was Brecht's act.

There was, however, a great pioneering in Brecht's "act," or artistic identity. He began the great movement toward writing plays in terms of production. No longer was the playwright to be a man at a desk with a typewriter. He was to become a theater person, as he should have been (and, indeed, as Shakespeare was). A play, after all, is not a play until you see it. On paper it can only be literature, and it is irrelevant whether or not it reads well. What matters is whether it plays well. Brecht created plays as living, theater things, and thus his concern with movement and masks and music. He began the great movement toward creative direction that is now going toward such things as the *Marat/Sade* that was written by Peter Weiss but almost equally created by the Royal Shakespeare Company's director,

Peter Brook. Or the company creation being practiced by the exiled Living Theatre, as it wanders across Europe with its wild production of *Frankenstein*.

What Brecht left behind him was a body of inconsistent works of art, many of them ruined by his insistence upon the rigid Marxist line. But there are enough masterpieces to make him not only a ranking playwright of our time but a genuine innovator who left behind him his techniques of production and a group of people trained in them. This is the Berliner Ensemble, probably the finest theater company I have ever seen.

Its current productions are not all satisfactory. *Schweik in the Second World War* is a minor and repetitive piece, saved only by some purely Brechtian interludes that have giant-sized Hitlers, Goebbels, and Goerings mouthing prerecorded mock arias. But *The Threepenny Opera* is being given its ultimate production, and an extraordinary actor—Ekkehart Schall—is proving again that for all its silliness of gangsterland Chicago, *The Resistible Rise of Arturo Ui* is a flamboyantly thrilling production. As for Schall, his performance is astonishing.

But the company's production of *The Selling of Brass* suggests that there are problems ahead. Like the Berliner Ensemble itself, the play is a dedication to Brecht (the playwright is a character in it). To use the Soviet phrase, this smacks of Cult of Personality. Brecht the playwright, Brecht the poet, Brecht the director: this is fine. But Brecht the god will destroy the company with sterility. How long can productions be based on how he designed them up until his death in 1956? As long as the actors, the directors, and the dramaturges who worked with him are there, memories and production logs can help. But what will happen after then?

A theater that is dedicated to a single playwright is necessary when his style is definite. It is why companies specializing in Shakespeare or Molière are so valuable. But when the theater is mummifying him, it courts death.

In the meanwhile, and as long as the company is so superb

today, it is stupid for American theater audiences to be unable to see it. Helene Weigel, Brecht's widow and the Ensemble's director, told me she would be delighted to bring the company to the United States if the State Department invited it. Whatever reasons the State Department might think it has for denying permission to visit, they do not seem possibly logical.

Arturo Ui (*September 15, 1966*)

A pattern has emerged at the Berliner Ensemble, and it is the pattern of production; an emphasis on what is happening; a concern with the stage rather than with the neat transferring of a play from script to theater.

The latest example is the Ensemble's production of *The Irresistible Rise of Arturo Ui.* Written by Brecht in 1941, when he was in Finland fleeing the Nazis, it is a mortally faulted play. In an ambitious design, he attempted to transfer the history of Nazi Germany to the thirties gangsterland of Chicago's suburb of Cicero. So Hitler becomes Arturo Ui, a stupid, cowardly crook who uses brutality to frighten the mayor (Hindenburg) and the businessmen (German capitalists) into servility, and who finally announces his plans to conquer Milwaukee, Pittsburgh, and the rest, now that Chicago has been taken.

Brecht's attraction to America and its gangsters was largely the result of James Cagney movies, and his knowledge of American things was limited to what he learned from the screen. Even at that, he saw these movies through extremely European eyes and never really understood what the United States was like. This strange, never-never-land America shows up in various of his works (*Happy End* and *Mahagonny* are just two instances) and is always a peculiar place inhabited by Europeans in Brecht-cartoon clothing.

Still, *Arturo Ui* manages to be enormously effective on the stage, and even very powerful at times, because so much can be done with it. Plays on paper were only working models for Brecht productions. Once he began to make a theater piece they could assume all shapes, all colors. They became alive. As theater, of course, must.

The present production was staged by Manfred Wekwerth and Peter Palitzsch, two of Brecht's disciples, and utilizes many of his Epic Theater techniques (subtitles, burlesques). More than that, it catapults the Brecht style (which was a style of production, of behavior, of movement and design, as much as a style of writing) into a Technicolor circus. The proscenium arch has within it another arch decorated with circus drawings and lined with red, blue, and green lights. The stage is a great circus tent. The sets are small, stark, and solid objects moved on the theater's giant turntable.

The production begins with a barker who indicates the evening's attitude toward the Nazi lunacy—that it was too bizarre to be real. That it was a circus whose clowns could murder. It is, he says, "a gangster show."

Hitler, Göring, and Goebbels are Warner Brothers gangsters in wild makeup. Everybody in this show is green-faced anyhow, all with strange and great color variations. They are dressed in extreme thirties pinstripes and double-breasteds. And they strut, crouch, wiggle, and sprawl in the finest Brecht style.

But certainly none of them is in the class of Ekkehart Schall, who gave an electrifying performance in the title role. This is a virtuoso part (as Christopher Plummer proved in the marvelous New York production), but Schall went beyond virtuosity. It was one of the greatest performances I have ever seen, especially so because it was not apart from the supporting company but came out of precisely its milieu. I am stunned by the interaction of this company with every performance I see. But as for Schall—with the screaming voice that suddenly becomes a gasp; with the near-epileptic fits; the puppetlike, jerky movement;

the grasping for the crotch as a nervous tic—it is a total performance, using the body, the voice, the mind. Not acting. Performing.

At the play's end, he steps forward to remove his makeup and warn the audience that the next time this happens they had better do something about it. In the Paris edition of the New York *Herald Tribune* on the very day I saw this production, I read a story about a protest march by Negroes on a lily-white Chicago suburb. The story read, "The massed whites began screaming: 'White power . . . black trash,' and waving swastika paper broadsides. Then came a rain of stones, rocks, bottles and cherry bombs." The suburb was Cicero, exactly where *Arturo Ui* is set. It's happening now, baby.

The Threepenny Opera (*September 13, 1966*)

The Threepenny Opera received its world premiere at the Theater am Schiffbauerdamm in Berlin. Although avant-garde in style, it was to become an enormous success and make its authors, Bertolt Brecht and Kurt Weill, world-famous. Now, thirty-eight years later almost to the day, it is playing there once more, although things are quite different (not the least of which is the strange division of the city). The house has since been renamed the Berliner Ensemble Theater for the company that the 1949 East German government sponsored for Brecht. And there he and the company became legendary not only for his art but for the company's finesse and devotion to his singular vision.

The production here is said to be nearly identical with the original and if that is so, the company's memory is as formidable as its ability. For sheer quality of performance, intermeshing of personnel, and maintenance of a consistent style of acting and staging throughout the production, it is extraordinary. I have never seen any company integrated so well with the possible exception of the Moscow Art Theater.

Following the cynical vaudeville of the play, this production is a weaving pattern of cartoons. Gestures are exaggerated; every expression is pasted on; movement is extreme and burlesqued. This is in the very fabric of the work. But Brecht had intended more. *The Threepenny Opera,* he wrote, "is concerned with bourgeois conceptions not only as content, by representing them, but also through the manner in which it does so." If this seems clear, in a vague sort of way, Brecht's lengthy explanation of it becomes so muddled that it winds up wrestling with itself on the floor. Nevertheless, and for all its confusion of theory, the work served as the first (and by Brecht's admission, the finest) example of his Epic Theater.

This Epic conception is more an assemblage of novel dramatic devices than it is a new idea of theater, but those devices were to mark nearly all of his subsequent plays. Titles flashed on a screen to reveal all plot surprises beforehand, presumably to leave us cold-blooded enough to think; songs sung in an artificial style; everything unreal. But these devices always fail to fulfill their stated purpose while working as effective play manners. As for this company's style of production, it, too, is not the general dramatic method it was meant to be. It is the style, totally mastered, of the singular and extremely original art of Brecht the playwright.

The *Threepenny* point remains confused in a maze of allusions to poverty, greed, capitalism, and general pessimism. Brecht's flaming idealism burns bright, but it destroys its fuel, leaving us with no idea of what he was really driving at. In miscellaneous writing, he misspells it out, but after all, the play is supposed to make its own point. *The Threepenny Opera* is bitterly comic and clearly on the side of the angels, but its assortment of complaints about the misery of the poor has little to do with any real world.

244

Dismissing then, as we must, the Brecht theorizing and the social comment, what is left is a bitterly amusing artistic achievement. So there is the story about Jonathan Peachum, who controls all of London's beggars and outfits them with crutches, artificial legs, and assorted pitiful equipment. His daughter, Polly, marries Mackie Messer (Mack the Knife), a burglar, arsonist, forger, and now a bigamist. Mackie is safe so long as his good friend Sheriff Brown remains on the payroll. But Polly's father, outraged at the marriage, threatens to upset the imminent coronation ceremonies by turning all the beggars loose at the processional. Intimidated, the sheriff arrests Mackie and has him sentenced to the gallows. The hanging is avoided by a mock-opera ending that has the queen give pardon and bestow an assortment of riches, all in sarcasm of the "real life" conclusion that would send Mackie to his grave.

This is accompanied by the wonderful Weill score, which was wishfully meant to be part of the Epic scheme by never becoming involved with the story. Following Brecht's instructions, the company sings the songs as isolated pieces—before a couple of lighted pinwheels dropped from the flies and with the small orchestra revealed on a platform at upstage center. These are supposed to disengage us, but the play is so good that we ignore them and accept the music as music for the theater. So go theories and good riddance.

Wolf Kaiser was a brilliant Mackie, gaudily cheap and stupid enough to run to the nearest whore despite a ready opportunity to escape. Norbert Christian skimmed the line between conventional businessman and idealist as Peachum.

The Caucasian Chalk Circle (August 17, 1965)

In the reading, Bertolt Brecht's The Caucasian Chalk Circle is an exquisitely written play, the work of an artist at the peak of his powers. In the performance it is a dramatic work of extraordinary strength, all the more extraordinary because that strength is born of classic structure (whose offspring is more usually beauty than fire). There can hardly be any question that the play is one of the greatest written in this century.

The production that the Minnesota Theatre Company is presenting produces that strength, projects that classicism, and blends them into a nearly perfect dramatic machine because of a remarkable combination of direction and performance. A combination that will happen rarely and that can only happen, I think, when a play like *The Caucasian Chalk Circle* is the subject. And for all of this, I can only thank this company for a tremendous event in my life.

The play, as most of Brecht, is in the form of parable, but it is more than that and really quite different from most of his earlier work. Because although it carries his usual bitter skepticism about the possibility of peace or justice, it suddenly allows, too, for human goodness—for genuine Christianity—something Brecht never before even admitted existed.

The title is drawn from a fable about two women, both claiming the same child. When the judge asks them to tug the infant from the center of a circle, one pulls and the other releases. The infant is awarded to the one who released since a mother would rather lose her child than tear it to pieces. It is similar to the Biblical story of the two harlots.

In the play, the child is the son of a governor who is decapitated after a revolt. Abandoned by his mother, who is more interested in escaping with her finery than with her son, he is rescued from the rebels by a kitchen maid. This is an act of purity, committed against all the rules of self-preservation. It is committed in a world where "motherly instincts can be a suicidal business"—a world where to be good is to ask for trouble.

From the moment she rescues the child, the maid suffers. When taken in by her brother, community "morality" demands that she marry since she claims the child as hers (which, in the only real sense, he is). And although engaged, she agrees to marry a dying peasant. But once the ceremony is over and peace is announced, he turns out to be a very alive draft dodger.

With still another revolution, the governor's wife returns in search of her son, and the dispute over the child is brought to the judge Azdak, a drinking, whoring, bribe-taking manic with a fantastic sense not of justice so much as of goodness. It is he who conducts the chalk circle test and it is the test that provokes the play's moral: "What there is shall go to those who are good for it. Thus, the children go to the motherly, that they prosper. The carts to good drivers, that they are driven well. And the valley to the waterers, that it bring forth fruit."

The reference to "waterers" concerns a dispute between two groups of Caucasian (that is, from the Caucasus) villagers before whom the play is given. Because of this structure, Brecht can bring Oriental stylization, "provincial" acting, and spectator reaction to his play. Combining all of these with greatly effective songs (written, and written well, by Herbert Pilhofer) and hilarious comedy, the result is consummate theater, at once ultrasophisticated and Biblically simple.

Edward Payson Call's direction was brilliant, launching the spreading spectacle across the big arena stage. Zoe Caldwell, as the little ball of a maid with sleeves rolled up to the elbow, gave one of the finest single performances I have ever seen. Ed Flanders nearly burst apart at the seams in the flamboyant role of Azdak—a wonderful job. The remainder of the very large company was superlatively controlled and absolutely on key—all to the credit of Mr. Call, who with them, and Lewis Brown's stunning designs, brought the roaring comic scenes full flush with helpless tears. All of the splendid fury of theater—real and important theater—is in this play and this production.

The Rise and Fall of the City of Mahagonny
(August 4, 1965)

"Nothing you can do will help a dead man." The city of Mahagonny is dedicated to irresponsible self-satisfaction. "We can't even help ourselves; you—never." Drums beat, trumpets blast dissonantly. "Every man for himself." The worst crime and the only mortal one is to be without money. "Nothing you can do will help a dead man." Men eat themselves to death, and love belongs in brothels where those on line chant, "Quick, fellow, quick." And drums march, chants roll, and friendship, humanity, and charity are mocked with cruel sentimentality. "Do nothing for love but only gain." While a simpleminded woodchopper is executed for not paying a bill. "Nothing you can do will help a dead man."

Bertolt Brecht wrote *The Rise and Fall of the City of Mahagonny* in 1927 as a multiple parody—of old-school opera, of human "fun." It is a parody of the theater that is designed to be entertainment, and it is parody of the entertainment that humans waste all their lives seeking. Both its design and its subject matter are "enjoyment." It is meant to be a "moral tableau" to show up the commercial character both of the entertainment and of the persons entertained.

As usual with Brecht, his extensive rationale for *Mahagonny* was very much apart from its art. And his theorizing on "epic opera" notwithstanding, this opera remains not a mockery of theatrical excitement but theatrical excitement iself. And, very wisely indeed, director Jean Gascon paid scant attention to the rationale in staging the North American premiere of the work here in Stratford, Ontario (let's ignore the fabulous insanity of having to wait nearly thirty years for it).

248

The result is a stupendously exciting production, as cuttingly red a piece of theater as I ever have seen. Staged with bursts of color that make Technicolored nightmares and moving in swinging, sliding patterns, it rings through the Avon Theatre with the savage blast of twisted trumpets.

Bitterness is in its very breath. Brecht was not yet a line-toeing Communist. Only a man furious with inhumanity. The city of Mahagonny, while based on an oddly European idea of America, represents everything that is wrong with Western civilization. Created by promoters as a place for moneymaking, it becomes a chaotic haven for animal freedom when a typhoon sidesteps it (Mahagonny needs no typhoons because it is fully able to destroy itself).

Its central lovers are avid lovers. Jimmy Mahoney is the woodchopper who pays one debt too few, and his girl is Jenny, one of the satin chorus of gum-chewing prostitutes. Their love is the sort that dies because she will do anything for her man except lend him money. Around them the aimless, self-destructive hedonism of the city plays its suicidal mockery of human "entertainment."

Louis Applebaum, the musical director, wisely chose to minimize Kurt Weill's musical parodies and instead played up the score for all its theatrical worth. Realizing that Weill's kidding of operatic clichés (Wagner, Rossini, Weber) was not that funny, he stressed the dazzling excitement of the score. But he made a major slip in allowing the orchestra full blast. For all of its furious contribution, there was much too much noise and a great deal of David Drew and Michael Geliot's superb English translation was lost in the din. Still, heard (and heard well) were Martha Schlamme's perfect Jenny, Thomas O'Leary's pathetically "manly" Mahoney, and Muriel Greenspon's loud, cruel, and hatefully greedy madame. Sliding steadily, in Gascon's constantly inventive and logical stage movements, and before Brian Jackson's extraordinary designs, they created a livid, rolling miasma of hatred pitched against hope.

At the end, with Mahoney sagging in the electric chair. With martial music beating in relentless waves. With the "ideals" of Mahagonny marching on placards (FOR THE EXPLOITATION OF OTHERS. FOR EXTERNAL VULGARITY. FOR THE NATURAL DISORDER OF THINGS). With acid dripping from the stage and brasses rasping against drums. *Mahagonny* ends. Brecht's theorizing has little application. It canceled itself out in its overwinding complications. What won—as what always wins—was the art itself. The opera is an experience of a lifetime.

Galileo (*November 29, 1968*)

The opening of the splashy new Alley Theatre here in Houston with Bertolt Brecht's *Galileo* demonstrated two facts: First, Nina Vance and her theater have been justly rewarded for twenty years of trailblazing with a lavish, handsome building containing two neat theaters and all the equipment a company might want. And second, the company remains what it was in the old house—a serious and capable group that can present any work, no matter how difficult, with professionalism and care. Whether the new inflated budget and institutional status will seriously restrict Alley's already less than radical programs remains to be seen, but in any case, if the play does not hold up it will never be due to the company's ineptitude.

Galileo does not hold up in production and never will, I think, because it is too much head and too little guts, and in that lies an irony. Brecht aimed for a theater of pure intellectuality—he considered "stage magic" a fraud, an easy way out for audiences. But this was all theory, and in fact the strength of his better plays lay in a powerful combination of thought and theater, hitting at both the head and the guts. *Galileo,* more than any other of his plays, fulfills Brecht's theories of minimizing theatricality and maximizing debate. As a result it is fascinating to read and talk about but sterile to watch. By demonstrating his theory, Brecht disproved it.

The moral is (and ironically, it is Brecht's own): Don't go against your nature. Here was a playwright consumed with the stage, trying to deny it for something strictly mental. Oddly, or maybe predictably enough, Brecht was not nearly the thinker he tried to be and *Galileo* is an intellectual mishmash. To begin with, this version of it had been altered in midstream. It originally celebrated reason as a sensual thing, comparing the hunger for knowledge with all bodily needs. But when the Atomic Age rolled around, Brecht decided to make his hero a villain who subjugated science to the state's needs, paving the way for bomb-building physics.

This hindsight revision distorted a play already twisted by contradictory and unthought-out ideas. The most irritating of these is a simultaneous idealism and pragmatism. Brecht thinks it is all right for Galileo to steal the idea of a telescope and claim it for his own because he needs the money. He further justifies it by showing how Galileo used the telescope for greater purposes (astronomy) than the real inventor (peeping). This is plain ends-justifying-means. It also smacks of the vast rationalization of which Brecht was annoyingly capable. The truth is that this Galileo is very much like Brecht himself.

As Galileo justifies his move from Venice's intellectual freedom to Florence's Inquisition because the living conditions were better, so Brecht justified remaining in East Germany and subjecting himself to intellectual tyranny and hypocrisy for the sake of a theater subsidy.

In any case, the play's attempt at intellectual dialogue is thus confused, and its elimination of conflict, climax, and emotion deprives it of dynamics and color. The Alley Theatre production is consistent with this, the stage barren and pale, the performances mental. Miss Vance, who directed it herself, was bound by its mechanics and suppressed by its lack of character interaction. I have no idea why she chose to have it played as terribly British, but that aside, she kept it as Brecht would have wanted—didactic—and that, of course, is its undoing.

Tony van Bridge nearly succeeded in making Galileo a man who enjoyed thinking exactly as he enjoyed food, believing in his eyes much as he believed in his stomach. He found no way to make the man a villain, the murderer of reason, and that is because Brecht himself found no way. Galileo recants rather than be tortured, just as Brecht would have. So the man remains a likable hero rather than the "criminal" the author says he should be.

Mr. Van Bridge did chuckle a little too often and affected a pointlessly gruff voice, but he moved as a man of nature. The company surrounding him was properly supportive and Nancy Evans Leonard made his daughter a pathetic victim of his thoughtless conceit.

As for the theater itself, the play was not the best choice for demonstrating its capabilities, demanding little movement in any direction except for the entirely gratuitous marketplace scene. Miss Vance calls it "a gentle thrust stage," meaning that it doesn't jut out into the audience as much as most such stages. Still, thrust it is, neither innovative nor striking, with all the advantages and disadvantages of such stages. There also have been built two unnecessarily permanent concrete structures at either side, serving mostly to hamper the stage as well as the sight lines. Two long runways go up the sides of the 700-seat theater, and they were used for silly, Radio City Music Hall processions. As for the building itself, it looks like a fortress for no special reason and probably would be handsome if you could see it all at once (which you can't). There is lots of red carpeting and lounging space inside, and that is nice, only I think more of it might have been made for the theater and its practical uses.

Pinter

The Room and *A Slight Ache* (*December 10, 1964*)

Harold pinter, by now, is well on his way toward becoming one of the finest dramatists of our time. *A Slight Ache* and *The Room* are two of his earlier plays, but in them the seeds of his greatness had already begun to bloom. In the production that opened last night (as "The New Pinter Plays") at the Writer's Stage Theatre they are performed superlatively, and for the sake of what Pinter has become, as well as for what he already was, it will be your very good fortune to see them.

Without getting into the irritating business of choosing a "better" of the two, take them in order. *The Room* is, simply enough, about a room. And what is inside it. This is a dingy flat, the grime of a dirty little village scraping against its walls, the harshness of metal dishes scraping against its shabby sink. It contains a working-class couple with not much in the way of cheer. The husband is a thick, crude, heavy-handed (and -hearted) truck driver, eating silently while his wife makes pathetically cheerful conversation. Soon the beginnings of fright are set in motion.

Pinter, of course, is a specialist in fright. He plants a hint about a threat in the basement ("Who lives down there?") and then abandons it for meaningless chatter. Soon he is back with another clue. Before long a landlord is there to talk in circular riddles, then a gum-chewing couple looking for a room, mentioning that the man in the basement told them this one would soon be vacant. The menace grows.

While the room is being swathed in mysterious tension, the small talk wanders in calculated paths. Pinter's greatest asset is his mastery of easygoing dialogue that steps all over itself in human confusion. The foolish, the repetitious, the obvious, the vacant. While unspoken fears lurk in the commas and silent question marks.

When the fear materializes—when the neurotic becomes the actual—the action comes tumbling over action and bang, the thing is over. *The Room* is an absolutely perfect one-act play, as rare as the perfect short story. Ward Baker's time-ticking direction is drenched in threat. Frances Sternhagen's cagey, frightened wife, Ian Jenkins and Margaret Linn's stupid couple, and Robertearl Jones' mysterious man in the basement are superlative. Clarence Felder draws a full-blooded characterization of a surly, dangerous husband without a word of dialogue until the play's violent conclusion, and even then, his words seem guttural monosyllables. Frankly, it is too exciting to even notice what he says at that point—and it doesn't make a difference.

On the other hand, dialogue makes all the difference in *A Slight Ache,* the second of the plays. Now we are in the country home of a "theological and philosophical essayist" whose writings range from space and time to the Belgian Congo (this is a typical Pinter joke, thrown in—as jokes should be thrown in— just for fun).

Again, we are dealing in panic. It is the purely neurotic fear that something dreadful is about to happen; that-man-is-staring-at-me fear, somebody-is-following-me fear. Pinter makes that man you *think* is staring at you *really* be staring at you; the somebody you *think* is following you turns out to *really* be following you. That is the dramatic scheme, a scheme worked for purely dramatic purposes.

In the case of *A Slight Ache,* though, the fears that materialize are the fears of a psychotic, a paranoiac. Beginning as a small-time sadist who enjoys trapping a wasp in marmalade and then murdering him with boiling water, the essayist moves from an obsession to an involvement with a ragged man who has been selling matches at the garden gate. His suspicions of plotting, and secret designs, finally lead him to invite the man in and treat him in every conventional manner, from the gruff to the obsequious. He is finally completely intimidated.

But Pinter, with an imagination that refuses to be limited, has other tricks in mind. The stable wife is as frightened by the mysterious as her demented husband. The mute match seller, in his unknown strangeness, brings out the panic and the basic in her. It isn't very long before she becomes obsessed with him, emotionally and sexually.

It must be said that *A Slight Ache* is also a slight nuisance in some excessive dialogue that hurts its tension. It is no minor flaw. But because of Mr. Baker's uncannily controlled direction (the movement itself is quietly tensile), and because of the excellent performances of Henderson Forsythe, Miss Sternhagen, again, and Ralph Drischell as the mysterious man, it is a play of great dramatic strength. Between the two there is enough exciting theater—enough strange pressure—enough of the irresistible pull into something-happening, for anybody who has been missing the thrill of pure theater.

The Birthday Party *(August 4, 1966)*

Can you imagine somebody writing a play about the terror of being an unsure person in a world of confident people? Such great artistic ideas are bound to appear painfully obvious (after an artist conceives them), and the playwriting of Harold Pinter has always been so elementary in conception and basic in dramatic method that it seemed as if the script wrote itself. This is the very definition of art. It has always been apparent that Pinter was a true artist—he fairly washes your face with it—but it is astonishing that this artistry was conceived and executed on a mature level from the start. *The Birthday Party,* his first full-length play, is seldom produced and, as best I can recall, has never been given a regular production in New York. The Theatre Group at UCLA is presenting a superb version of it, and it is an exciting theater experience.

It would be unfair to Pinter to say that the play was "about" anything, even something so broad as unsureness. Like the rest of his work, it is pointed primarily to the stage experience—for audience manipulation in terms of suspense, fright, excitement, climax, and emotional washout. Like the rest of his work, it takes fundamental dramatic tools and reverses them.

For example, in simple melodrama a man will hear dark, echoed, fearful footsteps stalking him on a lonely night. His fright is imaginary. Pinter makes those footsteps real—there is somebody following and there is a cause for fright. Our worst, weirdest fears are confirmed in a place where the illogical happens. Pinter takes the abstract and gives it the clothing of reality.

The Birthday Party applies this to the case of a person with all the usual exaggerations of the human mind, but a person for whom exaggerations have become lunatic. Stanley Weber, the central character, is paranoid, and his terrible fear of inadequacy, victimization, and solitude runs headlong into a Pinter world of imagined horror gone real.

Stanley lives in a boardinghouse which he refuses to leave, spending most of his time in bed. Intimidated by a threatening world, he keeps to his pajamas. Pinter introduces this with his now-familiar floating dialogue, which lazes around repetitious commonplaces to suddenly dip into sore spots and then float softly back. The mysteries, confusions, and illogics of ordinary conversation become increasingly apparent, and then Stanley's insulation from the threats of day-to-day life is threatened: into this place with a comforting, loving mother figure (the landlady) come two strange men.

Stanley's composed anxiety is almost immediately upset, now that his safety shell has been pierced. Fearing the worst (that they are out to "get" him), the worst happens. Goldberg, the leader of the two, is a glib, pinky-ringed small-time success whose social poise is made of the shallow collection of clichés, slogans, and sentiments that get most people by on the surface of day-to-day existence. It is the sureness that the unconfident person both despises and craves.

McCann, the other man, hangs on a common adjustment to daily pressures. As most weak people hook on to the strong, McCann sucks strength from the fast-talking confidence of Goldberg. And together they attack the frail Stanley with the threats, questions, accusations that the insecure dread.

Stanley, of course, is immediately defeated and breaks down, first with a crumble and then with a crash during his birthday party. They then take him away, presumably for psychiatric help, where he will be given the cheap confidence he needs to survive (but where, actually, the already delivered defeat will be sealed).

All of this, though, is subordinate to plain theatricality, and the story is furious with frights and confusions that exist only for dramatic purposes. In this production they have devastating power.

Mel Shapiro (who staged the lovely *Romeo and Juliet* for the San Diego Shakespeare Festival) has handled the excellent theater in Schoenberg Hall with an easy embrace of its size, especially in upstage and downstage movement.

Blessed with Michael Devine's near-abstract set of looming, slatted, intensified reality, as dramatically lighted by Gilbert V.

Hemsley, Jr., he drew a set of sliding, coordinated perform ances from an excellent cast.

Gerald Hiken's Stanley was brilliant, moving from weird humor to trembling fright, and at several points his tragedy was unbearable (the first act ends with Hiken beating a gift drum and, becoming unable to control his inside misery, thumping desperately with the sticks and then with his fists).

Harold Gould, as Goldberg, slid slickly with the facetious aplomb of all stupid men who have solved the superficial life problems that are so insoluble for the uncertain. Kelly Jean Peters, treated to a Technicolor set of sexual commonplaces by Mr. Shapiro, was excellent as a girl whose simpleminded stability made her perfect for Goldberg and infuriating for Stanley. The remainder of the cast was well up to the play's real challenges of mood and language, although they displayed the usual deficiencies in dialect.

I am not, however, about to complain. The play is a perfect example of the modern movement toward basic drama in the surrealistic style. More than that, it is real and true theater.

The Homecoming (January 13, 1967)

Without doubt, Harold Pinter is the surest, the most mature and artful, playwright presently writing for the English-speaking stage. He alone has found his style—his milieu, his artistic identity, whatever you wish to call it—and has proceeded to develop within it. With every play that style is deepened and refined; with every play it is put to more challenging use; with every play the work becomes deeper and finer.

Pinter's theatrical handwriting was definite with his very first one-act play (The Room) and has never varied. It has got only more certain, more defined, more ambitious, and more successful in its use.

The basis of this handwriting is the bizarre situation in the guise of the perfectly ordinary. In appearance, Pinter's plays are entirely plausible. Despite the impossibility of their situations, the characters behave as if all were normal.

The playwright sets surrealistic (that is, exaggeratedly realistic) situations in normal trappings. And once creating a bizarre premise, he proceeds to let everything follow natural, logical courses. In other words, the plays exist in their own dimension, proceeding normally *within* that dimension.

Perhaps examples would clarify this. One play (*The Caretaker*) is about a derelict who is given shelter by a gentle man and proceeds to become impossibly antagonistic, demanding, and greedy. Another (*A Slight Ache*) is about a strange match seller who never leaves the garden gate of a middle-class couple and is finally invited in to silently intimidate and eventually replace the husband. One (*The Birthday Party*) is about an insecure young man whose most neurotic fears are realized when a fast talker with the façade of confidence comes to "get him." Another (*The Lover*) is about the marital sex fantasies demanded by a reasonably sophisticated man.

In each of Pinter's plays the unreal becomes the real, lingering halfway between the naturalistic and the abstract. Sometimes a quality of imagination is introduced—that is, what we see onstage is not what is really happening but what a character emotionally believes to be happening. Stanley Weber in *The Birthday Party* imagines everybody to have the absolute poise he so frightfully lacks and reads it into everything they say and do. Aston, in *The Caretaker,* sees people as ungrateful while his brother Mick sees them as puny, and Davies the derelict behaves in these different ways to each of them. Certainly, these are neurotic characters and neurosis is a running Pinter concern. Weber is obviously a paranoiac, and Aston has been neutralized by electric shock therapy. In all the plays the troubled characters are clearly "sick." But this mental illness is again seen as only an extension of the behavior and emotions of those of us who are "normal."

It would be unfair to Pinter, however, to pin his plays down to such subjective material. They are primarily theater occurrences, designed to happen on a stage and involve an audience in their stories and moods. Pinter describes them as "basically 'well-made plays,' " which is typical of his modesty but not entirely untrue. As "well-made plays," they have stories with beginnings, middles, and ends, well-defined characters, suspense, surprise, and climax. But there is a great deal more to them than that.

Part of it is in the writing itself. In the use of the English language and the understanding of informal dialogue, word sounds, conversation rhythms, exact meanings, and real poetry, Pinter is peerless.

His humor is wonderful—ironic and dry, verging on the ridiculous and entirely within modern modes. For example, "What you've got to do is learn how to defend yourself, and you've got to learn how to attack. That's your only trouble as a boxer. You don't know how to defend yourself, and you don't know how to attack." The line is from *The Homecoming*, which opened at the Music Box Theatre last week, and the play is funnier than most straight comedies.

His manipulation of situation (and of audience) is awesome. Conversation will wander idly, poking into corners, leading character and listener astray with false clues, irrelevancies, and repetitions. But nothing is ever wasted; no dialogue runs away from the play. Everything is planned and coordinated, moving deliberately toward a conclusion that is always justified in terms of drama and idea.

The ideas implicit in *The Homecoming* are deep and multiple, having as their general reference the relationships between people. This is as it has been in every Pinter play. In this one, the characters are members of a family that pretends as most (all?) families do that fathers are paternal, mothers maternal, sons fraternal and filial. At some point each of them spouts the picture-magazine clichés of such family life. But in fact, they are frauds—their relationships are violent and hateful. Yet they are bound to one another, as all families are.

The commonplace situation that begins this play is the classic one of a son bringing his wife home to "meet the family." But we are in a Pinter family, one step away from reality. The father, a cruel, stupid, and coarse man, greets his daughter-in-law by saying, "I've never had a whore under this roof before" (adding, for a typical Pinter joke, "Ever since your mother died," which is meaningful itself since the mother was not the All-Britain Mother's Day Mom she is made out to be, but an unfaithful and perhaps unpleasant woman). The sons are equally violent—the youngest is a boxer, the middle a pimp who enjoys beating women, the eldest a professor of philosophy who has attempted to escape his background and become the model of the civilized man. His brutality is controlled but it is there. Their violence is a disguise for the masculinity they lack, and they all are finally subjugated by a woman who has the ultimate power over men—the power to grant or withhold sexual gratification. But that is getting into another vein of the play and *The Homecoming* is interwoven with them.

The play has its flaws, especially in the area of climax. On a second visit I found that its blackouts, which had first seemed to chop the play, were actually a careful and effective punctuation. In any case, it is an important and exciting work by the most original and talented of playwrights today.

Tea Party and *The Basement* (*October 17, 1968*)

Harold Pinter's extraordinary theater imagination, his craftsmanship, his consistency of attitude, his precision of language, and his terrific intelligence continue on their way. His two new plays—*Tea Party* and *The Basement*—which opened at the Eastside Playhouse, are examples of formal playwriting at its most perfect.

Like all of Pinter's plays since *The Birthday Party,* they take place in a world inflated with fake poise, with the air slowly leaking out. The characters are forever cool, hiding fright and insecurity under a mask of social confidence. Until sooner or later, somebody drops his mask, just out of fright that somebody else *really* is confident, *really knows* what's going on. Then, of course, he is through.

Tea Party is about a manufacturer of toilets who hires a secretary the day he gets a wife and finds them both ultraefficient, ultimately poised, and apparently alive to humiliate him. In fact, he only fears they are so—they really aren't but his fear is enough to make it as good as fact. They become that way with him—for him. Moreover, his wife's brother, sensing his fear, makes even more sport of it. As indeed, do his own twin sons. People seem monsters to the afraid and so become them. Since we are all in this boat, it makes all of us monsters and victims, and that is Pinter. What is unusual about this play is that for the first time Pinter comes out from behind his play's glasses and makes this point when the businessman says: "I believe life can be conducted efficiently. I never waste my energies in any kind of timorous expectation. Neither do I ask to be loved." This is a patent lie, an impossibility for a human being.

The play carries out the truth implicit in this lie by using physical deterioration as a metaphor for human withdrawal once insecurity sets in. The businessman claims to be confident, productive, and unemotional, but as soon as he imagines others to be that way he begins losing his sight and finally locks himself into a chair (into himself).

The Basement is no less weird, no less comic, no less chilly, no less perceptive, as it is no less delightful in its sense of wordplay. A man and woman intrude into the home and life of an apparent homosexual who is rather up-tight. Again it is Pinter time, with power angles, the effect of rudeness, the ease with which a person and his life can be disoriented, the ephemeral nature of confidence and the way it can be used and destroyed. And again, floating above it, is the coolness of a woman's sexual strength.

In this play the victim can be either man as it can be any man. First the intruder and the girl take over their host's home (for Pinter a host is always in the vulnerable position). They take the most outrageous liberties. Tables are turned and turned again and again. Force is used (thrown marbles, broken glasses) as physicality was used in the first play, to expose—if just for a moment—the pathetic, trembling animals who lie beneath shaved, powdered skins. And finally relief never—just continuation.

James Hammerstein directed both works with exactly the right frigidity, coping all the way with a basic burden: these plays were written for television and are involved with many fades over a variety of locations. Ed Wittstein needed two turntables to cope with the multiple scene changes, and the constant switching sometimes interrupted the flow. But parallel to this handicap was a tension created by exactly the same thing—the interruptions—so that things evened out.

Mr. Hammerstein drew splendid performances from his company, particularly Valerie French and June Emery as the icy secretary and wife in *Tea Party,* and the entire cast of *The Basement* (Ted van Griethuysen, James Ray, and Margo Ann Berdeshevsky). I wish that David Ford had been slightly more human as the victim in *Tea Party,* so that his collapse would have been in greater contrast to everybody else's composure, but Mr. Ford did extremely well nevertheless.

There is no more to say. It is exquisite theater.

British Theater

Marat/Sade (*December 28, 1965*)

IT is very difficult to believe that the play that England's Royal Shakespeare Company presented last night at the Martin Beck Theatre—this spectacularly theatrical poetic-dramatic tirade—is really the first by Peter Weiss. Nobody writes first plays like this. The grasping of the full, swelling idea of pure theater and the exploding of it into a living experience is something reserved for the master.

Mr. Weiss' play is masterful—a complete fulfillment of the theater's most demanding (and most rewarding) requirements. In its gathering of every dramatic element—language and sight and music and movement—and in its lush combination of them into a ballooning entity, it embraces its audience in a wild sensual-intellectual experience.

Its long title tells precisely what it is about—*The Persecution and Assassination of Marat as Performed by the Inmates of the Asylum of Charenton Under the Direction of the Marquis de Sade*. The Charenton Asylum, at the turn of the seventeenth century, used its inmates in theatrical entertainment as a bizarre pleasure for the aristocracy, rationalizing it as "therapy." The

Marquis de Sade, an inmate at the time, wrote and directed a number of these, and Mr. Weiss' play is about a performance of one of them.

De Sade's "play" is a retelling of the assassination of Jean-Paul Marat, a strange and fanatic post-Revolutionary reformer, by Charlotte Corday, an equally fanatic reformer. This in itself is a strange story. Marat was assassinated in his bathtub, where he was forced to spend most of his time because of an exotic skin disease.

It is a perfect situation for a discussion of the nature of freedom, which the play is primarily about. For as director-author De Sade represents the anarchistic individual freedom of egoism, Marat represents the opposite, mass freedom of socialism. The irony, of course, is that Marat is arguing freedom from the imprisonment of a bathtub, and De Sade is arguing freedom from the imprisonment of a madhouse.

The relative merits of these arguments, though, are subordinate to the production itself, although Weiss clearly sides with De Sade, who is drawn with idealized brushstrokes of humanism, idealism, and absolute morality. But the production is really all that counts and it really cannot be called a "play." It is, rather, a *performance*. It is a total theatrical occurrence—a demonstration and an experience. In the richest and finest sense, it is drawn to the rigid requirements of art—it is there to exist. And it exists, with all of its carefully drawn substructure hidden beneath the success of it.

Marat/Sade, set on a stage that has been deeply extended and designed with the forbidding gray brick of an institution, begins as the spectacle it is. A harmonium modulates eerily as the lunatics moan and stumble their entrances. In the center of this asylum bathhouse is the inmate who is playing Marat, already stuck in his horrible, black metal, prosthesislike tub. De Sade is nearby, directing with elegant precision. In stark contrast is the trio of aristocratic spectators, silken and stupid. We, the audience, are the remainder of the onlookers.

It is here—at the very beginning—that our shock begins: because we are reluctant to use terms like "lunatic": because we prefer to call asylums "mental hospitals": because we know that spastics and the palsied and the stuttering, drooling, and retarded are pitiful. Peter Brook directed this performance as a choreography of the grotesque—his actors are not playing psychotics. They are playing madmen, Bedlam style.

The point of this is rooted in the Theater of Cruelty, the bizarre and frighteningly theatrical dramatic scheme conceived by Antonin Artaud, the French theorist. It is, as far as I can recall, the first example of such theater on the New York stage. And if not all of this play is conceived for it, Mr. Brook has directed most of it for that theoretical effect. And the effect is overwhelming.

But that does not mean that *Marat/Sade* is pointless. In fact, its drive for human freedom is a blaze of idealism. Furthermore, its conception of politics and politicians as madmen, playing mad roles in madhouses, is massively pointed. And, projecting the idea still further, it includes us, the audience, in its lunatic world, making the very idea of rational progress a hopelessly frenzied confusion. While above it all towers the sheerly lovely purity of De Sade himself. Is he—this criminal, this masochist, this bizarre artist—is he the sanest of all?

It hardly matters. What matters is the totality of this conception, magnificently acted (particularly by Ian Richardson as Marat, Patrick Magee as De Sade, and Glenda Jackson as Mlle. Corday). Mr. Brook's direction is massive and incredibly musical, moving the action in a swirling whirlpool, going ever outward. Richard Peasless' music, while often eclectic, is a tremendous asset in its gaudy vaudeville. Above all is the language and the idea of Weiss. All is interrelated and entire. It is absolute theater. [I voted for *Marat/Sade* at the New York Drama Critics Circle as the best musical of the 1965–66 season. *Man of La Mancha* won.]

Not the Golden Age. Maybe Goldish
(*September 30, 1966*)

The London stage has acquired, only in the past couple of years really, the reputation of being the most vital, most up-to-date, most exciting theater in all the Western world. It is bound to be depressing, then, to go over there and find that *Marat/Sade* is not playing in every house. It is depressing for only as long as it takes to regain one's perspective. In fact, the London stage *is* terribly exciting in a very realistic, very plausible way.

But certain facts about it must be got straight. There is an awful lot of theater available in London, and it covers a broad range of quality, in both material and performance. The bulk of the major productions on the West End (which is equivalent to New York's Broadway) is trash, from potboilers to inane little comedies that would never last a weekend in New York. For example, there is a comedy called *There's a Girl in My Soup* that has been running since June. Forget the title—the English have some peculiar tastes in language. I wish the play could be as easily forgotten. A comedy in the least sense of the word, it is rather an assemblage of machine-tooled parts, similar to the dozens of such "plays" that work the American summer circuits each year. The only encouragement is that London's theater situation is so healthy that even such nonsense can be carried awhile. [Needless to say, it was subsequently produced in New York and received the reviews necessary for a season's run. So much for my commercial judgment.]

On the other hand, there are full-scale productions of Bernard Shaw, Oscar Wilde, even Victorien Sardou, playing to very healthy runs. About such presentations several points should be made. First of all, English actors, directors and designers are not genetically attuned to high style despite their reputation. There are many productions of period works that are sloppily performed and shabbily presented. A revival of Wilde's *An Ideal Husband* stars Margaret Lockwood and Richard Todd, two good drawing cards for the middle-class London theater crowd. The Lockwood-Todd popularity notwithstanding, they have no sense of the high Wilde style. Nor do the cardboard sets and tacky costumes help matters. Or, as another example, M. Sardou's *Divorçons* (retitled, *Let's Get a Divorce*). Sardou, a well-forgotten but wildly prolific playwright of the late nineteenth century, wrote in the Beaumarchais tradition, whipping up overplotted trifles and stocking them with what he thought was terribly clever, unbearably witty dialogue. Assuming that Angela and Robert Goldsby's translation was accurate (and there was every reason to hope it wasn't), the barrage of determined raillery had little style and less humor. The French are notoriously overimpressed with their own wit.

Director Robin Midgley was evidently seeking the high style of comic opera—say, Mozart or Rossini—but he worked under the considerable handicaps of misunderstanding that style and having a cast largely incapable of it in any case. This presented somewhat of a problem.

Only one member of the company had any appreciation of the manner and that was the enormously popular Fenella Fielding, who is broad, pure, hoarse-throat English to the point of parody. Miss Fielding is wonderful and always has been. I am not sure I would call her an actress—she is so restricted to a special style, a special kind of role, a special kind of theater. Perhaps, rather, a performer, but she belongs in a repertory company specializing in Congreve-to-Sheridan-to-Wilde—not a tacky little pickup troupe.

On the other hand, a production of *You Never Can Tell* did

marvelously with the seldom-produced Shaw comedy. It is apparent that Shaw is not going to date, only because his style and humor outweigh his messages (news that would positively kill him). This play is very, very funny, and it was wonderfully played, bright and alive. It is the perfect example of a kind of adult, literate humor entirely absent from the modern theater.

However, the erratic quality of these productions does not outweigh the simple fact that they *exist*. And that there is an *audience* for them (the Shaw ran 300 performances). Moreover, other classic comedies are being produced on their heels. Certainly, Wilde and Shaw are practically English folk favorites, and the people who go to the revivals are not about to buy tickets for serious or original drama, but it hardly would do to complain about their taste. Better *An Ideal Husband* than *The Impossible Years*.

So much for the mass theater—the 95 percent of the productions. It is the remaining 5 percent that has given the British theater its reputation. The percent that accounts for the development of John Osborne, Harold Pinter, Peter Shaffer, Arnold Wesker. And now a still newer generation—John Arden, Henry Livings, James Saunders, Joe Orton. The percent that is constantly looking for, constantly producing, new plays. The percent that is prompting classically trained, modern actors—the vital old guard like Olivier, Gielgud, Mills, Redgrave; and the exciting newcomers like O'Toole, Courtenay, Finney, Geraldine McEwan, Vanessa Redgrave. The percent that is working a steady shuttle between movie production and the stage (luckily for the English, both films and plays are produced in London, making combination activities possible). The percent that is aware of new stage developments and is looking for still newer ones.

That doesn't mean that everybody is churning out masterpiece after masterpiece. John Osborne's newest play, the one-act

A Bond Honoured, is an artsy-craftsy bore. Arnold Wesker's last few works have been harshly received. Pinter's *The Homecoming* was given a less than enthusiastic critical reception. Also, these playwrights are beginning to bridle at the royalties available from repertory theater productions as opposed to straight West End presentations. High prestige sometimes loses its glitter beside low income.

But that does bring us to the repertory theaters, and both of them—the National Theatre of Great Britain and the Royal Shakespeare Company—are ambitious, well financed, idealistic, and talent-laden. The National Theatre is performing a series of brilliant productions of classics to packed houses. The Royal Shakespeare Company is having its troubles with a group of badly chosen new plays, but there is little doubt that things will improve. Most consequentially, both of these companies have few worries about potential audiences.

Finally, there are the smaller resident theaters, and remember—all of them in London itself. The Royal Court Theatre has disappointed many of its early supporters, who pine for the days when it introduced playwrights like John Osborne to the decaying London stage of ten years ago. But the Royal Court still presents uncommercial, experimental works and is governmentally supported. Other companies like the London Traverse Theatre Company at the handsome little Jeannetta Cochrane Theatre work together to produce offbeat new plays by authors such as Marguerite Duras and Orton.

This all contributes to a ferment, a variety, a life. The overall quality is highly inconsistent, and it is a long way from *There's a Girl in My Soup* to the company-created Vietnam "show" that Peter Brook is presently preparing with the Royal Shakespeare Company. But it is precisely that great spread that gives London theater its life. Seeing it for what it really is—not a miracle but a genuine, achievable vitality that runs across audience and theater lines—makes it all the more impressive.

Othello *(September 26, 1966)*

Laurence Olivier's *Othello* is the definitive one. Among Shakespeare's major tragedies, definitive performances in central roles are impossible—the characters are too complex, open to too many interpretations. *Othello* is an exception because the main role is comparatively simple—as simple as the play itself. For here is a tragedy that moves smoothly along a direct track, its plotting uncomplicated, with effects following causes step by step. Certainly, it is not as deep as *Hamlet* or *Macbeth,* but in its own way it is a practically perfect play that holds within itself the very soul of tragedy. It is this soul that Olivier has found, and his is the *Othello* of a lifetime.

The main theme of this terribly sad story is the human conflict between self-control and emotions, a battle that always concerned Shakespeare. Of course, it is the classic story about jealousy, and as stories go, it is a marvelous one. Shakespeare is seldom given his proper credit as a storyteller in the rush to rummage through his philosophical implications. This is a play that is clearly told in a consistently lovely stream of poetry. It is interesting, it is serious, and it is deeply moving. These are the basic involvements of drama.

The enormously successful production that is being given by the National Theatre of Great Britain at the Old Vic is straightforward, the company being perfectly professional and the direction sensible. Except for Olivier's astonishing performance, there is nothing to make it any more than very good. Maggie Smith's Desdemona is "of spirit so still and quiet, that her motion blush'd at herself." She is the perfect, unfaulted, sweet, pure, and impeccable wife. Now what can you do with that? Frank Finlay gives Iago a whine and a proper meanness of

276

person, but he still has only Shakespeare's excuses for his impossible villainy: an upset over Cassio's receiving the lieutenantship instead of himself and a conviction that Othello had seduced his wife. These hardly justify the intensity of his evil. Iago will always remain a primitive villain (except for the occasional playing of him as a homosexual, which gives the play a much more interesting caste).

With a work so simply written, the proper playing of it should be expected. John Dexter's staging laid it out as demanded—neat and proper (although moving into a surprising and impressive spiral from murder of Desdemona to the conclusion). With a merely capable title player, this would have been a respectable production of the "festival" variety, and no more.

But this was Olivier giving, perhaps, the performance of his career. His makeup is Negroid and his accent (except for a single lapse) African. More than that, he has actually *become* Negro, assuming the physical characteristics, the bodily structure, and the movement mannerisms of the race. What does "acting" mean, if not that?

But, as well, this is part of his interpretation. Olivier is not only pretending to *be* Othello in the way he looks. In looking like him, he is analyzing him. Othello is a primitive in the clothing of civilization—a giant precursor of Joyce Cary's *Mr. Johnson*. When things are going well for him he is a lord of a man. But once his emotions are attacked, he returns to his genuine identity, and that is a raw and a very physical human. This happens in a thunderous bellow of animal pain that leads into the epileptic fit. And ever after that, Olivier is at the brink of foaming over. He becomes Iago's tool, to be reduced to pure flesh with every reminder of Desdemona's presumed infidelity. In this creation of the basic human animal, Olivier reached a monumental peak. He is the greatest actor alive on the English-speaking stage.

It is a pity that Shakespeare missed this opportunity to explore racial attitudes. His first-scene concern with interracial marriage is, disappointingly, never resumed. But the play remains superb and this production is a fine mounting of it. The Olivier performance makes the occasion a landmark for the theater of our time.

A Flea in Her Ear (September 29, 1966)

The National Theatre of Great Britain has taken a thoroughly asinine comedy by Georges Feydeau and translated it into what is probably the funniest play on the current London stage. It is still another example of the most modern trend in theater: creativity by the director and an emphasis on production rather than on fidelity to a script. Whatever arguments may be made over this, and there are some currently raging, the simple fact is obvious: *A Flea in Her Ear,* if played straight, would be a stupid farce on the Minsky level. As directed by Jacques Charon, it is hilarious.

To be sure, there is an excellent translation on hand, and the company took the unusually wise step of commissioning a professional playwright (John Mortimer) to do it. This produced a considerably more adult kind of humor than Feydeau's, but still the play is too broad and too simpleminded to stand alone. M. Charon then set it before Art Nouveau designs and started it spinning at triple speed. He kept his cast French in style, for the play remains terribly French (as it should), but the tone was impeccable and the manner was high.

A Flea in Her Ear is a conventional boulevard comedy, its plotting thick enough to be the minestrone of drama. A lady is worried about her husband's recent bedroom disinterest and fears he has outside interests. To test him she has a friend write an anonymous love letter arranging a tryst at the local lovers' hotel, planning to meet and trap him. The friend's husband, a murderously jealous Spaniard, accidentally sees the letter and recognizes his wife's handwriting. Meanwhile, the faithful husband passes the tryst along to his friend and everybody converges at the hotel, where there is a porter who is the husband's double. Take it from there.

There are revolving bedroom walls and, of course, dozens of doors to be run into, run out of, and generally slammed, all of this surrounded by André Levasseur's green-bright sets. The company dashes through them like thoroughbreds, managing to conceal the clumsy humor that remains at the root (as well as in the lines; for example: SHE: Married couples come here. HE: Not at the same time).

So the stage becomes a marionette show, everybody jerking, jumping, and spinning and everything artificial and showy. Even the unpleasant dependence for humor upon a character's cleft palate becomes bearable because of the thoroughly unreal and lickety-split vitality (there is no sense, anyhow, ignoring plays because of bad taste in such matters).

The performances were marvelous and I might say that a cast obviously having a grand time (or at least seeming to) can do wonders for a production. Frank Wylie was almost unbearably funny as the ready-to-kill Spaniard. Somebody told me that Andalusians lisp, and I'm not sure whether or not I was being put on, but Mr. Wylie's was hilarious, as was his whole lunging, matadorial manner. Robert Lang, playing the double role of the dignified husband and drunken porter, managed to handle them splendidly despite the hectic costume-changing that such theatrical hanky-panky demands. Geraldine McEwan was splendid as his wife although, strangely, she played the role in high English (in the Joan Greenwood-Glynis Johns-Fenella Fielding style) while everybody else was doing French.

But it made little difference. Everything was so spinning, so reeling, so physically, visually, vitally funny, that minor inconsistencies were washed away beneath the primary watercolors. Such is the accomplishment of a superb company and an inspired director. This is the theater.

The Dance of Death (October 27, 1967)

In *The Dance of Death*, August Strindberg isolated a marriage on a bleak island, leaving the husband and wife to tear at each other in the love-hate frenzy that he saw in all marriages. It is an awesome and frightful play, written by a savage, bitter, and emotional man at the peak of inspiration, driven by neurosis into an artistry that was, and remains, incredibly modern.

In *Antony and Cleopatra*, William Shakespeare coolly detailed the excitement of the sexual passion and its eternal journey through game-playing, thriving joys, and physical exultation, leading inevitably to the triumph of the woman over the man. It is not Shakespeare's greatest play, but it is surely one of his truest.

These plays and their ideas are presently being produced at Expo 67 in Montreal by two of the three finest theater companies in the English-speaking world (the National Theatre of Great Britain, the Royal Shakespeare Company and the Stratford, Ontario, Shakespearean Festival). And their male leads are being played by Laurence Olivier, far and away the greatest English-speaking actor alive—and perhaps ever—and Christopher Plummer, the finest actor on the North American continent. It is a thrilling coincidence, providing endless theater comparisons—in plays, in themes, in ensemble performance, in individual acting. If you are interested in genuinely great theater, there would seem no finer opportunity for seeing the best.

Regarding the plays themselves, although *Antony and Cleopatra* appears to be another Shakespearean pageant play with a large cast, a historical background, and an episodic structure, it really is involved with only its lovers. Everything—the fates of empires and wars and subjects—is subservient to the romance itself, and once the final posture of that romance is set, all other questions are answered. As long as Antony is strong, manly, and in control of Cleopatra, he can deal competently with his rather trivial political competitors in Rome. But his strength exists only while Cleopatra believes in the romance. With that belief, the love affair thrives and gives him joy and confidence. But since Cleopatra's interest is not in loving as much as it is in playing at passion, her belief is adolescent and doomed to die. When it does she becomes the bitch she has been all the time. Capable of being hotly erotic, she is just as capable of putting the screws on Antony and ultimately degrading and destroying him. He, ensnared by passion as only the male can be, sacrifices everything to her. And of course, the more he sacrifices, the less interested and so the more powerful she becomes. By the time the play reaches its unavoidable end, she is cruel enough to have her death falsely announced to him, just to see his reaction. His reaction, simplemindedly enough, is suicide, since Antony turns out to be an idiot. In many ways it is *A Man Destroyed,* another example of the cliché that is a cliché because it is so classically true.

But that is the story of a sexual passion. The constant push-pull between man and woman is far more complicated than that, rooted as it is in the complete difference between them, not merely biologically but emotionally and intellectually. A male-female struggle of another sort is the one that continues once the sexual passion has been resolved in favor of a permanent relationship (I had hoped to avoid that word but, like all things you try to avoid, there it is). "Permanent relationship," in nearly all cases, means marriage, a situation that could not be more unlike a love affair.

The Dance of Death, I will grant you, does not see marriage through the eyes of the man most likely to be a counselor.

Strindberg's troubles with lovers and wives are well known, and his hatred of women is almost matched by his obsession with them. *The Dance of Death* sees marriage as just that macabre dance—mortal battle, black, grotesque, and brutal. And yet inescapable, not because of any legal or moral reason but because married people can't help being stuck, marooned, and obsessed with each other. It is a sick attitude, obviously. But it also glitters with a single part of the truth, blown up and splattered against a driving theatrical force as conceived by an honest-to-God artist.

As *The Dance of Death* begins, Edgar and Alice have already spent twenty-five years in the "miserable existence which is our marriage." They are "welded together," married because, as Alice says, "he took me" (sexually and, in effect, actually). Now they are living together and alone, friendless because in one way or another Edgar's candid cruelty has divorced everybody from them (even their children have been sent away). Edgar is stupid though not unfeeling, at least when it comes to his own pain. Alice is brighter and consequently more cutting and vicious. Yet each of them returns, no matter how great a wound has been inflicted on the other. If there is any sense in this, or significance, Strindberg sees none. "The meaning is that we are unable to see any meaning and we must submit." If Shakespeare sees any happiness, or love, possible in the mating of a man and a woman—and of course he does in other plays— Strindberg sees none. The sexes, though physically and emotionally fitted to each other, are, by the very same token, physically and emotionally antagonistic, as far as he is concerned. They can be one person and still they are forever two. He and Shakespeare are looking at the very same coin, but they are seeing different sides.

In fact Shakespeare, being cerebral and apparently well adjusted, was able to see all truths, able to accept contradictions and vaguenesses. Whereas Strindberg, being ultra-emotional, could not cope with such frustration. Shakespeare could acknowledge the blessed and cursed. It drove Strindberg into a frenzy.

In these productions the plays are being performed by companies bred alike—trained for the classics, well drilled in ensemble performance and individual technique (vocal, physical, intellectual), and conditioned to accept the director as the master. The companies, by and large, are not personality performers but anonymous artists, dedicated to playing *characters*—to *acting*. Yet the National Theatre of Great Britain is doing a brilliant *Dance of Death* while the Stratford Shakespearean Festival of Ontario, Canada, has mounted an overproduced, undisciplined, and boring *Antony and Cleopatra.* How can that be when not only are the male leads being played by superlative actors but the entire companies are deep and experienced?

The main reason is that the National Theatre—perhaps because it is younger but more likely because its leaders are more vital—has managed to maintain the freshness and play-for-play individuality that has long since disappeared from the Canadian company. Stratford has become an exhibition hall, displaying perfectly mounted, unerringly played, and absolutely sterile productions in virtual glass cases. Mr. Olivier's Edgar is an astounding performance—a character seen more deeply than any of us could ever hope to see ourselves. The mania, the pain, the groping for love, and the confused intelligence seep through a completely realized exterior to reveal a man alive, kicking, and bleeding. Mr. Plummer's Antony, on the other hand, is a magnificent actor fatally given a field day. There is show, there is flashy speechmaking, there is a magnificent voice, but there is no Antony. Only Plummer. Byam Shaw has staged his *Dance of Death* as a theater whole—a company work. It may not be surreal enough for my sense of the play, but there is no denying its brilliance. Michael Langham directed *Antony* for glorious pictures and then gave Plummer and Zoe Caldwell complete freedom.

Now Miss Caldwell happens to be a great actress, but like

Plummer, like Olivier, indeed like any actor or actress, she must submit to a director to be effective, and that director must be strong. Mr. Langham, inexplicably weak, left her and Plummer to do their things, and they might as well have been in separate plays in separate theaters. Despite the ingredients in *Antony and Cleopatra* for lush love along the banks of the Nile, Plummer and Caldwell were off in a theater-ego never-never land of their own.

What this all boils down to is that whatever the play, whether Strindberg or Shakespeare, it is not merely a trained company but overall conception and theatrical vitality that brings it to stage life. If the struggle between a man and a woman is as infinitely varied as there are kinds of men and kinds of women, and if two playwrights as divergent toward copulation (the union of men and women) as Shakespeare and Strindberg could make such insightful and exciting drama of it, then great companies and great actors should be able to produce great theater from the work. Only it isn't that easy.

As You Like It (*July 11, 1968*)

Theory and performance. Critic and practitioner. Academic and professional. Those on one side have traditionally been separate from those on the other, each position feeling superior.

The reason Jan Kott, the Polish academic critic, has attained great publicity is not only because his analyses of Shakespeare's plays are perceptive and refreshing but because they deal with performance as much as they do with literary meaning.

Although Clifford Williams says his production of *As You Like It* for the National Theatre of Great Britain "is not designed to demonstrate specific ideas advanced in [Kott's] essay," his disclaimer cannot deny the obvious. In the essay,

"Shakespeare's Bitter Arcadia," Kott says that *As You Like It* is about "the universality of desire which cannot be contained in or limited to one sex." The essay goes on to suggest that all female roles be played by male actors, as they were in Shakespeare's time. Of course, this was the theater convention of the time, but Kott believes that Shakespeare was capitalizing on the convention to make an erotic point.

Where Williams and Kott diverge is precisely in the area of eroticism. Kott is interested in the confusion of sex as the ultimate in erotica. Williams thinks that male actors in the female roles will have a desexing effect, emphasizing "the infinite beauty of Man in love, taking place in an atmosphere of spiritual purity which transcends sensuality in the search for poetic sexuality." There is a serious difference here, but Williams' directing remains the result of Kott's theory. The misbreeding is but one of the reasons for the production's peculiar quality as being fascinating to watch but tedious to endure.

The look of this *As You Like It* is not ambisexual, as Kott suggested; it is not nonsexual, as Williams intended; it is entirely homosexual. The roles of Rosalind, Celia, Phebe, and Audrey are not played by actors trying to look like girls—they are played by actors trying to look like queens. Moreover, the males in the play are characterized as either fags or fag parodies of males as empty-headed studs. The look of the production is pop art and sadomasochistic, both of which have homosexual connotations, and the music is pop-rock head music, which unfortunately has come to be associated with such ideas. There is an enormous difference between such homosexual staging and the stated theories of both Kott and Williams. Again, this tears at the production's underpinnings.

The ironic but predictable result is that the sexual confusion which prompted Kott to suggest all-male casting in the first place practically disappears. It is indeed odd that Shakespeare has Rosalind, fleeing to Orlando in the Forest of Arden, decide to masquerade as the boy Ganymede. It is also odd that Orlando consents to woo Ganymede while thinking he is a boy. But as Williams has staged things, Rosalind, when disguised as Ganymede, does not seem to be a boy, or even a girl dressed like a boy. Ganymede simply seems to be a drag queen. What is surprising is that Orlando does not notice it. There is no sexual mixup; everybody is a fag, plain and simple.

As for the rest of the homosexuality in this production, it is even more perplexing having no theory at all to back it up. It is true that Rosalind—in the Shakespeare—wears boys' clothing. This would not account for Williams' making Duke Ferdinand a sadomasochist fag or Touchstone a Midlander queer.

In short, there is a great difference between wholesale homosexual staging and the theories of Kott or Williams. And the reason is that theories are simple while a complete production is complicated. Neither of them really thought out the practical effect of an all-male cast.

Well, how does this work out as a production? Not very well, I'm afraid, though there is a certain novelty and an occasional note of revelation when the play coincides with the theory. *As You Like It* does give some substantiation for bisexual ideas, and when it does, the actors in drag underline it. But just as often, this production descends into cheap laugh-mongering at the expense of the fags.

The principal character has become Rosalind, naturally, because it is Rosalind upon whom the theories have been built. She is the one who whimsically disguises herself as the boy Ganymede, and she is the one who convinces Orlando to love "him" as if "he" were Rosalind. Since she is being played as a fag we see this romance as a homosexual game, a humiliation of the heterosexual. Ronald Pickup, who plays the role, is not very certain about how to do it, undoubtedly a reflection of the director's uncertainty. For most of the play, Pickup is effeminate rather than feminine, whether as Rosalind *or* Ganymede. Certainly, his relationship with Celia (whom Charles Kay plays as an absolute queen) is entirely fag. At least it gives some reason for Celia's being in the play. But toward the end, Pickup softens the queerness into something quite close to girlhood. By the time Shakespeare's touching quartet arrives, he can read Rosalind's "I for no woman" with a double meaning both effective and moving. And from then to the end he is wonderful, reading the epilogue as it has never been read before ("If I were a woman I would kiss as many of you as had beards that pleased me").

Hadrian the Seventh (July 15, 1968)

Peter Luke has found the soul of a man who never meant to bare it. His play *Hadrian the Seventh* is an artful dramatization of the heartbreaking, unintentionally autobiographical book by Frederick Rolfe. If your soul is your pain—and in so many ways it is—then Rolfe's book wept the ache of a man so lonely, so bright, and so neurotic that his life could be fulfilled only in a fantasy that swept the pain away in a miracle of dreams come true. Where Mr. Luke's art lies is in the insight and the compassion that he added to the fidelity of the adaptation.

Hadrian the Seventh is about a man whose consuming ambition was to be a priest, but whose paranoia prevented it—so in describing someone who is his own worst enemy, it is basic tragedy. Luke has changed the main character's name to Frederick Rolfe, which is accurate enough, since the novel used only a pseudonym for the author. Like his character, Rolfe's devotion to the Catholic Church and his mission to the priesthood was thwarted by an insecurity that made him defensive to the point of impotence. Fearing constant rejection, he would be hypercritical and caustic, eager to love but fearful of exposing himself. The play is written with a love for this man, and an understanding of his agony, that would have thrilled him. It is one of the gentlest and most pitiful psychoanalyses I have ever seen—one of the most complete renderings of a human's heart.

So it is a terribly moving play, as well as an enlightening one, not only about the human soul but also about the nature of religion and religious organizations. It is not perfectly written by any means, and much of it is verbatim from the novel in Rolfe's precise style. But its main flaw could be corrected with one simple snip of the scissors. Its other weaknesses lie mainly in an exclusive concentration on the main character to the detriment of the others, but I think the play's strength remains true and clear. It is being beautifully produced at the Mermaid Theatre (in London), made hallow by Alec McCowen's magnificent performance in the title role.

Hadrian the Seventh begins in the shabby room where Frederick Rolfe has withdrawn from a society that has frustrated his every wish. He has already been ejected from two seminaries on grounds never quite made clear because we get only his psychotic side of the story. He has knocked about in various jobs, forever rejected and forever retaliating with hatred and biting, erudite wit. Now, hounded by creditors, he goes under and hallucinates a visit by a cardinal and an archbishop. They have decided to grant him his priesthood.

From this point forward, *Hadrian the Seventh* portrays the ultimate gratification of the paranoiac. Every imagined abuse is corrected, every suspicion justified, every grand delusion fulfilled. The priesthood is only the first step. Rolfe is asked to go to Rome to participate in the election of a new Pope and he is elected to the Papacy, choosing the name Hadrian because the only previous English Pope was Hadrian IV.

He becomes a wonderful Pope, benign and intellectual, informal but strong, liberalizing the Catholic Church beyond the greatest hopes of its present-day reformers and demanding a real religion, an abandonment of materialism, and an honesty of devotion from the Catholic hierarchy. But even within this grand and impossible fulfillment, Hadrian remains the paranoid, for whom life could not possibly be satisfying. Torment remains; imagined enemies will lurk in the shadows. Along with the realization of his best dreams comes the realization of his worst nightmares.

But there is still more in this play's grasp of tortured soul. The paranoiac has an awful insight into his own problems. Hadrian knows just how mad he really is, understands his own religious fanaticism, knows exactly how miserable he has made himself. Mr. McCowen's performance is a devastating projection of this misery—from the beginning ("Why, oh, God, have you made me so strange?") to the sense of his own development ("The affect on my soul has been ghastly—I have lost faith in man—I have lost the ability to love") to the outright paranoia ("They'll see—one day I'll be vindicated").

On a stark stage that sets off the brilliant colors of Catholic pageantry, Peter Dews has directed this production to support McCowen, which weakens it, but then the script is so absorbed with Hadrian-Rolfe that perhaps this was inescapable. Secondary characters are barely developed and hardly exist, but then, of course, the play is existing in Rolfe's mind. The playwright's mistake (and this is where the scissors should be applied) was in returning to the shabby room at the end of the play, making it an it-all-was-a-dream thing. This is not only a cheap and unnecessary structural cliché, but misses a greater strength. Hallucination is quite real to a sick mind, and if the play were allowed to proceed as a fantasy it would be quite clear that it was the imagining of an extraordinary madman, occurring within his tortured brain.

The ending could easily be excised, and without it the play's power would be stronger. The similarity of it to Ronald Ribman's *Journey of the Fifth Horse* is quite striking—the compassionate analysis of a rejected man who uses arrogance as a defense. But the force of truth and love remains powerful enough to excuse similarities. Besides, and this is important, *Hadrian the Seventh* is a true story. Knowing that—sensing the truth of its evidence anyhow—you bear with it. [I found the play's Broadway production a good deal weaker, due to Mc-Cowen's self-indulgence, Dews' underlining of homosexual aspects, and the script's not uncommon quality of having enough substance for a first visit but not a second.]

Problems in Criticism

THE reviews in this section exemplify problems in criticism —interesting ones, I think. They include second thoughts, nonverbal communication, definite reactions, separating a director's work from the playwright's, panning and objectivity.

The most common of the questions asked a critic is whether he ever changes his mind about a play, and if so, does he change it in print. I have sometimes wished to rewrite a review, but not because of errors in judgment. Rather, because the writing was sloppy or because interesting points of detail had been omitted in the rush of deadline or in a too hasty scanning of notes.

Arthur Miller's *After the Fall* is the one play of which I think when someone asks this question. I've seen it three times and have reviewed it twice. Each time I was quite excited and moved. Yet the next day always brought a second thought that the play was self-indulgent, pompous, and pretend-intellectual. Seeing it again only dispelled that suspicion. The play, I'm convinced, is an excellent one, only I'm never going to be sure the next morning, and these two thoughts comprise my feelings about it.

Part of my technique as a critic is to write a review so that it reflects the look, the feel, the *cant* of a play and its production —not merely in what I say but how I say it: the kinds of words, the lengths of sentences, the tempo, the sounds, and so on. Jean Kerr's *Poor Richard* did not succeed at what it was trying to do, but it was written in a careful, intelligent way reflecting a particular style of education-sophistication (that includes things like wit, common sense, and so on). Also, of course, Mrs. Kerr is married to the critic Walter Kerr, and though my acquaintance with them is by no means close enough to endanger objectivity, that point of reference did exist.

These various matters affected the review. The style of writing was meant to reflect Mrs. Kerr's style. The line "all work and no play" is her kind of *line*. "The rake has all the lines" is an obvious play on her book title *The Snake Has All the Lines*. The phrase "situation drama of an act" is a mild parody of Mr. Kerr's reviewing style, and "nudging our partners with our elbows" refers to a silly trade stir, some years ago, accusing Mr. Kerr of being influenced by his wife's elbow nudges. (Intracritic references have no relevance to a play, but reality demands that you admit knowing the playwright's relationship to a colleague. This was my own way of admitting it.)

Certainly, I mean to articulate my opinion (and believe I do), but there is more to writing than the specific meanings of specific words. As it is, words are overused and for every dozen only one or two ever count or mean anything. On the other hand, the pace, the tone, the rhythm, of a review can put the reader in just the mood of a production—sometimes more specifically than can descriptive prose—and I believe my review of *Poor Richard* achieved this purpose.

James Goldman's *The Lion in Winter* presented me with a critical crisis. I have always depended on having a definite reaction to a play and am very lucky as a critic to have things work out that way. Lucky if for no other reason than that I seldom have to write a qualified review, which is the kind that frustrates many readers. I have no interest in the reader who only wants to know whether a production is "good" or "bad," and most people think that "criticism" equals "opinion" and that "opinion" equals "liking" something or not. But almost anybody wants a piece of criticism to be an appraisal of value concluding in some assessment (I use accounting terms to emphasize the commercial nature of such criticism and I hope I didn't have to spell that out).

In the case of *The Lion in Winter*—and it is the only case I recall—I was rather frightened to find, as I rushed from the theater toward my deadline, that *I really didn't know whether I liked it or not.* Didn't know *what* I thought of it or *how* I felt about it. Naturally, the harder you try to think of what you *thought* of something, the more uncertain you grow. I finally realized that my reaction to *The Lion in Winter* was uncertainty itself. A real enough reaction. But I thought of that too late. The review as printed (and by what was never said) is an example of ultimate qualification.

One of a critic's most difficult problems is sorting out the differences between a director's work and a playwright's. It is an important responsibility, especially when a good script has been spoiled by a bad director or when a director has camouflaged weak writing with creative production.

Abe Burrows' staging of the comedy *Forty Carats* made this responsibility unusually easy to fulfill and yet strange because the direction distorted a weak script. It also made the production one of the most peculiar I have ever seen. It perfectly demonstrated the techniques by which a director can twist a script so that, though the dialogue is the playwright's, the play, in effect, is not.

Still another problem in reviewing is the *pan*. Good criticism has traditionally been associated with nasty criticism (generally called "acerbic"). Elegance, presumably the heritage of critical writing, has always been a baroque glibness of which this acidity was an essential part. Critics today (especially beginners, provincials and professional bad boys) still aspire to such writing, and too many readers enjoy it, identifying it with intellectualism. Such writing is archaic, ornate, egotistical, and a camp of "clever." While perhaps apt (though I even doubt that) when critics like George Jean Nathan and Alexander Woollcott were practicing, today it seems fourth-rate duplication of relics. Those who try their hands at it are invariably clumsy and unoriginal, harping on key words like "banal," "pretentious," "tedious," and clichés like "As————as it is————."

But then, a New York critic is presented with an avalanche of inadequate productions, most of them atrocious and many tantamount to sieges on the idea of theater. If they must be reviewed (as they must if one is a daily critic), why not with humor?

Ironically, the productions that most deserve condemnation least deserve the effort of wit (and I wonder whether wit is worth the effort). That is, the target isn't worth the ammunition. Another point: Why have fun at the expense of even a bad production? Finally, masturbatory clever-nasty review is an ego device, designed to make the critic look good, which is not merely vain but inappropriate and silly. The critic's responsibility, presumably, is the consideration of theatrical productions and not a demonstration of his personality. Masturbation is just a lower form of breast-beating.

I am including my review of *Fire* to exemplify my style of *panning*. I'd like to add that it is much more difficult to praise, and doubly so to qualify.

The final problem demonstrated is that of objectivity when confronted by a person with whom you are personally involved. A critic is bound to develop friendships with people in the theater—people whom he must review. Though these people always say they expect you to be objective, they are not so forthright after the fact. I have lost a number of friends because of honest opinion.

My first confrontation with such a problem led me down the path of dishonesty for the only time in my career as a critic: rather than denigrate it, I ignored the performance of an old college friend. He didn't speak to me for years, and even now can only manage a hello or good-bye (mostly good-bye). Since then, I have managed to entirely forget knowing someone when I am reviewing him, but though that's good for criticism it sometimes makes you wonder what sort of human being you are to coldly reject the work of a person whose home you visited only a week earlier.

Though not so personal, the same problem occurs when reviewing a work whose point of view means a great deal to you, either positively or negatively. The play *MacBird* concerned things about which I felt very strongly: the war in Vietnam and the Lyndon Johnson administration. My attitudes weren't as extreme as the author's, but then she was writing parody, and parody must be exaggerated (one of the play's problems was confusing exaggeration with overstatement). One is naturally inclined toward plays with which one agrees and disinclined toward plays with which one disagrees. Theoretically, it's possible to admire a play whose attitude you resent just as it's possible to like a play whose style is not your own (*The Subject Was Roses*, for example). I wonder. In any case, *MacBird* represents the problem of intellectual objectivity.

After the Fall (*January 24, 1964*)

Arthur Miller cut up his brains last night looking for an answer—an answer to the confusion of life—for himself and for all of man. That is important.

It is important because it was his *brain* he cut up and not his "heart." It is important because he came out of the confusion with only a less indefinite uncertainty. And it is important because when he *did* come out it was not with despair but with a leniency toward himself and a forgiveness for all of us.

Mr. Miller's harrowing look into his own insides happened last night at the ANTA-Washington Square Theatre, where his play *After the Fall* opened. And if anybody there was uncomfortable about being present at so calculated a self-surgery, it was more the chill of being *forced* to look at something really naked than it was the more shallow feeling of embarrassment.

After the Fall is a confession. A man called Quentin comes forward to tell about his life—the audience represents perhaps a friend, or a psychiatrist, or God, or probably just the audience—mankind. And all of Quentin's life that was concerned with his essential being is told—that is, everything up until the present, when he is about to marry. As Mr. Miller says, "The action of the play takes place in the mind, thought and memory of Quentin, a contemporary man."

Quentin's story seems to be Arthur Miller's story. At least, the facts of Mr. Miller's life that have been publicized are there and it must be assumed that the rest of it is also factual. And once you accept the confession as being Mr. Miller's own, you can forget it and take it on a universal basis.

There are three wives—the first is a middle-class woman offering him middle-class accusations (Why don't you talk to me? Where were you all night?). The second is Marilyn Monroe—a neurotic child who needs more love than anyone can provide and is hell-bent on self-destruction. The third is a German archaeologist, forgiving even the Nazis their murders. (A piece of a concentration camp hangs high over the stage—a symbol of forgiveness.)

The three wives are three roads that Quentin has tried in search of an answer to the feeling of guilt that he cannot escape. With the first wife he sought justification through thought;

with the second through love; with the third through forgiveness.

Wandering over these hazy roads that have so far proved misguiding is Quentin's past. His problems with investigating committees; his relationships with friends who are weak, who betray, who always need. His materialistic mother, wanting "success" for him; his father, always crying, "Where's he going? I need him—where are you?" His brother telling him "the family's behind you."

And perhaps the major revelation, the core of the play really, is Quentin's recognition that he has been spending his life judging people and now he must judge himself. Or else mankind—we, the audience—must judge him. That is why he has come. The judge is now on trial.

There is much, much more to this staggering drama—and some of it is confused. But if any one of us dared to sit in a bright light and examine his life—has he lied, has he been hypocritical, has he said he loved when he really hated? Who would not dare to admit to confusion? Mr. Miller has had the frightening bravery to spill that confusion out—to admit to it and be not nihilistic but driven to look for a positive relationship with life.

Jason Robards, Jr., as Quentin, handles the enormous central role magnificently—a strike at the heart with a fist (the Jewish self-punishment on Yom Kippur); beginning a lighthearted race only to, instead, crumble—and a staccato delivery that can only be the voice of a man speaking to himself [as well as, it turned out, the start of a ruinous acting mannerism]— "Why do I feel like an accomplice? Why is the world so treacherous? Is it altogether good to be not guilty for what *another* does?"

Mariclare Costello and Salome Jens are excellent as the first and third wives, and Barbara Loden is superb as the second, wanting limitless love at a time when Quentin thinks limitless love is the answer to life (only to find himself incapable of giving it and her insatiable). The remainder of the cast is superb, aided to an incalculable degree by the timeless tension of Elia Kazan's direction.

This is a difficult play to see, and it is not easy to take all at once. But it is a brilliant work, brilliantly executed.

Poor Richard (December 3, 1964)

There is a rare intelligence afoot in *Poor Richard* and with it an uncommon sense of language, for the Broadway stage or anywhere. But the new Jean Kerr comedy that opened last night at the Helen Hayes is meant to be funny, and though it is crafty about it, it is all work and no play.

It is a handsomely polished piece of theatrical craftwork that has had its every word, its every line, written, rewritten, and thrown away to be substituted with another line, written, rewritten, and so on. Such supreme care is a depressing waste when, no matter how smooth the surface, the table won't stand.

It is about a poet who has written a collection in memory of a wife he loved and didn't know it. It takes him three acts to find out, as well as to fall in love with the pert little ingenue who promised she would marry him after the curtain had barely risen.

There are a number of good things about this plot as well as a number of bad. It is good because it is about poetry, and Mrs. Kerr is about poetry. She loves the English language truly and treats it as if she does—by using it well. It is good because it has a leading character who would believably be both articulate and witty. And it is good because its adult situation is in keeping with Mrs. Kerr's very adult mind.

It is bad because so little is happening that the entire second act could be chopped out if it weren't for a couple of facts that it provides for the story (the facts are incorporated in a single character—the poet's sister-in-law—who has that weird look of being a theatrical mechanism). It is bad because it is all so easily mockable by the playwright's cold, realistic, all-mocking eye.

Nevertheless, good and bad, it would serve well enough as a vehicle for comedy if it weren't that Mrs. Kerr does not believe in filling the tank, preferring to get three dollars' worth, let it run out, and then get some more. What happens is that the jokes come in bundles, good bundles, frequently funny bundles, bundles that are too carefully wrapped perhaps, but most of all, just bundles. And between them is empty space, and if that second act must pop up again, it is an entire empty space in itself—a situation drama of an act that is neither terribly interesting nor terribly uninteresting.

The good lines are mostly given to the poet, a marvelously talented young man who is going to pot (see title). He is a charming devil, sought after by womankind. With a supporting cast to play straight man, he is in a setup situation. The rake has all the lines. "Your mind is all made up—like a roomette on the Pennsylvania." "I have not forgotten you—it would take at least ten minutes to do that." "She has gone and tampered with what used to be a breathtaking ignorance."

Alan Bates plays the role wonderfully and is especially impressive despite the stiff competition given by a really first-rate cast. Mr. Bates can fumble in his cardigan pocket for an address book as if he really didn't know it was there. He can rattle off his wisecracks and wittier lines so naturally it almost disguises the fact that they really aren't spoken lines but written ones. He has all the physical grace the man would have without being stagy, and if it weren't that Mrs. Kerr avoids sex humor as if it were syphilis, you would think he had a good sense of it.

Gene Hackman is the good-guy-no-girl, the decent editor who loves the ingenue—an annoyingly stock role. Mr. Hackman seems to be the only extant actor who can play a funny straight man. Saddled with a full-blown stand-up comedy routine on being average ("I'm the guy that———" jokes), he survived to be a tremendous asset to the play.

Joanna Pettet gets thrown a line or two as the determined young girl, but these are mostly contrivances that are intended to strike a jab of Truth—"Marriage is the only place you can say, 'Move over, my arm's asleep.'" Even though we aren't nudging our partners with our elbows, she acts as if we are. Miss Pettet is a fine actress.

But she and *Poor Richard* have the ring of the typewriter bell, right down to the careful mechanical tendernesses about little girls in the park. Too careful to be funny, too slim to be pointed, too uninteresting to be interesting, it is a bad good comedy.

The Lion in Winter *(March 4, 1966)*

The Lion in Winter is a play that is trying very hard to be of quality—to be formal and fine; perhaps it is trying too hard and perhaps its author, James Goldman, was not quite up to it. Or perhaps, and more likely, one does not write a formal and fine play by simply trying to. Mr. Goldman's play, which opened last night at the Ambassador Theatre, has a quality that is artificial, a finesse that is self-conscious and inconsistent. Every once in a while there is a patch of cotton in its damask.

That is not to say that *The Lion in Winter* is a bad play or that it is badly written. In fact, it is a very interesting play, very well written and written by an author with a genuine talent for language. But it can never really become what it is aching to become because Goldman is too intent on keeping the language, keeping the manner. He cannot resist the impulse for what he fancies is a good line, even when it is inconsistent with tone or with what has happened before. And he cannot help but write a family drama, even when he is determined to write a historical play.

The trappings of classicism are in abundance—the play is set in twelfth-century France, at the castle of King Henry II of England. There, at Christmastime, he is entertaining his queen (except for such occasions, for the past ten years she has been locked in a tower).

He is also enjoying his beautiful twenty-three-year-old mistress, his junior by twenty-seven years, and is trying to break the news to his three sons that he will name the youngest as heir. The play is concerned with the conflict between the king and the queen over this selection, since the eldest is her favorite.

But while the guise of the play is the inner, personal relationships that spur the direction of history, its identity really lies in the husband-wife conflict. In fact, *The Lion in Winter* bears an uncomfortably close relationship to Edward Albee's battling lovers of *Who's Afraid of Virginia Woolf?*

There is no mention of the Albee play in Mr. Goldman's, anachronism forbidding, but there is mention of its other parents, *King Lear* among others, as if the acknowledgments would forfend any accusation of being derivative. No such luck, for whether or not Goldman mentioned *Lear,* that influence exists too. There is, after all, a king who is planning to give up his kingdom. There are, after all, three possible heirs, two of whom are greedy. Unlike Lear's Cordelia, Henry's John does not truly love him, but in a sense that makes the play even *more* derivative, as if Goldman set out to see what would have happened to *Lear* if all *three* daughters were no good.

I use the term "no good" because it is such colloquialisms that keep creeping into the play's determined (and generally successful) rhetoric. Goldman can write a good, literate crack like, "She smiled to excess but she chewed with real distinction," but he cannot resist the crass ("Like a democratic drawbridge going down for everyone").

The playwright's inability to resist temptation extends to his very construction. The queen, for example, seems in and out of love with her king, and although this is part of her carefully conceived character it seems as often because of the author's inspiration for a line here, and a contrary one for a line there. While many of these conversational turns were indeed fairly inspired, they should not all have been used. The logical development of a plot cannot be undermined by an author's weakness for the bright line.

The production is designed as if it were as classic as everyone had intended. Will Steven Armstrong's sets revolve handsomely and ingeniously to reveal various chambers in various moods, and his costumes are elegant. Noel Willman directed everything in the smooth, gliding manner that typifies high drama. And the performances he drew from his cast made it seem as if *The Lion in Winter* were impeccable. This whole business of a classic look is artificial, of course, but it sometimes works, and with the magnificent Rosemary Harris making the queen a fascinating, bitchy, desperate, abandoned woman, it occasionally made things seem as if they were what Goldman wanted to think they were. Unfortunately, Miss Harris also showed Robert Preston up for the personality actor he is. Mr. Preston's professionalism, which is fine for the ordinary play, is lost in its reliance on personality when it comes to serious real acting. Like Goldman's play, it is the modern masquerading as the antique. *The Lion in Winter* has many qualities, but at its heart it is in disguise and I think it knows it.

MacBird (*February 23, 1967*)

MacBird, like most collegiate political satires, is so carried away with its own point of view, and so impressed with its own nerve in taking it, that it can tolerate no restraint or discipline. The play, overlong, overdone, its humor outgrown and its attitude muddled, opened last night at the Village Gate.

The opening had been long anticipated. Barbara Garson's comic treatment of *Macbeth* was a surprise paperback best seller. Its attack on President Johnson, personally and politically, had been delightedly embraced by those unhappy with the present administration. But it is not a professionally written play, and its basic identity is crudely cartooned, fitted to move along broad, outline-thinking patterns.

MacBird means to parallel *Macbeth,* substituting characters in the Kennedy-Johnson history. Duncan, King of Scotland, is John Ken O'Dune (Kennedy); Duncan's sons are now Robert and Ted Kennedy; Macbeth and Lady Macbeth, of course, are MacBird and Lady MacBird.

Miss Garson's other characters could not be fitted into *Macbeth* so easily, and so they were simply inserted: the Egg of Head (Adlai Stevenson), the Wayne of Morse, the Earl of Warren, and so on. Some of the other characters in the printed version have been deleted in this production, those representing Arthur Goldberg and Robert McNamara in particular, apparently because Miss Garson's treatment of them was so overdrawn as to verge not so much on the libelous as the ridiculous. I think, though, that considering the play's sloppy attitude toward both truth and interpretation, the deletions were gratuitous.

The analogy with *Macbeth* is taken only so far, just through Act One, really. For that period, Miss Garson manages to apply the play's general plot quite neatly to the Kennedy election, the choice of Mr. Johnson for the Vice Presidential candidacy, and his itch for greater power after the election. Many of the speeches are acceptably paraphrased, and the writing is a fair enough approximation of the Shakespearean style.

As the parallel with that first act progresses, Miss Garson reveals a working knowledge of *Macbeth.* Most of her script is in either blank verse or rhymed couplets, and whatever ability this required, she possessed.

However, the shadowing of the *Macbeth* plot could be taken only so far, and insistent on its own point, *MacBird* had to abandon the story for its own purposes. The Lady Bird-Lady Macbeth parallel is almost nonexistent. There is a childish re-wording of well-known Shakespearean catchlines ("There's something rotten in the state of Texas," and so on).

As for the play's treatment of Johnson, it embarrasses the cause of anybody truly concerned about the current administration. Whether or not Miss Garson thinks that Johnson actually plotted the murder of President Kennedy, her play says so. Whether or not she thinks that Lady Bird pushed for this, her play says so. Her treatment of the other characters is not so wild-eyed (Senator Morse is a red-flanneled Don Quixote, Adlai Stevenson is a sellout), and so who knows just how much of this she meant to suggest and how much was exaggeration for the sake of a point? It doesn't matter much, since this kind of political satire is predictably excessive.

Director Roy Levine began the evening with a great deal of energy and theatrical force, making much more of the production than was actually in the script. He placed a working emphasis on strong speech, lighting, and movement. But his invention dribbled out midway through the first act, and except for a halfhearted processional at the second act's start it never appeared again.

Stacy Keach gave a rather good physical impression of Johnson, and his vocal imitation was briefly amusing in the recitation of Elizabethan cadences. Mr. Keach went about his work with force, but his mockery was not even up to the points made by comedians who work with the Johnson line. William Devane so incredibly resembled Bobby Kennedy that it was difficult to believe it was not the Senator himself. Moreover, Mr. Devane never stopped his act, beautifully flashing the Bobby smile that suggests a myriad of hidden mental tickings. The other actors were sure and disciplined, and Mr. Levine often moved them definitely across the Gate's big stage. Unfortunately, he made a dreadful error in trying to use humor against a background of the Kennedy funeral drumbeats. Those rolling drums are much too familiar, much too awful, to be used this way.

But even more unfortunately, the legitimate and important political complaints of the adult intellectual community are dealt a real blow by the ludicrous attitudes taken by *MacBird*, and Johnson's position is only strengthened when the criticism of him is so absurd. *MacBird* is as trying politically as it is theatrically.

Forty Carats (*December 27, 1968*)

The attitude of *Forty Carats* is so tacky, the writing of it is so distorted, and the direction of it is so subversive that it doesn't even seem worth being labeled the repellent thing it really is. Billed as a comedy, the thing that opened last night at the Morosco Theatre is more an architect's rendering than it is a play, and any resemblance between it and either the theater or reality is neither coincidental nor desirable.

It is difficult to tell just who is responsible for what. Its source is a French play by Pierre Barillet and Jean-Pierre Gredy. Jay Presson Allen adapted it, Abe Burrows directed it, and the number of cooks is reflected in the number of broths, because this isn't a single play but several, each having a different point of view, mashed into a genuinely irritating, unintended reflection of a genuinely irritating way of life.

The story is weird considering that somebody must have thought it amusing at one time. A forty-year-old career woman meets a twenty-two-year-old boy on a Greek island and they have an affair. She returns to New York to find him dating her seventeen-year-old daughter. The flame rekindles and he wants to marry her. The daughter, meanwhile, falls in love with a forty-five-year-old man and they want to marry. One of the mother's ex-husbands is still around, is still (presumably) charming, is still in love. But the marriages proceed and that is the play.

Now if you think that is bewildering as the basis for a comedy, I submit the play's attitude as a topper. As Mr. Burrows has directed it, these autumn-spring marriages are foolish. His reason is that young people are detestable—they go to noisy places like the Electric Circus, they wear silly mod clothes, and they are altogether unfeeling, unsophisticated, and unworthy of true love. But what are *his* people? They are the golf-club, suede-jacket, nightclub people—men's cardigan sweaters with balloon sleeves. The crummy, plastic, show-business mentality with its hideous, greeting-card morality and sequin values. That, my dear, is the credo behind this play, only I'm not sure that anyone but Mr. Burrows knew it.

Because the play is not entirely written that way. Digging down into its layers of plastic, you find a guess who's coming to dinner of mixed generations. There is even a big speech about conformity ("Who are these people whose opinions mean so much to you?"). But when you surface, the play doesn't really approve of that at all. The young people are staged as little beasts, the old ones who want to marry them as foolish. Only the ex-husband is admired by this production, and aptly enough, he is the only one in a three-piece suit (just as aptly, his three-piece suit has no cuffs on the trousers, marking the guy —and the production—as strictly from Miami Beach).

I think it a devastating irony that this three-piece man is played by Murray Hamilton, who had exactly the same role in *The Graduate*. If you will remember, there was a *Mister* Robinson, he was it, and the character was the film's villain, representing just the cheapness, the motel values that in this play the character champions. In short, *Forty Carats* stands for all that is ugly and fraudulent and even sick in this country.

As I said, I don't think that its authors meant this, and I doubt they were even aware of it until Burrows took over. Not that they had much of a play anyhow. Mrs. Allen didn't even seem to be writing a comedy, her dialogue is so serious, but as a play this one has exactly the defect of her earlier *Prime of Miss Jean Brodie*. It is hopelessly episodic, running about 30 lines to a blackout, each of those blackouts preceded by a dumb curtain line ("Would you like to move a little further out of town? Like Cleveland," or "And you're definitely not to come up to my apartment," followed by, "We'll talk about it at your place"). There are also bewildering snatches of dialogue ("I can provide you with every luxury you've ever dreamed of. Plus many more you've never heard of"). Moreover, though female dialogue is natural, the male is plasticene.

What all of this adds up to is canned life—canned seductions, canned marriages, canned theater—a representation of the Broadway Comedy that could well be mounted on fake walnut. Should be. With the canned audience for which it is made.

Because of the extraordinary confusion of the play's intentions, the cast was hard-bound to act anything at all, which compounded some real incompetence. Marco St. John and Gretchen Corbett (who played the youngsters) were obviously fouled up by the production's sheer dislike of them, but did little to make one disagree with that. Mr. St. John could not unglue his arms from his sides, and Miss Corbett seemed desperately intent on making sure her miniskirts didn't reveal her panties. Julie Harris tried very hard, in a Method way, to understand the motivations of the mother, which would have been a neat trick considering the play's refusal to make her simply in love. Miss Harris also tried very hard, in a Method way, to play comedy, and like all Method actors, failed because of sheer overseriousness. Oddly—really not so oddly—only Mr. Hamilton succeeded. His slickly, hard-nosedly, and misguidedly moral ex-husband came off as just the creep that is supposed to be a hero in the swimming-pool life of this play's mentality. What made his role bizarre was the play's hurtling toward a re-marriage, when instead, Hippolytus and Electra do indeed marry their Phaedra and Agamemnon. At that point, the whole business turns just weird. Not as weird, though, as it is unfunny and cheap and plain ugly.

Fire! *(January 29, 1969)*

Fire! is that lowest of theatrical lives, the philosophical alle-gory, and it may very well be at the bottom of the heap. The John Roc play that opened last night at the Longacre Theatre has a set fit for an *Aïda* tomb scene and a script that should be buried there.

Mr. Rock's play is a script in the worse sense. It is all writing. No theater, no characters, no action. And the writing flows like a backward toilet, regurgitating its stuff until the lid pops. Pur-ple prose? Enough to keep a half-dozen Holy Rollers burning away with room left for a couple of national anthems. Mr. Roc likes to use words like "cerebellum" and "subjunctive," but only when he is at a loss for flatulating paragraphs. "You talk about blood. There are other juices—sperm and spittle. Some say they're both the same." I would really like to know who says that. Or, "What is the end of reason—cant or incantation?" Cant or incantation?

There is a definite feeling in this play that its author has no idea what his words mean. If the play is confusing, it is ob-viously because there is no self-comprehension—of words, of sentences, of plot. Only of point, and that point could not be more ridiculous: having buried God, men are throwing them-selves on the funeral pyre, burning themselves up in amoral, pragmatic, scientific lovelessness. Whenever I hear "man" or "mankind," I know it's time to put down the magazine and turn on some music.

Fire! is set, naturally enough, in limbo. A group of people (read that as "mankind") have gathered there for the purpose of—well, for the purpose of being in this play. They are supposed to represent different aspects of men, but the author hasn't heard of the word "characters."

Anyhow, only two of them count. The hero, who still believes in God and looks reverently into a long spotlight to prove it. And the villain, who has just escaped from a kiddie television series with his beard, his boots, and his wrist strap. This bad guy is trying to get everyone to vote for "fire," that being the furnace of our own invention. You bet, it really is a hellfire and damnation play, complete with a trapdoor down which a fag-devil descends. No kidding.

I am actually telescoping the action, but if the telescope were shut we'd all get an eyeful of, as one of the characters say, "pus and putrefication." In any case, the first-act climax has the good guy flat on his back, being either castrated or lobotomized by what looked like a rat (?) of striking versatility. Come the second act and he is a vegetable, while poor old wrist strap is still trying to get the poor bugger to say "fire" (there's a fetish for you). Much to my relief, the dreaded word was finally uttered, allowing the electronic music to resume, the lights to darken, and the exit doors to let in some air.

In summer camp there used to be an expression: "gliffitz." It was defined as a five-pound-capacity manure bag stuffed with ten pounds' worth. I never could quite understand it until last night. Mr. Roc has a strange capacity for finding words (like "ignominy") that have no right-sounding pronunciation, and his dialogue follows that lead. Alliteration, the most embarrassing of all figures of speech, drizzles steadily (from "quake and quavered" to "remainders, remnants, and residues"), accompanying its partner, the epigram ("The master of us all is masturbation"). The humor is restricted to putting down the fag, at least the conscious humor.

Charles Werner Moore stated it all as a combination of hysteria and moving statues, so that everyone stood still while screaming. Some of the acting was so atrocious that it entered the heady realm of camp. Peter MacLean, for example, played the bad guy jumping up and down as if about to shout "Shazam" (at which point, at least, he might have lost his Boston *a*). On the other hand, Rene Auberjonois—one of the best actors in America—tried to apologize for his dialogue with some very pretty, if irrelevant, bodywork. Give him credit for not betraying embarrassment. And the same can be said for Carolyn Coates as a character entirely devoid of purpose.

Is *Fire!* a disaster or just a theater heartburn? Both, but more crucially, it exemplifies the appalling naïveté, the intellectual and artistic vulgarity, that has given Broadway drama its reputation as the trough of American culture.

Off-Off Broadway

Six from La Mama (*April 12, 1966*)

On Second Avenue at St. Mark's Place there is an umarked door that opens into a couple of flights of stairs that are filled, on almost any night, with gabby, eager theatergoers wearing anything from levis and leather jackets to Mamaroneck uniforms. They are waiting to enter a long room filled with tiny tables. It has a stage at one end, and upon that stage, for not a very long time, have been appearing new plays, one each week, by new playwrights. Ellen Stewart runs this place on something less than a shoestring and something more than dedication, collecting one-dollar dues from each audience member because the theater is a club—The La Mama Experimental Theatre Club—and it is one of the major reasons for the booming off-off Broadway movement dedicated to experimental plays.

Last night producers Theodore Mann and Paul Libin brought six of the plays produced at Miss Stewart's theater up one step to off-Broadway's Martinique Theatre. It seems likely that the step will not be a good one for Miss Stewart and her playwrights.

The reason it will not be good is that her theater was honestly designed for experimental plays—the playwrights were young, only feeling their way, and admittedly unsure of themselves; the directors and actors were not much more experienced; the productions, physically and structurally, were not presented as professional. It was (and remains), in a very true and constructive sense, a workshop where young theater people could begin to build the theater of tomorrow. It was a place dedicated by Miss Stewart to the abstract plays that are surely going to spur the new theater.

When these plays are moved to off-Broadway, they are set into a professional arena for which they were never intended. There they must be judged by professional standards that were never sought. By professional standards, they represent beginner work by playwrights talented to varying degrees, one of them with a possibly shining future.

The first, William Hoffman's *Thank You, Miss Victoria,* suffers from the most common elementary playwriting problem: the inability to write more than one character. It is about a decadent young man who is given a functionless executive position in his father's business. A brittle hipster, he seems furiously poised, and contemptuous of women. It is because they are weak. He is revealed as a pathetic sexual masochist when he answers a female sadist's personal ad in a girlie magazine. Michael Warren Powell is often very funny in a style closely modeled on Lenny Bruce, which is helpful since Hoffman's lines for him are modeled on the Bruce style.

The second play is by far the most original and exciting, an exercise by Lanford Wilson in stage methods, using sound patterns, movement, intertwining time and song to paint a picture of a hillbilly town, its people and its rhythm. In a sense, it is a modern *Our Town* or *Under Milk Wood,* although without the hokeyness of the former and with far greater theater sense than the latter (which was originally written for radio).

It finds loved life in a dramatic collage of back porches, cars, everywhere.

To be truthful, it is frequently unintelligible, and intentionally so, in its concentration on feeling and the beat of human conversation; but a play need not necessarily be intelligible on a literal level. The problem with *This Is the Rill Speaking* is that it is often unintelligible on a dramatic level. That is, almost as often as not you cannot really *feel* it. Therefore, it is precisely the kind of play that should be performed in experimental theater. Precisely the kind of play that should *not* be performed as a finished work.

The final play on the first evening's bill (three more will open tonight) is Leonard Melfi's *Birdbath*. This is the most conventional of the three, a realistic play about a poet type who works as a cashier in a greasy spoon and takes home the pathetically shy waitress to find her an oppressed and tortured soul. Its occasional moments of interest are not helped much by Tom O'Horgan's sloppy direction which managed to muffle the bizarre denouement by having the girl speak the lines incomprehensibly. On the other hand, his staging of the complex Wilson play was excellent.

The company itself is generally superb—proof of the importance of repertory performance. The five young actors in this troupe play major and minor roles in each of the plays and are far ahead of most of their contemporaries in their craft. Mari-Claire Charba particularly in *The Rill* and *Birdbath* showed herself to be an actress capable of really becoming somebody else—and what else is acting all about?

But their work is being unfairly exposed to a test it was never meant for, and La Mama's important role will be severely hampered by the denial to it of the freedom of experimental theater.

About *America Hurrah* (*November 11, 1966*)

There is an excitement to an original, consummated production like *America Hurrah* that makes all the drudge nights, all the insipid musicals, all the old-fashioned Irish melodramas, all the television comedies, well worth the wading through. Just when you are almost ready to forget what thrills the theater can cause—what points it can make and what effects it can produce —a real playwright with a real director and real actors will come up with real theater.

Jean-Claude van Itallie's plays are one-acters and small in form. But they are not small in conception. They are written by a playwright who knows how to handle a stageful of people —how to write for them and how to juggle them. They are written by a playwright who, unlike too many newcomers, has fully polished his writing technique. But in addition to being a true writer, Van Itallie is aware of the newest uses of the stage. Refusing to restrict his work to words, phrases, sentences pursuing one plot line or another, he works in terms of rhythms, poetry, and music; in terms of movement and choreography; in terms of sound and color and noise. The result is a play of today's theater.

I mean "today's theater" if the theater were as up to date as popular music or the movies. Since our theater is still trapped by a style created thirty years ago, *America Hurrah* might almost seem far ahead of its time. It refuses to sit still before a realistic box set and tell a simple story. It wants to *move,* and it does.

The first play begins with a vicious impersonation of personnel methods practiced by modern business. As is to be the playwright's method throughout the evening, there is no broad satirizing of the impersonality or the cold and presumptuous questioning of today's job interviewers. The language is realistic, just as the other plays' attacks on television mentalities (both the program and the programmers) and the motel phenomenon (both the owners and the customers) treat the subjects exactly as they are. But in the *use* of this accurate dialogue, Van Itallie employs overlap, tempo, and all stage tools to create living theater creatures that make important statements about things we all may see but have not seen with a special perspective.

The result is theater at its giddiest and most serious. Theater that uses strange plastic masks, vocal-choral effects, dance shapes, musical rhythms, giant dolls, stark and inventive sets. Theater that sets a madly comic top to spinning, only to lash through with nasty truths about anything from American miliary tactics in Vietnam to unfriendly pedestrians on the city streets.

A playwright such as Van Itallie, and plays like his, could never possibly originate in our reactionary Broadway theater, or even perhaps off-Broadway. His work would never be understood by the backward minds that reign there. Moreover, the kind of staging that encouraged his style of writing is not Broadway's. It is the staging that is developing in America *despite* the general ignorance, and only because young, creative people care enough about the theater to work at new things at the price of income and recognition.

America Hurrah and its author came out of Open Theatre, a shoestring group of enthusiastic directors, writers, and actors who were justifiably disgusted with the idiotic standards of mainstream New York theater. Willing to work for no salary on theater that excited them, they sacrificed the ordinary chorus, touring, and *wow-even-Broadway* work that interest most uninspired theater people.

Open Theatre first produced *America Hurrah* at Ellen Stewart's Café La Mama, although in somewhat different form.

La Mama is an experimental theater club that lends its facilities to playwrights in need of a staging, even if their plays are unpolished. It gives them a chance to see their work in a theater and before an audience. Miss Stewart's only stipulation is that they be dealing in modern theater modes.

The opportunity for a playwright with the talent of Van Itallie to work with so unusually knowing and advanced a director-teacher as Open Theatre's Joseph Chaikin is one he could never find in a graduate school, an ordinary drama studio, or anywhere. But ironically, as La Mama's work with Van Itallie was paying off Sunday night at the Pocket Theatre, Miss Stewart was preparing to go before the Actors Equity Board of Governors to defend the very existence of her operation.

Equity's regulations require any theater that charges admissions to pay its actors off-Broadway scale. La Mama charges a one-dollar fee, which does not even cover its basic costs.

It is perfectly arguable that actors should not be allowed to work for sub-Equity salaries. There are too many stagestruck youngsters willing to do anything to get into the theater, and too many unscrupulous producers ready to take advantage of them (the kickback and alias are still very much in practice). But blanket regulations are as stupid as the automated personnel procedures which Van Itallie bitterly attacks in his play. La Mama is not a hustling, penny-ante music tent. It is a serious and terribly important place dedicated to keeping our dying theater alive by allowing some stage for the young, the innovating, the just-beginning. The fact that something so polished and electric as *America Hurrah* was helped by it should be proof enough of its value.

Exactly why the big foundations have concentrated on institutionalized resident theaters to the exclusion of La Mama has always eluded me. While waiting for their—or somebody's—help [Rockefeller and Ford Foundation help came a few years later], Miss Stewart's idealistic creation must not be ended by blind policies. She and her playwrights need professionals. If

Equity commits this artistic murder it will lose any right to consider itself a force for the theater's benefit.

Public Privacy (*December 8, 1967*)

The problem of whether or not to review off-off Broadway productions is a sticky one. The whole purpose and value of off-off Broadway lies in its laboratory, amateur status as a place for learning how to fly, free from commercial pressures and make-or-break criticism. Nobody expects polished work and nobody pays polished work prices. A critic can very easily harm this life-giving periphery of our sterile theater by publicly reviewing such in-progress work.

But the lure of publicity is almost irresistible, and even more irresistible is the need to be judged. When any one of us does anything, we want somebody to say what he thought of it— "how he liked my stuff." It is a reasonable enough desire.

In the final analysis, a critic must decide for himself just which off-off Broadway productions should be written about. There are two that I would like to mention because they represent a variety of styles that makes our professional stage seem even more monotonous than it is. We tend to think that variety means musicals, comedies, or dramas, but as a matter of fact this isn't variety at all. Most musicals look like most musicals, most comedies look like most comedies, most dramas look like most dramas. Off-off Broadway you will find a diversity that makes these categories almost meaningless. It is a diversity born of freedom—a diversity that is the proof of eagerness, invention, and productive creativity. It is life.

I saw two off-off Broadway productions last weekend, and each was very striking though they could hardly have been more different. The drama was relatively conventional. Called

Line, it was written by Israel Horovitz, a young playwright whose work I first saw at the Eugene O'Neill Foundation's Playwright Conference last summer. Mr. Horovitz is an extremely talented writer whose stylistic inclination runs to qualified surrealism and who makes personal points within a comedy context. He is quite funny, likes to play with the English language, and has a native sense of theater. He is also rather a bit more professional than off-off Broadway though still in need of finishing.

Line is a just slightly rough work, and if it were polished only the slightest bit more it would probably be an unqualified success. It runs an hour, is nearly always interesting, is frequently funny, always intelligent, and if its point were not so explicitly explored might be intellectually meaningful. The play is set on "a line," referring to both a line of people and the line behind which they are standing. We are never told what the line literally is for, nor does it make a difference. It could be for anything—people do wait on them. Metaphorically, it represents the accumulation of people hoping to outdo each other at whatever it is they want.

Mr. Horovitz created five distinct people to be waiting on his symbolic line, and just being able to create them proves his talent. What is theater if not a playwright's being able to conceive real, special, individual people? Not many playwrights can do it. Horovitz's people include a first-on-liner—the man who waits overnight and inevitably loses position anyhow. This man, a big, dumb beer drinker is immediately tricked out of first place by a young, psychotic composer who turns out to be the play's and the situation's moving force. Another person joining the line has a simpler, more mundane set of tactics. He believes in sticking with second place and being under the belly of the champion, where he can eventually kick him and get on top himself. The final two people on line are a married couple, the woman coarsely sexual and her husband a born loser. He is long since accustomed to being in last place, and her life is the story of a woman using sex to get ahead only to find that she is being used herself. The men just turn over and toss her out, and, in fact, all the men on line do.

The play, then, follows the metaphorical position-changing, almost everybody having a chance to be in front and then being tricked out of it, while the young man is spending what he hopes is the last day of his life, hoping to achieve first place as a composer by outstripping Mozart (who is in first musical place) in dying at an earlier age—that is, at younger than thirty-five.

It is a quite well-written play, although, as I said, not without flaws that make it slow going from time to time. And it was very well directed at the La Mama Experimental Theatre Club by James Hammerstein. The cast was excellent, entirely professional, and thank goodness Actors Equity has given special dispensation for such productions. John Cazale showed a special acting strength and intellect as the underdog. Even Mr. Horovitz, taking the composer's role in a last-minute emergency, turned in a fine job.

Line, a worthwhile and original play, was a million miles away from *Conquest of the Universe* playing only a ten-minute walk away at the Bouwerie Lane Theatre. Here was wild, free-for-all theater, so exuberant one could hardly keep from being carried away by it. Post-pop art, post-camp, and so thoroughly obscene that it was nonsexual, it turned out to be the absolutely modern equivalent of burlesque, vulgar in the best, most down-to-earth, basic-theater sense.

I won't even begin to describe the plot, which is a travesty of science-fiction cheapie movie spectaculars and entirely unfollowable. John Vaccaro's staging of Charles Ludlam's script allowed a freedom bordering on anarchy, and the stage activity capitalized on it. Imagine, if you will, a jester popping up among the vinyl Venetian-Martian-Saturnian trappings with jokes like, "The soldier turned up at his wife's bedside with his discharge in his hand." Or "guest star" Taylor Mead soaring out over the audience on a swing, decked out in green Mary Martin-Peter Pan tights, singing (more or less) "I've Got to Crow" straight-faced (more or less).

I won't tell you that *Conquest of the Universe* is professional theater, and to be honest its best quality is its antiprofessional attitude. Yet there is a theater intelligence behind it. More important, though, there is a theater excitement—a giddiness of spirit and a joy of invention that make its spontaneity worth almost any price of amateurism. As it happens, the production is well turned out and there is nothing chintzy about its looks. Expectably, the music is provided by a rock group in the best, most modern spirit, and expectably too, I suppose a good part of it drags. But the moments of hilarious obscenity and nearly reckless good nature are worth it all. The company is called The Playhouse of the Ridiculous, and the best thing about *Conquest* is just how entirely ridiculous it is—and knows it is. It's been so long since people could enjoy the ridiculous.

Futz! (*June 26, 1968*)

I tell you there is a theater life and it is being lived all around this town. *Line* and *Conquest of the Universe* were two good chances to talk about it and so I have.

At a performance of *Futz!* the other night at the Theatre de Lys, Sally Kirkland, the actress who plays the narrator, was indisposed. Instead of replacing her, the company played the role itself, but not in a simple, choral reading of the rather large part. Actors and actresses stepped in and out of the narrator role, making these lines part of the theater cantata that *Futz!* is. Their familiarity with the lines and with some very complex staging (both vocal and physical) made immediately obvious the versatility, the work-under-any-conditions and the self-

324

creation of The La Mama Theatre Company, which originated *Futz!* with its author, Rochelle Owens.

I first saw *Futz!* at La Mama more than a year ago, and it had been in the repertory who knows how long before then. At that time it was a complex theater organism, extremely moving and exciting. Since then, sheer performance has polished the production. But it has also been tinkered with to the extent that its artsy-craftsy elements—which were always considerable—have now become almost overwhelming. From time to time the incantation, the determined ritualism, the fancy dance movement become self-parodies. And still *Futz!* is a generally tremendous theater experience, winding a tricky way between compassion, good humor, idealism, and a condemnation of America's wicked moral hypocrisy.

There is a great deal to be learned in comparing the script with the presentation because, as is often La Mama's way, much is in the production that is not in the play. There is so much improvisation and group creation that a number of Miss Owens' implications have been obscured.

As a script, *Futz!* is verbal—there is only one stage direction and it reads: "Stage directions are either performed by the actors or verbalized by the narrator. This is left to the decision of the director." Everything else is either dialogue or descriptive material read by the narrator. "The decision of the director"—Tom O'Horgan—has been to fill the short (thirteen-scene) play with dance and mime and song and incantation.

If you eliminate these additions, you find a play filled with implication when it isn't wordplaying in simple derivation of James Joyce. The story is clear enough. Cyrus Futz is a farmer who is in love with Amanda, his pig. Marjorie Satz, the local tramp, is offended by Futz's preference for the sow and turns the town against him. Meanwhile, Oscar Loop—a religious fanatic and near-psychotic—rolls in the hay with Anne Fox and they discover Futz doing the same with Amanda. Oscar is frightened by this vision of "something very evil" and murders

Anne, for which he is subsequently executed. Meanwhile, Marjorie's brothers slaughter both Futz and Amanda.

The story is told in flashback and flashahead, pretty well under control, and except when O'Horgan makes the choral arrangements overcomplicated it is fairly easy to follow. The points it makes, though, are not so simple once you get beyond the basic one of an America enforcing a hypocritical morality and interfering with individual rights. The whole business of animal love runs deeply through the play—is animal love "good?"—we so often describe sex as best when it is at its raunchiest. Or is animal love "bestial"? Are we animals or aren't we? Just how much difference is there between a sow and a woman? And what is the difference between love for one and love for the other? Who is the pig, the incestuous tramp Marjorie or Amanda? Remember that in urban jargon, an unattractive girl is called a pig. In fact, Marjorie could be Amanda, both "pigs," both innocent.

But *Futz!* does not exist only for these points. Miss Owens is a spirited playwright, and when her spirits get high she will stop any line of thought to horse around with word jokes (many of them unfunny) and side comments when she finds her own stuff ridiculous. Very often you get the feeling that *Futz!* is a play out of control—alive but careening.

That is a feeling you never get about the production. It begins with a stunning film (new since last I saw the play) that makes both humans and other animals beautiful in the forest and then has one slaughtering the others.

Peace (*January 28, 1969*)

The original musicals produced at the Judson Poets' Theatre by Al Carmines (music) and Lawrence Kornfeld (direction) have worked out for themselves a tradition for whimsicality, raunchy naïveté, vaudeville, and a refreshing scorn for serious points. In applying this tradition to an adaptation of Aristophanes' *Peace,* however, Carmines and Kornfeld have missed a great chance. This rarely produced comedy has an astonishing relevance to today's peace (or war) movement, and without stretching anything, a real point might have been made while producing a delightful, forgotten play. But the Carmines-Kornfeld habit would not be broken, and *Peace* (at the Astor Place Theatre) might as well be any of their other musicals.

Except that it is better rehearsed and more handsomely (or at least slickly) produced. This professionalism has not destroyed the amateur quality that gives the Judson productions their spirit, nor has it helped sustain patience. As usual, the spontaneity, the broadness, the eager entertaining, and the intellectual farce are fun for a while and then the whole business begins to get on your nerves. The pity is that after having learned so much, Carmines and Kornfeld have learned so little. They still cannot sustain a work through a full evening, and the reason is simple—they refuse to plan it.

As *Peace* begins, there is an attempt to follow Aristophanes' plot line, even while having Hermes played as a screaming fag in silver lamé. The gods have had it with the world and in disgust have decided to let it go to pot (so to speak). Peace has been locked up. But this is as far as Tim Reynolds' book goes in the direction of coherence. For no apparent reason, it has been set as a minstrel show, though that didn't stop Carmines from using music that ranges from mock opera to mock art rock and finally to his favorite—the ricky-tick.

These, however, aren't criticisms, since the show makes no attempt to have reasons for anything. In fact, the main point is that there are no reasons, just as Carmines revels in his eclectic composing—it is *supposed* to be derivative. That's okay, it's all okay. The irony is that this outlook is very close to Aristophanes', far more so than the sobriety of a classical production. It was a real chance for easygoing, legitimate Greek comedy. Instead, it is just another Judson's musical—the best I've seen, but still the same business.

The music is the best part of it, nostalgic, mimicking, boisterous, wonderfully arranged in chorus numbers, and always well sung. With Carmines himself expanding at the piano with very full and galloping arrangements, it is a richer kind of musical sound than the average Broadway musical with its pit orchestra and superamplification.

The uncredited lyrics must have been by Carmines and Kornfeld because they have the same old ring ("Way down upon the old plantation/Where Trygaeus lives") and one song reads, in its entirety, "Plumbing has been raised to such an art/ That they don't need plungers anymore."

Kornfeld directed with a sculptural simplicity tremendously superior to the usual ragged clowning in these musicals. Rather than struggle for constant choreographic movement, he kept his company neat and striking, locking them in handsome and basic shapes. The effect was cool in every sense, and in effective contrast to the barrage of bathroom jokes. At least it demonstrates that this kind of high-low comedy doesn't demand a supersloppy production.

But Kornfeld could not handle individuals as strictly as he did the group, and solo numbers or dialogue sequences were haphazard and unconnected. David Vaughan was very funny as Hermes, particularly in a mock-pedantic explanation of Aristophanes. And Julie Kurnitz was powerful as singer and personage playing a darky, though all the voices were especially good.

It's nice to see such disciplined performing and directing in a Carmines-Kornfeld musical. And it's good to see this delightful stream of wacked-out theater moving closer to the general public (if the cognoscenti resent sharing the secret, they can move one step further out to the Playhouse of the Ridiculous). But until a way is found to organize these productions without eliminating the chaos so essential to their nature, they will always begin as refreshment and conclude as irritant.

What's New

Revolutionaries—The Living Theatre
(September 9, 1966)

ONE of the most significant, if not *the* most significant, American theater developments is not even happening in America. Julian Beck and Judith Malina's Living Theatre has been in exile since July of 1964, wandering the face of Europe with a gypsy band of actors and developing a theater attitude that surely leads to the future.

First, a brief history. The Living Theatre began conventionally enough, with a production of Christopher Marlowe's *Dr. Faustus* at the off-Broadway Cherry Lane Theatre. It grew slowly during the next twelve years, moving uptown to 100th Street and finally settling into its own theater on 14th Street. There it had its greatest success with the premiere of Jack Gelber's *The Connection,* and continued in repertory with increasingly unusual plays. These culminated with Kenneth H. Brown's *The Brig,* a strange combination of photographic reality and pure stage. *The Brig* was a fact-for-fact duplication of life in a Marine Corps prison, seeing in those facts the choreography and musical rhythms of absolute theater. It meant, in that relentless beat of military inhumanity, to reveal the unbelievable machinery that men have created to destroy themselves. And while it did not quite work (it became only boring in its repetition) it was the beginning of a new view of the stage.

But in October of 1963, the Bureau of Internal Revenue charged the company with nonpayment of admissions taxes and locked the theater. Malina and Beck chose to sit in for three days and were arrested for "impeding federal officers in the performance of duties." They were sentenced to thirty-day and sixty-day prison terms respectively and soon left the country.

In fact they were *driven* from the country by a cultural attitude that would not support genuine innovation or criticism—the very same attitude that murdered Lenny Bruce.

In Europe they became wanderers, roaming with the company and performing *The Brig*. Interrupted only by the departure of Beck and Malina to serve the sentences, they performed at the price of near-starvation conditions. London, Paris, Antwerp, Basel, Berlin.

Then an extraordinary accident occurred. Invited in October of 1964 to play a benefit performance for the American Students and Artists Center in Paris, they were asked for something new and, floundering for a choice, began working with their own acting exercises. Out of this came *Mysteries—And Smaller Pieces*.

This was not a "play." It had no script and virtually no dialogue. It was created by Beck and Malina and the company itself. A series of eight, nine, ten scenes, it was based on the writings of French theater theorist Antonin Artaud. Artaud's intention was to reach an audience through shock. To draw a plain, physical, agonizing, almost hysterical gut reaction. It is his Theater of Cruelty.

Beck and Malina, who are now here in Berlin, describe *Mysteries* as "a series of theatrical events which explore all of the physical senses, simultaneously tracing both the physical defects and physical glories in man's present estate." Their work, then, has a "content"—a literary meaning—and since they are of the it's-a-groove, intellectual school, it is bound to be less than thought out. But it is in the sheer theater of it that the value lies.

The final scene has twenty-five people dying of the plague, the deaths taking as long as each actor finds necessary. Then six of them rise to bury the others. This has come after such things as ten minutes of blackout during which there are sensations: female voices, constellations of light, and odors of incense.

The Paris production drew an excited response, and the work was performed in Brussels, Rome, Vienna. Beck told me there were fistfights in Rome. In Vienna "we were closed because of a hysterical reaction; further performances were forbidden. They were, I think, very frightened."

Now committed to the creation of its own works, the company decided to do a version of Mary Shelley's *Frankenstein* in September of 1965. This was "a spectacle like *Götterdämmerung*," according to Beck, "based on the attempts by man to improve his own state—attempts that backfired just as Dr. Frankenstein's did, and which resulted only in the creation of destructive monsters." It is an excellent analogy.

While *Frankenstein* has some conventional dialogue, and even some lines from the original Shelley, it is a free-form work. More than three hours long, it uses overlapping languages (as in simultaneous translations) and continued Artaudian effects, as well as various ideas suggested by Beck, Malina, or members of the company. One of these is the reading of the Jewish military burial passages from the American Army regulations. There is, as in *Mysteries*, the use of ceremony, ritual, incantation. There is also the gore—electrocutions, hangings, garrotings, gas chambers, and other entertainments.

The monster himself is a part of it—an 18-foot amorphous shape played by a group of actors. And later in the play the action occurs within his head—a giant scenic head. The dialogue is limited and much of the sound is just sound—on tape and in partly extemporized chanting by the actors. This music continues throughout the production as "mystical chord."

If this is difficult to imagine, it is because you have never seen anything like it. It is a new kind of theater, away from any sense of a "play" or a "script." While directors in American resident theaters are assuming greater and greater creative responsibilities, Malina and Beck have taken the great step into full creation.

In productions such as *Mysteries* or *Frankenstein,* the Living Theatre intends to entirely eliminate both the playwright and the director from the theater. It is after a communal theater where the company creates for itself, using the final equipment of the stage.

The implications of this are enormous, but Beck and Malina do not mean to ignore the play as a literary creature. In fact, they are presently preparing a production of Brecht's version of Sophocles' *Antigone,* using Brecht's script, word for word. This may not evolve as an *Antigone* that Brecht would recognize [it didn't], but does that matter?

I don't think so. The only thing that matters is the production itself. If it is not Brecht's *Antigone,* then it is the Living Theatre's. And if it *is* Brecht's, fine, too. Playwrights will not die and there will be theaters and directors and actors to translate their work from the script to the stage. Some of this will be good theater—as good, in its way, as this new, self-created theater.

As for Beck and Malina and the Living Theatre, it is ironic that they are working out of an American intellectual-theatrical framework for the benefit of an America that has closed its doors to them. However simplistic their ideas and however muddled their philosophizing, they have dived more deeply into the idea of theater than anybody working in their own country. Europe has accepted them and they are now self-sustaining—far more successful than they ever were in New

York. They have commitments through May of 1967. Why should they ever come back?

Beck and Malina realize that they must eventually return or else die of artistic sterility in an alien environment. They are basically and irrevocably American and know it. As long as they are away from their artistic home they will be refugees and fugitives.

They say that if they return they will never again work in ordinary theaters. They want to play small towns and city streets. This is as unrealistic as nearly everything they have done, but they are extremists in all things. The artist who creates in wild unconvention will not turn around and be conventional in nonartistic matters. The Becks' artistic and intellectual commitment has forced their exile upon themselves since, by giving in, they could well have functioned in New York. But by giving in, they would not have created what they have created. It is a bewildering and probably insoluble problem, but one thing is clear—they belong in America and should be there. Whether that will ever happen is unanswerable, but it is terribly like our country to reject its most original (and so most valuable) artists.

Mysteries—And Smaller Pieces (*September 18, 1968*)

The Living Theatre has returned to find a theater that is just beginning to assimilate the ideas it was developing five years ago and a country as oppressive as it seemed to be radically predicting five years ago. It is exciting to find the company so far advanced in technique and inspiration. It is frightening to find America so far gone.

Just five years ago the Internal Revenue Service attached the property of the Living Theatre because of $20,000 in unpaid taxes. Rather than give up its theater—in a real way, its beliefs —the company locked itself inside for a play-in. They were arrested, and their leaders, Julian Beck and Judith Malina, were indicted for "impeding federal officers in the pursuit of their duties." Since then, the Living Theatre has wandered across the face of Europe. Beck and Malina served short jail sentences in New York.

Today, clashes between young idealists and the government are an ugly commonplace. Today, a cry for pacifism and a rage with the military is ordinary (when the Living Theatre closed it was presenting Kenneth H. Brown's *The Brig*, a brutal demonstration of American military discipline). In fact, today is so barely caught up with the Living Theatre of 1963 that Rochelle Owens' *Futz!* is only a current off-Broadway success and it was on the Living Theatre's schedule (though never produced) five years ago.

Now there is so great a disgust with the American establishment that the country is on the brink of a dozen revolutions. Indeed, the pacifism that colored the Living Theatre's anarchy (and still does) has been superseded by anger and even violence. Perhaps the youth of America have finally caught up with the pure-burning, innocent, and occasionally naïve goodness of Judith Malina and Julian Beck, but our theater still trails in its shadow. We do have the Open Theatre, which owes an admitted debt to the Living Theatre, and its *America Hurrah* has an obvious foundation in the work of Malina and Beck. But the success of *Hair* proves just how middle class our idea of advanced theater is.

So the Living Theatre has returned to find an America that, in effect, sent it into exile. Yet, for all the stupidity and mistreatment they caught from this country, Beck and Malina have always insisted that they and their theater were American and always expected to return. Now they have returned, if tem-

porarily, beginning a six-month tour with an engagement at the
Yale School of Drama.

As if it had been planned for all the five years, the opening
production represented everything that the Living Theatre believed, theatrically and philosophically, and at the same time
drew an extraordinarily vivid profile of America itself from the
audience. I have seen many companies try for audience involvement. I have never seen—as I saw last night—an audience truly
involve itself to the point where it made its own statement. By
the time the evening was over there had been outcries from furious young revolutionaries, frustrated old conservatives, bewildered liberals, and hateful black militants. And a kind of theater existed—with inspiration, craft, and discipline—that had
not existed before in this country.

The production is called *Mysteries—And Smaller Pieces.*
Created by the company, it is based on an essay called "The
Theater and the Plague," written by French theater theorist
Antonin Artaud. The essay compares the theater with a plague
that "releases conflicts, disengages, liberates possibilities, and if
these possibilities and these powers are dark, it is the fault not
of the plague nor of the theater, but of life."

The evening began with a single actor standing at the edge of
the stage, staring at the audience until it squirmed, giggled,
made wisecracks, and finally began to chatter. This went on for
a long, long time—maybe ten minutes. Then a singer began a
song in the dark, a repetitious, irritating, and purposely exasperating song. Now the audience was really involved, not just
jokes but near-conversations.

Finally actors arrived, and movement was military and immediate, with close formation drills and lots of foot-stamping.
This led into a stage once again emptied, except for Julian
Beck, long-haired, in black, very ascetic, sitting in the middle of
the stage. A member of the audience joined him, meaning to be
cute. Beck put an arm around his shoulder and had him sit

337

down too. Then Beck began to chant, "Stop the war . . . stop the war . . . stop the war . . . ban the bomb . . . stop the war." The audience plunged in, chanting along with him and then partly chanting against him. Soon the theater was a mass of confused sound. You could hear Beck no longer but you knew what he was saying: Ban the bomb . . . stop the war. Then the company formed a great circle around him, and one by one, then in bunches, members of the audience joined them. Soon the stage was filled with audience and actors while others cried out against participating (that, of course, was participation too). The company itself was forever cool.

That was the *Mysteries* part, and never in my life have I seen anything like it. Then *Smaller Pieces,* a group of theater exercises dealing with the senses. One, a series of living, comic snapshots, was very funny, and another, about playing at being animals, was delightful. The evening concluded with Artaud again —an exercise in death, onstage and all over the theater.

Now perhaps some of this was silly. Maybe. But there was an audience-theater that I had never experienced before. There was a mix of truth and art that I never saw before. An excitement. And it was all put together by a company whose preparation and discipline might well have been forgotten in the surprise and originality of its work.

Think, then, that this production is the company's oldest. That there are newer ones to come. Even while away from America, the Living Theatre has been the leader of our country's stage invention. Even while away from America, the Living Theatre has been the voice of peaceful revolutionaries, knowing no answers but opposed to all violence. Now it is home for only a while because official America is still rejecting it. It is accepted in Europe because Europe is more in love with the idea of America than America is.

Paradise Now (*September 30, 1968*)

I think the main reason the Living Theatre so often accomplishes the incredible is that its ambition is as blithe as it is awesome. The company's newest—and most notorious—production, *Paradise Now,* means to create nothing less than the revolution as a stage production. And when I say revolution, I mean *the* revolution: the absolute replacement of the present morality, politics, personal values. The production means to do it by including more than just the audience in the action (as it already had done with *Mysteries—And Smaller Pieces*). With *Paradise Now,* the participants include the local police department, the local fire department, and members of the community who have not bought tickets to the production. In brief, *Paradise Now* makes *reality* the theater. In many ways it is a dazzling success, and it is immeasurably advanced in technique and conception beyond any comparable stage undertaking. The crucial reason for this success is the absolute naïveté that prompted the company to attempt it in the first place.

I saw *Paradise Now* Friday night at the Yale School of Drama as the company neared the end of its engagement (it begins a three-week schedule at the Brooklyn Academy of Music tomorrow night). The previous (opening) night, members of the company had been arrested by the New Haven police for disturbing the peace and indecent exposure (leaving the theater and marching down the streets wearing nothing but loincloths).

As a result of that, the company was a little uptight because its founders, Judith Malina and Julian Beck, were still on probation for a five-year-old arrest on a similarly theater-oriented charge. This pressure, too, was part of the production, but I

339

suppose I should first give you some details about what *Paradise Now* is.

It is the revolution within a theater context. As you enter the auditorium, the stage is jammed with sympathetic members of the community who have learned from previous Living Theatre productions that they are part of the action. Things begin as members of the company wander through the house whispering, "I can't travel without a passport." They do this for about ten minutes, building in volume as they say it to individual spectators. A crescendo is reached, and after screaming it en masse, they climax with a moan. Then the audience is left to its reaction as another slogan begins in whispers: "I don't know how to stop the war." The crescendo is duplicated and then the process begins again: "You can't live if you don't have money" —and, "I am not allowed to smoke marijuana." And so on. The basis for the revolution is laid—laws restrict individual freedom and most of the time they are arbitrary and foolish.

This opening sequence is called "The Rite of Guerrilla Theater," and it is the first of 23 sections that conclude with the exit into the street and a beginning of change. These sections are mapped out on a diagrammatic program that relates them (rather simplemindedly) in a mystical way to both Hebrew and Indian philosophy. At the bottom of the program is a summary of the production's point: "This chart is the map—The essential trip is the voyage from the many to the one—The plot is the revolution."

Paradise Now took four and a half hours to play Friday night (though the length can vary) and had the superficial appearance of absolute chaos. In fact the program is extremely well controlled by the company, and just when you think the wandering is aimless, a move to the next point on the program is made. This might be the company's removal of clothes to signify abandonment of accepted restrictions. It might be a yoga exercise or a representation of mass sex and the importance of personal touch. Or an Indian chant-dance or an exercise in bigotry. The audience is part of the show from the very beginning, complaining, being involved by company members in conversation, even intimidated by direct accusation. Soon enough, a crowd of people were massed outside, along with the New Haven fire department (concerned about fire laws) and the police (looking, really looking, for trouble). The theater very quickly seemed in a true-real state of siege as the audience actually discussed the possibility of challenging the police. In fact, then, this was revolution just as the program said. Strangely, though, it was not the revolution that campus radicals are after—and one of those radicals made it quite clear on-stage. The radicals are committed to violence, the Living Theatre to pacifism, and this is the company's main problem in reaching its most likely supporters. Its other problem, of course, is the frustrating childishness of its love cure for complicated situations. But what must be remembered beyond all is that its revolution is in stage production as well as reality. As a production, it is often very long-winded and silly. But it is also extraordinary.

Which One Will You Pursue? (November 3, 1967)

The difference between being a participant and a spectator, speaking generally, is the difference between having fun and watching someone else have it. For the playwright, it is the difference between writing *from* a point of view and writing *about* it. And it is a crucial difference. I am hardly about to say that all plays written *from* a point of view are good while those written *about* a point of view are bad, but I would just as soon see the former. They are more likely to be ardent, more likely to be honest and convincing, and more likely to reveal just what the point of view is. They are also less likely to be teachery and condescending.

It is easier to demonstrate with examples. *Hair* opened recently at the Anspacher Theatre and *The Beard* at the Evergreen. Both are involved with the hippie phenomenon. *Hair* is about hippies, and there's no mistaking that. Its characters have long, straight hair, wear beads and flowers, smoke marijuana, and behave more or less the way the press says they should. *The Beard* has only two characters, and neither looks like a hippie. They are Jean Harlow and Billy the Kid, and they talk about sex. Yet *The Beard* is truly hippie and *Hair* is fake. You'll learn—understand—more about what attitude is behind the hippie movement, and behind general young-person thinking today, from *The Beard* than what the liberal, instructional *Hair* could possibly begin to describe.

This is not because the authors of *Hair* are middle-aged, though I must admit I half expected that. James Rado and Gerome Ragni, who wrote its book and lyrics, are young guys with young attitudes. Though they are theater-trained, their work has been with more innovating things (like the Open Theater or *Hang Down Your Head and Die*) than the tired stuff of the theater establishment. Their composer, Tom MacDermot, is a formal musician, and while his training may have kept his rock score from matching the exuberant, creative drive of today's fast-growing pop music, it is in fact the youngest and freshest part of *Hair*.

No, it is Rado and Ragni who have made this "hippie musical" a spectator rather than a participant affair by making it *about* hippies. Hippies are explained and justified. They demonstrate what they think, and their parents (the establishment) are put down as squares. I use this archaic language because it is the outsider language of the play.

The Beard has music, too, though it is not part of the play. Because Michael McClure's work is brief, the producers have filled out the evening with a wonderful light-sound show that is exactly *of* the hippie phenomenon. Swirling colors and melting sounds growl and flutter through the sculpted Evergreen Theatre to draw you out of your seat and into a soft tunnel of experience. Finally a small group (autoharp, tambourine, guitar) plays McClure's music, which he describes as postpsychedelic "cowboy shiva." Then the play begins.

The Beard is written out of a fundamental hippie philosophy, perhaps best stated in the John Lennon lyric, "Nothing is real/Nothing to get hung about." The only things that are real are the things that are *real*, and high on the list is the physical grandeur of pure sex. Billy the Kid and Jean Harlow are its only characters, drawn beyond their superstar, supersex, super-American folk status into a pop eternity where they live, beautiful and golden, in a blue-velvet eternity. And there they take the oldest and forever game of man-seducing-woman and woman-seducing-man through the cheap language that the streets apply to sex. A language that comes through as obscene and then funny and finally as the realest, *only* language of sex. Because it is so royally obscene, this language takes on a strange kind of fundamentalism, and because McClure is a poet, its rhythms and sounds grow musical and rhythmic. Finally the sex itself happens, and it is gorgeous, glowing, "Star! Star! Star!"

I am not about to tell you that *The Beard* is a successful play. Though repetition is its device, the device does not always work, and sometimes it becomes merely tiring. While both Billy and Jean are hopelessly funny exaggerations, and while a great deal of what they say is wildly comic, McClure has not been able to go beyond his wonderful, visual-poetic idea of them.

But whether *The Beard* or *Hair* is successful or not is not my point. My point is that *The Beard* conveys completely and successfully an attitude that hippies represent, in extreme, of modern America. It is art coming out of attitude. Whereas *Hair,* in attempting to describe and explain the attitude, tells less than nothing about it. In fact, *Hair,* while presuming to be about hippies, is really the nonhippie only talking about the hippie. Its own attitude, really, is of the prehippie, liberal generation, and there is nothing it can do, nothing it can say, that seems true.

If we are not to be old, intellectually speaking, we must grow with time. Youthful ideas such as hippieness are reserved for youth and there is nothing so ridiculous as an older person trying to act like a child. But the child's language, fresh though immature, must be understood by the adult if he is to stay alive, and for the stage's sake, such vitality is essential, for life, for effectiveness, for growth. It is understood only in conversation, only in participation, and that is why *The Beard* is more artful, more significant, and more important than *Hair*.

America's New Music (*January 2, 1968*)

At the midtown New York studios of Atlantic Records the lights are out in a control booth while little red and green bulbs glow in the darkness, and the big reels slowly revolve on the eight-track Ampex tape recorders. Out on the studio floor, The Rascals are dramatically spotlighted. One of them is hidden behind a three-sided wooden enclosure, built to resonate his drumbeat, and all you can see of him is the top of his head, the long straight hair swinging with the rhythm, his drumsticks flashing through the air.

At a dance bar called Wheels, on Second Avenue near 83d Street, the New York Rock and Roll Ensemble is moving through a tremendous, driving, melodic, musically fascinating set. It is impossible to resist dancing, and the floor is packed. Several members of the Ensemble are Juilliard students. The group is the talk of some of New York's more tuned-in musicians.

At the Café Au Go Go on Bleecker Street, the Butterfield Blues Band begins a session at just past two and doesn't stop until four in the morning. By that time, the packed house of hip-hugged, straight-haired, glitter-eyed youngsters has been shot through with pounding rhythms and ripping blasts of trumpets and electric guitars.

Autosalvage is recording its first album at RCA Victor's studios on 24th Street. Sitting around between takes, the young musicians talk about their far-out sounds. Then one of them walks out on the floor to "lay on" another guitar track. His stuff is Bachian, the fingerwork formidable, the music terrific.

Arlo Guthrie—son of the legendary folk singer Woody Guthrie—is working his way through a performance at the Bitter End, also on Bleecker Street. Everybody is waiting for his eighteen-minute talking song, "Alice's Restaurant," and he finally gets around to it. Guthrie has three or four stories to tell with the song, but the most popular one is about a draft board questioning a boy's moral fitness for war because he was once arrested for littering. Guthrie is mesmerizing.

The Rascals, the Butterfield Blues Band, Arlo Guthrie, Autosalvage, the New York Rock and Roll Ensemble, are all moving on the excitement, the creativity, and the public acceptance that has made pop music not only the most vital and influential art in American culture today but also the reflection of young people's attitudes. It is the first hint of what this country is going to become when the whole under-twenty-five population —already half of America's total—takes over.

When the first rock-'n'-roll record—"Earth Angel," I guess—moved out of the Negro "race music" milieu to make the white Hit Parade, something began that was to become a creative explosion. Only who was to know it? All we realized was that pop music had changed and most people resented it. The beat was monotonous, the melodies banal, the chords repetitious, the lyrics inane at best and vulgar at worst. Then advances began— the Everly Brothers with quick-changing time and catchy chord

345

progressions; Elvis Presley's driving, true-musical, Nashville sound.

The Beatles (need I say?) were responsible for the biggest advance of all—not only because of their innovations, though these were abundant; not only because of their early capitalization on recording-studio technical possibilities, though this was an enormous influence; but because they were so fantastically popular that they could sing almost anything and get an audience.

The Beatles were guaranteed acceptance—acceptance of abstract poetry, dissonance, electronic sounds—all new to record buyers' ears. They could get mass audiences to love what concert hall audiences rejected in composers from Stravinsky to Stockhausen. They popularized chamber arrangements ("Yesterday"), baroque orchestrations ("Eleanor Rigby"), electronic sounds ("A Day in the Life"), fantasy lyrics ("I Am the Walrus").

With the release of *Sergeant Pepper's Lonely Hearts Club Band* last spring, they ushered genuine art into American-English popular music. The album shot to the top of the charts, as any Beatles album will, but never had such serious music been so commercially successful. As with virtually all groups now, the Beatles had written all of their own music (in itself a formidable development).

And as most groups, they had spent as much time in the engineering booth as with their instruments. But never had a pop album abandoned the scheme of individual song collection for an entire work of related art songs. *Sergeant Pepper* studied the idea of love and of being lovelorn on a broad level, mocking the sentimental, weeping for the genuine. It abandoned conventional values for the mysteries of abstraction and the trueness of pity:

> See the people standing there who
> disagree and never win

346

And wonder why they don't get in my door.
I'm painting my room in the
  colorful way
And when my mind is wandering
There I will go.*

Throughout this article I may write about music and may even try to describe it to you. But there is no describing it, and that's the best thing about it. The only way to hear music is to listen to it and ignore the people who try to explain it to you. If it reaches you, it is yours. You needn't know the first things about counterpoint, about theory, about harmony, to get stoned on it.

But musicians have to know about these things to compose the music. Or do they? One of the most striking things about the new music is that it is invariably written by the performers. Most of these musicians are young and untrained, and yet they write these terribly complicated things. How do they do it?

Most of them feel that if they had been trained, they would never have the freedom to go outside the bounds of conventional music, classical or pop. And there is some truth in that—I doubt that Leonard Bernstein, who wants to, could compose unique rock music. He can—and will—be influenced by what has been done, but his very discipline (and his age) will hold him back.

On the other hand, the most talented rock composers are studying composition and harmony, so they can do more with the sounds they already hear: Paul McCartney of the Beatles and Brian Wilson of the Beach Boys (he composed most of their wonderful, surreal *Smiley Smile* album). This will become more and more common, and it remains to be seen whether the education will stimulate or hamstring the booming creativity. It seems to me that training will inevitably make great talent even greater.

* "Fixing a Hole" (Lennon and McCartney). Copyright © 1967 Northern Songs Limited. Used by Permission. All Rights Reserved.

With the success of *Sergeant Pepper,* there was no ceiling on what pop music could be. Album buyers' ears were educated to new sounds while the teenies kept their little Top Forty records in the nursery. An album as far out as the first by the Vanilla Fudge, with its roaring trips into pure sound and its unbearably building fugal motifs, could have cuts running over eight minutes, unplayable by those spastic disc jockeys, and still hit the top five on the sales lists. The Association could record "Requiem for the Masses," the Electric Prunes its "Mass in F Minor," the Bee Gees and the Left Banke whole albums of baroque rock; the Chrome Cyrkus could be commissioned to write a score for the Robert Joffrey Ballet; Frank Zappa could compose and record a rock symphony (mock-titled, as is his style, *Tribute to Lumpy Gravy* and unfortunately, still unreleased). [It later was, as *Lumpy Gravy.*]

The LSD-inspired imagery of the groups' names—the Strawberry Alarm Clock, Moby Grape, Clear Light, the Jefferson Airplane, the Grateful Dead, the Buffalo Springfield—reflected in the open poetry. And their kinds of music reflected the individualism: hard rock, folk rock, sunny rock, raga (Indian) rock, acid rock, baroque rock, and the music so individual that categorization was impossible.

And curiously, it had all turned white. Except for some soul singers (Ray Charles, James Brown, Aretha Franklin, Otis Redding), rock was being almost exclusively written and performed by white singers. And the new sound was pure white. Nobody knows why, but there it is, and ironically, because the whole thing started with Negro music.

But in any case, a very special thing had happened—something I can't recall having happened in any other art, fine or popular: the most artistic had become the most commercial. In every other field, it is virtually the worst that is the most successful—in books, in the theater, even in the movies, where things today aren't bad at all. But nothing like pop music.

For example, the Doors, while hardly the most inventive

group in America, do perform the new kind of music with the new kind of attitude. The message they transmit is sex, pure sex.

Jim Morrison, the group's singer, slides on stage wearing tight black vinyl pants and a matching jacket. He says nothing. He plants both boots on the microphone platform, curling his knees around the shaft. He cups the microphone in his palms and opens his mouth around it:

> . . . Come on baby, light my fire
> Come on baby, light my fire,
> Try to set the night on fire.*

It was the No. 1 song in the country and, I mean, what do you think he's talking about?

The Doors do their thing, and it is an effective one. Some of the other groups are more creative, more ingenious, more musically sophisticated: the fresh Lovin' Spoonful, the rocking Cream, the adventurous Beach Boys, the wonderfully sunny Harper's Bizarre with its musical games.

The poetry-lyrics, sometimes political, sometimes philosophical, sometimes just dreamy, come out of the folk-rock singers. Bob Dylan, of course, started it all when he first went rock to a horde of booing fans at the Newport Folk Festival. Donovan and his wonder-beautiful ballads; Simon and Garfunkel, the Mamas and the Papas, Tim Buckley, and Richie Havens.

Today it is commonplace for a composer to say that modern pop is sophisticated and valid. Bernstein introduces it on network television. David Amram writes about it in *Life*. Ned Rorem reviews Beatles records in the *Village Voice*. With these mass media acceptances by certified cultural authorities, the music has officially arrived. And, as usual, by that time it didn't need the introduction.

---

* "Light My Fire." Copyright © 1967 by Nipper Music Co. Inc./Doors Music Co. All Rights Reserved.

Now the new music is reaping the benefits of this acceptance. And standing at the head of it, generally unknown to the public, are two young men. You have probably never heard of them. They are Frank Zappa and Van Dyke Parks.

Zappa heads The Mothers of Invention (to be abbreviated, with affectional obscenity, as "the mothers"), a group that never has, and probably never will, have a hit single. His music changes restlessly, from noise for the sheer sake of it to relentless parody. "This is Frank Zappa sockin' it to ya."

And this is what he personifies for most modern rock musicians. He takes nothing seriously—nothing is worth taking seriously. Everything is absurd, even himself and his music, and he purposely comes on wildly bearded and foolishly dressed (or undressed). Nothing can be respected because everything is corrupt and dirty and dumb.

The high spirits and final freedom of pop music are rooted in this attitude of reverse idealism—though Zappa's admirers refuse to take it as far as he does, and, indeed, if they did they could never get anything accomplished. Most of them wonder whether Zappa will ever achieve his potential, and feel pitiful because he is more capable of doing something magnificent than they.

The other legendary figure among rock musicians is the twenty-five-year-old Van Dyke Parks, a composer-orchestrator and apparent genius from Los Angeles. Parks is mentioned in terms as hallowed as Zappa, but he is going to be more significant because he takes his music seriously, is more productive, and has been developing. He represents the pure-American basis for this modern music and has moved it over the line it was fast approaching—the line separating it from classical music. It was pure music, all his, from the very beginning, going beyond ordinary song constructions in search of fresh harmonic systems, strange modulations, and new combinations of instruments: "Come to the Sunshine" and "High Coin" for Harper's Bizarre; "Heroes and Villains" and "Vegetables" for the Beach Boys; variations on Donovan's "Colors," and finally his own album, *Song Cycle,* composed, orchestrated, and sung by Parks.

Song Cycle wanders through Hollywood, Laurel Canyon Boulevard, Vine Street, Palm Desert, with a combination of love and contempt—love for the area and its musical identity, contempt for its reactionary attitudes. The music is humorous and affectionate, while growing special sounds from pure-American roots. And the lyrics run from a disgust with Southern California's Communist-baiting and superpatriotism to warnings of racial troubles ahead:

> Strike up the band
> Brother hand me another bowl of your soul
> The song of the forgotten South
> Just don't hang us up here
> Jews don't hang us up here
> The unknown is at hand
> And not far from my heel
> The tar baby feels for the Czar*

Parks' *Song Cycle,* like the spirit of the new pop music and the young people behind it, loves America and what it promised to be, hates it for some of the things it has become. Though it sometimes sounds as if it has no hope left for a country that has done and become so many dumb things, the hope and love remain. The music of America, the feel of America, the land and the high spirits of America remain good.

A university instructor was telling me recently about his students. "They believe," he said with solemn excitement. "They really believe. Corruption and cynicism and materialism aren't going to be accepted anymore—nobody is going to say, 'Well, that's the way things have to be,' anymore. These kids honestly

---

* Used by permission of Dyke Parks, of Found Farm Ballads (publisher, B.M.I.).

believe what they've been taught and they mean to live their lives that way. And we'd all better watch out." [How extraordinarily accurate was that prediction.]

It's true. You'd better watch these young people, because they're going to demand decency and not settle for pragmatism. They're going to reach for beauty and intelligence, and you won't be able to sell them plastic. They know trash from the worthwhile and you can't buy them. Not with money, not with respectability.

Their disinterest in cheap values, cheap work, cheap leisure, cheap existence is making its first mark in the music they listen to. It is represented by the people who make that music. It is a new insistent, pure shining idealism. Nobody wants a Buick anymore. Listen to the music.

Rock Theater (*May 8, 1968*)

Last weekend at Fillmore East, a singer named Arthur Brown made his entrance from the rear of the house, carried aloft by four bare-chested young men, his headpiece flaming and his body swathed in robes. Arriving on the stage, with a rock group blasting behind him and a light show flashing on the big screen, he dropped the headpiece to the ground and removed his robe. Wearing a shiny foil mask, he swung first full face, then left profile, then full face, then right profile. And while he did, he sang—yelled out—and danced, his long, bell-bottomed legs flapping like string beans in the wind. And the mask glittering, evil and weird, in the dazzling light.

The weekend before, a rock group called the Iron Butterfly lighted five torches, turned up the synthesizer (an electronic device that creates artificial sounds), and left the stage. The machine began pouring out rhythmic, shattering music-sound, so physically painful that many in the audience were forced to protect their ears. With nobody at all on the stage, the sound built and the torches flamed until it all passed away together. The effect, purely gut, visual and sonic, was extraordinary.

Fillmore East is a big old movie house that has been taken over for weekend concerts by serious rock groups. In no way does it present itself as a place for theater events. But theater does not merely include productions that present themselves as theater in the conventional sense—a comedy, a drama, and so on. Obviously, these two events at Fillmore East were all the things of the theater and were far more exciting, as theater, than most everything presented on New York's ordinary stages. The Joshua Light Show that backs each act is strikingly beautiful and unfailingly original.

What is happening at Fillmore East is the theatrical fulfillment, or the beginning of one, for the pop music blast that has been expanding over the last year. Like the music, it is deeply involved in hippie influences; and like the music, it matches fundamental artistic appeals—rhythm and color—with a whole set of personal attitudes: moral and political and philosophical. All of this is represented at these concerts, and along with it the group participation that dancing has pushed into so many other areas. At Fillmore, the musicians sometimes have a tough time outdoing the audiences in originality and color of costume. The house is filled with catch-styles—beads and bell bottoms and long, stringy hair. But the variations in color and material are endless, and in any case, almost everybody is moving and alive, whether dancing while seated on the floor or just moving restlessly with a cigarette back in the lobby.

Still, it is the performance that is the main theater event. The groups are becoming more and more aware of visual effects to expand their performances. Jefferson Airplane begins its act with a love-your-neighbor movie short, and then its glittery model airplane zooms along a wire over the audience's head. The movie then switches to a pilot's view of takeoff and the amplifiers detonate a jet blast. Then the lights are on and the Airplane is singing.

Blue Cheer works in hard rock, the hardest I've ever heard, exploding out of twelve massive amplifier-speakers for an exercise in pure sound. ("Blue cheer" is the nickname for a type of LSD. While Traffic, one of the newer and more sophisticated English groups, moves in relatively quieter musical-dramatic circles.

The following afternoon, a sunny Sunday, the Airplane was out in Central Park with two equally big-time groups—the Grateful Dead and the Butterfield Blues Band—giving a free concert for thousands of hippies and hippie-influenced people (and almost no teeny-boppers). Mind you, each of these groups draws big money for any date. But free concerts in the park, whether San Francisco's Golden Gate or New York's Central, are part of the striking openness and difference of these performers. Creating, as they are, a bright and intense young audience, the theater of their work is bound to influence our deadening stages, and we are lucky for it.

Getting Laid Onstage *(March 27, 1969)*

The recent nudity thing in the theater has led to where it was inevitably destined: explicit sexual acts on stage, police arrests, court injunctions, television cameras, and newspaper reporters. It is where the producers wanted it to lead, and it is where the news media wanted it to lead. Predictably, when it finally happened it was a pathetic display on everybody's part, culminating Wednesday in perhaps the most disgusting exhibition I have ever seen in a theater.

Crowded into the little Free Store Theatre in Cooper Square were a handful of people involved with the play *Che,* and more

354

than a hundred newspapermen and television newsmen. The lighting, ordinarily subdued for the production, was turned all the way up to help the cameras. The occasion was a press conference and special performance, called after ten actors and production people had been arrested Tuesday night on charges of "consentual sodomy, public lewdness and obscenity."

At the press conference, Lennox Raphael, the author of *Che*, said that the sex in the production "symbolizes the ideological struggle between America and revolutionary movements." Then the performance began, and with it, a still larger performance. In any production, the audience is part of the performance. When nudity is involved, especially today, when we are unaccustomed to it, the audience's shock-embarrassment-whatever is even more a part of the performance. When the audience is all reporters, many with cameras, almost entirely male and of a stag-movie mentality, it turns a play into a quite larger phenomenon.

But there is still more. After all, these newsmen were invited to the special performance by the producer. They weren't drama critics but reporters. The publicity-mongering, the degradation of both sex and theater for such crude purposes, couldn't have been more flamboyant. Nor were these particular reporters and photographers, vulgar as they were, as despicable as the razor-cut executives who gave them the assignment before going off to their civilized lunch appointments. Theirs is the true degeneracy.

What was going on at the Free Store Theatre was degenerate enough, not onstage but among the newspaper and television people. Onstage the play proceeded, and I'll get to that in a minute. Around its perimeter the cameras ground away at the first hint of sex, shutting off whenever the conversation was political (which was most of the time). Lady photographers moved in on actors for close-ups of male genitals—close enough to dampen the lenses, which they would have deserved. The male reporters responded with fraternity-house wisecracks

("Please, fellers—no hand-holding during the performance"). All of this represented, with gross clarity, America's obsession with sex on the lowest possible level and proved, if you didn't know it already, that no mind can be in a gutter but that gutters can be in the mind.

Mr. Raphael's play itself wins no medal for style. Coming on as a revolutionary dialogue between Che Guevara and Uncle Sam, it is plainly diverted by sexual hanky-panky. It means to be absurdly coarse about sex in the style of the Playhouse of the Ridiculous, but Raphael's writing is much too heavy-handed for that. The result is long stretches of revolutionary nonsense interspersed with sex scenes that are meant to be funny and aren't. (Only once is there a serious sex scene and it nearly works.)

The play is set in a plastic land where Uncle Sam is naked except for a striped top hat and a sash and Guevara is fully clothed. Behind them is "Mayfang," a science-fiction girl in silver lamé except for the plastic bubbles on her naked breasts. The men converse in one-sentence dialectics. Uncle Sam says things like, "Your perception illuminates," or "Shower me with your sins." Guevara's responses are just as underground newspaper: "You shall reap the glory of my innocence," "Love is bereft of innocence." If you dig under all this garbage, which hardly requires any depth, the play's point is a love-hate and somehow sexual relationship between America and revolutionaries, the purity of revolutionaries, and the rape-murder of that purity by America.

As for the sex, it begins with fondling and gets progressively detailed, though there is a minimum of four-letter language. Guevara finally drops his clothes, but only after a long honeymoon with open-fly surgery. The science-fiction girl stays fully dressed, but another girl appears about halfway through the one-and-a-half-hour, intermissionless production. And she does enough for two. From her entrance until the end, the play is mostly sexual, though it never works as pornography (much to my disappointment). There is a great deal of fellatio and cunnilingus, homosexual and heterosexual. None of it really happens because—understandably—the actors were unable to achieve erections under the circumstances. So the intercourse scene itself had to be faked, to the obvious disappointment of the audience, which spent all this time craning with cameras for better angles and clambering all over the seats (I wonder where they expect to show the film). There are sex scenes between two men and a woman (rather than two women and a man, as most men prefer to see it, flattering their egos as it does).

The performances were quite good in that the actors and actresses did what they had to do without visible embarrassment and read their lines quite clearly. Edward Wode's direction was atrocious, keeping the dialogue so unvaried that it droned off into nonsense. He refused to move the company and could muster up no imagination for the sex scenes. The murder of Guevara, which was the play's crucial event (among maybe three plot developments all told), failed to give the production a climax, which I suppose was apt, considering the sexual futility. And the only point proved was that even with a tacky and pretty innocent play-production like this, our news media—the official frauds of "fact"—will drag anyone into their pigsties.

The New Theater Is Here. Isn't It? (*April, 1969*)

The body has made it to Broadway. Bare-assed actors and actresses are no longer shockers in avant-garde productions but even show up—very much so—in your run-of-the-mill Broadway flop. The schlocks know box office when they see it (undressed). There isn't a single *well-made* play on Broadway. Four-letter words sprinkle stage dialogue the way "son of a bitch" used to. The Living Theatre sold houses out with productions that had virtually no dialogue—productions that couldn't be fit into the old classifications of musical, comedy, drama. Actors are streaming into the audiences and encourage the audiences to stream right back. Playwrights are creating productions in the midst of rehearsal instead of submitting finished scripts. And a letter, signed "Eleven New Dramatists," arrived at my office reading: "We fear we are drifting into the most superficial posterish kind of playwrighting—Instant Theatre. The playwright needn't do his work anymore—let the newspaper do it, or the nude actress, or even the 'participating' audience itself . . . as our theatre gets increasingly non-verbal, it becomes shallower, certainly less brain-scratching and, ultimately, less emotionally affecting."

The irony is that such "changes" are negligible, as habitual meaningless, and vain (both senses) as the kind of complain (and the way it is expressed) of these "Eleven New Drama tists."

Something is going on all right, Mr. Jones. You couldn't mis it unless you were President. But what, exactly, is it? Is there a pattern? Is the Majestic Theatre disappearing? You mean Ar thur Miller *isn't* a genius?

It is a time of change and the watchcry is "revolution." The talk is of the *new*—new politics, new morality, new music, new theater. The past became camp—the thirties, the forties, th fifties—finally, the present. Even change itself. Some of us clin to the rock of reason, taking these revolutionary cries as symp toms of progress within the old order. Not sensing that "order is suspect, that "progress" is sometimes another word for re trenchment, and that "reason" is only the name of what we ha always considered intelligent.

Well, none of this is terribly original. We read about the ol order's death every day, see it buried on every picketing plac ard, hear it damned in every art-rock lyric. So what if Margar

Farrar retired as editor of the New York *Times* crossword puzzle? Won't Will Weng do?

Well, Will Weng is no Margaret Farrar. Things just aren't the same anymore. George Abbott and Comden and Green can't get away with it anymore. Miller is stuffy, Williams has lost contact, and Albee's an intellectual pretender. And for that matter, the innovations of off-off Broadway theaters, coffee-house theater, communal theaters, and your whole *avant-garde,* with all the well-intentioned, desperately artistic amateurism—all of this is just as much a part of old times as *The Dark at the Top of the Stairs* or, for that matter, *Hair.* What has worked can no longer work. The world is hardly about to collapse, but doors—our eyes—have been opened. Everything has been revealed as existing within quotation marks. And who did it?

Andy Warhol and Marshall MacLuhan!

Is that possible? MacLuhan, a professor of English literature who can't (or won't) write a coherent, grammatical paragraph? Warhol, in leather?

Together—or simultaneously—they opened our eyes to look at things a different way. A way that, not knowing it, we had learned already.

The medium is the message.

A can of Campbell's soup.

I would like to be a machine.

The surface is everything.

Pop art led us back to the top. There, everything is what it seems. There, the fact is its own comment. What more could James Reston have said about Lyndon Johnson than what Lyndon Johnson said about himself? And, in turn, what more could Reston have said about *Reston? Forty Carats* is canned theater for canned audiences. Need *I* say that? *Forty Carats* says it. Who must notice that Lincoln Center is really an architect's rendering: white cardboard buildings with little men in fedoras and little ladies with flower hats walking along lanes edged with little paper trees. Why, there it is!—the rendering itself!

The plays of Harold Pinter are geometric planes. They are set in places that could well be the primary structures of modern sculpture. They are constructed that way. What people find spooky about them is their strange, steel environment. It is foolish to ask for meanings in such plays because Pinter has dismissed the idea of meanings (in *Tea Party* a child of post-adult maturity asks, "What does 'mean' mean?"). Words are but arbitrary symbols for intangible ideas.

In Pinter's plays the words are fixed, the people are fixed, the continuum is fixed. In *The Homecoming,* a man subjects his daughter-in-law to a torrent of abuse. She gazes at him. There is no stage direction to suggest her reaction. Pinter says she *has* a reaction. You go back to see the play again. No reaction, and still Pinter insists. In fact, she *does* have a reaction, only you haven't been looking the right way. The reaction is her gaze, coupled with what you think she is thinking. Complicated? No. Just a big change from the spelled-out-for-you serials that have passed for drama ever since Henrik Ibsen decided that life was about social diseases.

Recently, a production of *The Homecoming* was given by the Watford Repertory Company in suburban London. Pinter himself played Lenny (the bitter middle son). Terence Rigby, who played the younger brother—the prizefighter—in this production as well as those in London and New York, compared Pinter's performance with that of Ian Holm (who played it originally), saying, "Holm was intellectual. He played the part with his head. But Harold is cold. He's *tough*. And *that's* his Lenny."

The *plays* of Pinter are tough. They abandon interpretation as so much fake talk. They insist on the straight line, the clear space, the precise word, a (c)leanness of space, people, events talk. The fact is all that matters. Not the fact you'd like with accessory answers, explanations, and denouements. Facts aren' that way—*life* isn't that way. If you want to see, look to the surface. That's what's there.

The surface is a frightening place. It is a place of no sentiment, no easy feelings, no trim, no justification. Where everything is fundamental. Samuel Beckett's *Come and Go* (called "a dramaticule") is a play of 121 spoken words. Its three characters are women whose hats are pulled down to cover their faces as their silences are pulled down to cover their feelings and thoughts. The play's strength is in the unspoken. Each character leaves and returns. While one is gone, the others discuss her:

RU: How do you find Flo?
VI: She seems much the same (*Ru moves to center seat, whispers in Vi's ear. Appalled*). Oh! (*They look at each other. Ru puts her finger to her lips.*). Has she not been told?
RU: God forbid.

This sequence is repeated for each of the ladies while they play musical chairs. The series of anti-informations is the play's substance much as it is life's. What is it we haven't been told? (Nothing.) At the play's end the women entwine their arms, join hands, and one says, "I can feel the rings." That is *all* she can feel of the other two. Not the hands. Not the person. The *rings*. Rings that mean nothing. Rings of the material.

Beckett is getting at what Pinter is getting at, which is no surprise, since Pinter has admitted the influence. Pinter's plays, though more verbal than Beckett's, have always been severe and are becoming more so as he settles—like an iceberg—into his sense of himself. Like Beckett, he emphasizes uncertainty by limiting himself to only the certain and showing how it is not enough and yet all we have to go on. All there is.

Now you aren't going to catch those Eleven New Dramatists complaining about Beckett and Pinter, who certainly are writers. There's no mistaking Beckett's poetry: "Astride of a grave and a difficult birth. Down in the hole, lingeringly, the gravedigger puts on the forceps. We have time to grow old. The air is full of our cries. But habit is a great deadener. At me too someone is looking, of me too someone is saying, He is sleeping, he knows nothing, let him sleep on" (*Waiting for Godot*).*

That's more human than Pinter, but what do we mean by "human"? Too often we mean "sentimental," and Pinter despises sentimentality and is even frightened by its threatening temptation (Remember Goldberg in *The Birthday Party?*). His language is stripped, and the rhythms—like words and punctuations and sentences—are kept to geometrica. So that even when a thought is soft, it is clean: "All it is, you see . . . I said . . . is the lightness of your touch, the lightness of your look, my neck, your eyes, the silence, that is my meaning, the loveliness of my flowers, my hands touching my flowers, that is my meaning" (*Landscape*). Here is Pinter at his most self-revealing.

It may seem a long leap from this to the movie *2001* and still further to the off-off Broadway Play-House of the Ridiculous, but they all have something very important in common, something that Eleven New Dramatists fail to grasp: a refreshed sense of life, a new dimension for looking at things. In their letter, those playwrights cited *Rosencrantz and Guildenstern Are Dead* and *Hadrian the Seventh* as plays of "thought-verbal superiority." Actually, they are plays, merely, of a familiar type, as much a part of literary ritual as a phrase like "thought-verbal superiority." And ironically, they are as unoriginal as their styles. Peter Luke took most of *Hadrian* verbatim from the Frederick Rolfe novel. *Rosencrantz and Guildenstern* is neatly divided between the situation of *Hamlet* and the language-attitude of (Well, what do you know?) *Waiting for Godot*. Though *Hadrian* is affecting and *Rosencrantz* stimulating, it would be foolish to insist that literary drama—and this very specific kind of literary drama—will always be high theater and vice versa. The idea of literariness has changed, as Beckett and

* Translated from the original French text by the author. Copyright © 1954 by Grove Press. Published by Grove Press, Inc.

Pinter demonstrate, and so has the idea of truth. Indeed, words themselves, like Campbell's soup cans, have become self-reflective, the meanings habitual, the tones ritualistic, the combinations formulated thought. Do we ever notice that the conversations we have, the speeches we make, are identical—with each other's, with those we spoke before? That is why Pinter and Beckett have taken to a frugal precision in the use of words. *Words mean things besides what they "mean."*

2001 is a movie of few words, and those there are don't make much sense (only after reading Arthur C. Clarke's novel do you understand what was meant—to be embarrassed by it). Taken literally, the movie is incomprehensible. But to grasp the sense of *2001*, you must abandon old notions of comprehension. Stanley Kubrick, its director, pictured the unity of man and his universe, needing no story, no point, no literary content to make a statement because the statement was the image. Nor did attuned audiences need a plot or literary coherence to grasp its purpose.

As with the plays of Pinter, as with the duplicate realities of Warhol, as with the bands of color of Frank Stella or the primary structures of sculptors like David Smith and Don Judd, *2001* must be viscerally understood, not explained. You don't ask a hamburger what it means but it can mean more than a lump of meat. A hamburger has come to be an object that looks like what hamburgers are supposed to look like. The way motels look like pictures of motels, and lamps look like pictures of lamps, until everything becomes a replica of a prototype: our parties are reproductions of parties, our lives are reproductions. It is why Warhol would like to be a machine.

The power of *2001* lies not in its words but in its pictures, so many of which are as geometric, as basic, as the primary structures of Smith and Judd or the elementary patterns of Stella. Kubrick's film is as primary as atoms and solar systems, minuscule-infinite. It is the first I've seen that justifies the use of a large screen and one of the few that justifies a screen at all (most movies could be novels).

The Playhouse of the Ridiculous, on the other hand, is an avalanche of words—restructuring the language, challenging meanings, applying this new dimension to the cause of comedy. Organized by Ronald Tavel, with John Vaccaro as house director, this off-off Broadway company presents postcamp spectaculars, degenerate-naïve, so outrageously obscene, so exotic-idiotic, that you are relieved of the burden—reminded of the hopelessness and artifice—of nineteenth-century rationality. Tavel has stated it impeccably—he has gone "beyond illogic into pre-logic."

Tavel, who collaborated on the early Warhol movies, specialized in baroque plotting, preposterous puns, confused gender, and the ultimate extension of sexual deviation (we are yet to suspect where the current movement to ambisexuality will lead—probably nowhere). Vaccaro contributed supergaudy staging, slapstick humor with massive companies, and constant genital humor—grabbing, squeezing, pinching, pulling off, sticking on, or in, or up, or out. The Playhouse presented a string of productions, including Charles Ludlam's interplanetary extravaganza *Conquest of the Universe*. The highlight of this production was the effeminate, blankly smiling Taylor Mead, costumed like Mary Martin's Peter Pan, swinging out over the audience and singing "I've Got to Crow." Tavel and Vaccaro have since gone their own ways; while Ludlam organized the Ridiculous Theatrical Company and stocked it with the likes of *Turds in Hell*, Tavel extended his work to other theaters (*Gorilla Queen* and *Sins of Lutetia* at the Judson Poets' Theatre, *Boy on the Straight-Backed Chair* for the American Place Theatre).

Such not-quite-nonsense is like Pinter, Beckett, and Kubrick in replacing traditional (and often spurious) "intelligence" with deromanticized fundamentalism, a postexistential fundamentalism most richly expressed by today's fantastically thriving art and music.

The relationship between pop (and post-pop) art and today's music is fascinating and exciting. The most modern of the new art songs are "pop" in the same sense that art is "pop." That is, they rise to surfaces. This is the key to Tiny Tim's popularity as much as it is to the work of the Beatles, Harper's Bizarre, Van Dyke Parks, Harry Nilsson, and Randy Newman. It is where Bob Dylan went after realizing that the wind was more important than the answers (?) blowing in it. It is the same vision as that of modern painters and sculptors—a vision so far ahead of the movies and especially the theater that the difference becomes not merely progressive but dimensional. (Small wonder that young people are not attracted to the theater.)

What we presently call avant-garde theater demonstrates how vast that difference is, if only in that our avant-garde is but a duplicate of all past avant-gardes. The stage has, for the past five years, been giving directors ever greater creative roles. A play, after all, exists only when it is produced. Until then, it is only a script. Academics will argue this point, but take my word for it, or better still, look for yourself. Brecht understood this thirty years ago, creating his plays as productions. Broadway choreographer-directors (Jerome Robbins particularly) did this of necessity, and it's one reason why the Broadway musical is the only current stage form that will have any lasting significance.

Meanwhile, the theater, sluggish creature that it is, is only now discovering such directing. Directors like William Ball of the American Conservatory Theatre in San Francisco, and Peter Brook of London's Royal Shakespeare Company, are creating theater pieces such as *Tiny Alice* and *Marat/Sade* (respectively) upon bases of writing and staging. Theater companies are working communally with playwrights—Joseph Chaikin's Open Theatre particularly—so that productions like *America Hurrah* and *Futz!* become the joint work of playwrights, actors, and directors. Other of these companies are dismissing playwrights entirely—the Living Theatre, Jerzy Grotowski's Polish Lab Theatre, Richard Schechner's Performance Group.

Some of these companies are edging toward a primary structurism in the theater, but for the most part they are held back by outmoded senses of meaning and message (our whole idea of *depth* has been a trivial and sad pretense). They talk a great deal about ritual and masks as if these were sufficient for a whole kind of theater. Concepts like ritual are, again, merely duplicates of some original, whimsical idea of *art*.

As for the current innovations, I only wish there was as much to them as there is written about them. *An actor going into the audience—dressed or not—is no big deal.* A complaint about American policies in Vietnam is Ibsenism whether the actor is wearing clothes or not. Guerrilla theater is tacky propaganda by costumed middle-class intellectuals of whom Che Guevara was this generation's original. Such specific devices and purposes are archaic, pathetic, simpleminded imitations of the idea of innovation.

So you see, the stuff you read about in Sunday supplements and drama sections—the nudity, the audience involvement, the language—well, that's only the specific detail at the bottom of the column, after you've subtracted the sense of what's going on. It is "news," "feature stories," in the sterilized, journalism-with-a-green-visor sense. It is pure Warhol, just as those productions are without realizing it, and no less so than *Forty Carats*.

Meanwhile, music and, most of all, art continue. Where they will lead is very much a mystery and perhaps a little frightening. The stage trails hopelessly behind with just those few exceptions I've been talking about and some I haven't, like Michael McClure's *The Beard,* John White's *Bananas,* or the movie *Head.* Yet, even in our theater, the ground is beginning to shift. Young audiences, so hopelessly lost as customers, are looking back now that movie art is no longer a novelty. The stage is a little unsteady on its feet, but our eyes are changing, and when that happens, everything is dragged along sooner or later. *That's* what's new.

Backword

One Step Backword

A theater critic's seat is always in the orchestra, but his place is really between the audience and the performance. In a sense, he is trapped in that place, belonging neither onstage nor in the house. He must protect the do-ers from the see-ers, he must defend the idea of theater from both. He cannot sit back and let the production come at him, because he must ask it certain questions. But if he cuts himself off from emotional response, he abandons the essential theater experience. He must understand the workings of the stage and yet leave the craft to those who make the show. He is responsible to the audience, he is responsible to the production makers, he is most responsible to his own vision of the theater and must write to *that* responsibility.

This nowhereland isn't intimidating, but it does represent the critical island that floats between the stage and the seats. Such isolation is necessary and helpful. It makes it possible to concentrate on stimulus (the production) and reaction (its effect) at the same time.

One Step Inword

Ideally speaking, a critic's judgments are definitive. I believe in an absolute value of art. That is, I believe that a painting, a piece of music, a film, a theater production have ultimate worths. They are either good or bad (by *good* I mean however you define the term: *integrity* or *value* or *art* or whatever you like). Definitively, there is a correct opinion of a given work. The ideal critic is into this truth—knows he is right and *is right*.

I believe that I was *right* about every production I've ever reviewed. Of course, I also always believed, on finishing a review, that it was the most beautifully conceived and written piece of criticism possible to the occasion. I found, as you may have, that this was far from so. There is some crude writing in this collection. I still believe that the judgments were true.

One Step Downword

There are two gaps in criticism. One is between those who criticize the theater and those who make it. The other is between academic critics and professional critics.

The first gap exists because theater people are concerned with causes and critics are concerned with effects. That is, the makers worry about construction while the consumers worry about intellectual-emotional content.

Critics think that a playwright and his director understand what a play was supposed to be about and how it was supposed to feel. But the playwrights and directors seldom understand. *They* think that critics should know what it takes to create theater, but critics seldom know. Because of these disappointments, there is no interplay between critics and theater people. Critics have no working influence on theater makers and are read exclusively for commercial effect. Criticism should identify a piece of work and conclude its birth.

It would be nice if a critic actually gave a viable idea once in a while.

The second gap exists because professional critics are concerned with the theater as production while academic critics are concerned with the theater as dramatic literature. The professionals—involved with fact—believe the academics are interested in words rather than action. The academics—involved with theory—believe the professionals are interested in only the surface level of theater. Both are partly right, and a proper critic should, at least, combine these traits. There is too great an ignorance, in professional criticism, of critical instruments, critical methodology, historical background, and dramatic lines of development. There is too great an isolation, in academic criticism, from the electric effect of working theater and the need for a play to exist as a production if it is to exist at all.

These two ought to get together.

One Step Unword

The final article in this collection ("The New Theater Is Here at Last. Isn't It?") represents my point of view at the moment of this writing. I think that essay-criticism, which purports to state and substantiate a point of view in logical sequence, has become a *replica* of such criticism. It is the sort of criticism that has been written for the last hundred years—in style, in purpose, in material. Perhaps—probably—it was always replica.

We have developed for ourselves a system that we call *logic,* which we have presented to ourselves and accepted as meaning what we have decided the word "logic" means. We have invented the essay as the form in which this logic can be applied to manufacture "statement." We have developed and accepted "good English" and "good sense" and "insight." We read a combination of words, accept them as representations of thoughts, descriptions of plot, comments on acting and direction, conclusions, jokes, and whatever. If this is written as an accurate facsimile of what criticism has always been, we call it criticism.

What happens when these concepts are challenged?

There must be another way of doing what we call *criticism* because what we have accepted as criticism is only "criticism." A professional can produce this "criticism" with the same facility as a machine produces Coca-Cola bottles. Critical work, like the too many words we use, has become a duplicating process. Events, situations, and things repeat themselves and are repeated in images created by history, experience, habit, advertising, photography, and finally (ultimately) television. We are shot through with pictures of everything—even of thoughts, because we always thought of thoughts as sentences. In criticism —in everything—this cannot go on.

Whether such another way is possible.

Index